· BUSHWORLD ·

·BUSHWORLD·

ENTER AT YOUR OWN RISK

Maureen Dowd

G.P. Putnam's Sons

New York

G. P. PUTNAM'S SONS
Published by Penguin Group (USA) Inc.
375 Hudson Street, New York, New York 10014, U.S.A.
Penguin Group (Canada), 10 Alcorn Avenue, Toronto, Ontario,
Canada M4V 3B2 (a division of Pearson Canada Ltd.)
Penguin Books Ltd., 80 Strand, London WC2R 0RL, England
Penguin Group (Ireland), 25 St Stephen's Green, Dublin 2,
Ireland (a division of Penguin Books Ltd.)
Penguin Group (Australia), 250 Camberwell Road, Camberwell,
Victoria 3124, Australia (a division of Pearson Australia Group (Pty) Ltd.)
Penguin Group (India), 11 Community Centre, Panchsheel Park,
New Delhi – 110 017, India (a division of Penguin Group Books India (P) Ltd.)
Penguin Group (NZ), Cnr Rosedale and Airborne Roads, Albany,
Auckland, New Zealand (a division of Pearson New Zealand Ltd.)
Penguin Group (South Africa), 24 Sturdee Avenue, Rosebank, Johannesburg 2196,
South Africa (a division of Penguin Group (South Africa) (Pty) Ltd.)

Penguin Books Ltd., Registered Offices:
80 Strand, London, WC2R 0RL, England

G. P. Putnam's Sons
Publishers Since 1838
a member of Penguin Group (USA) Inc.
375 Hudson Street
New York, NY 10014

Published simultaneously in Canada

Dowd, Maureen.
Bushworld : enter at your own risk / Maureen Dowd.
p.   cm.
A collection of the author's columns originally published in The New York times.
ISBN 0-399-15258-X
1. United States—Politics and government—2001–   2. Bush, George W. (George Walker),
1946–   3. United States—Foreign relations—2001–   4. Imperialism.   I. Title: Bush world.   II. Title.
E902.D69   2004   2004048798
973.931'092—dc22

ISBN: 0-399-15258-X

Printed in the United States of America
5   7   9   10   8   6   4

This book is printed on acid-free paper. ∞

Book design by Claire Naylon Vaccaro

For my mom,

who thinks all the Bushes are swell

Contents

■

WAR OF THE CHADS
IN WHICH THE HIGH COURT PURLOINS THE THRONE FOR THE BUSH DYNASTY

OEDIPUS WRECKS
IN WHICH THE FAMILY DRAMA AESCHYLATES

WASHINGTON'S TRANSIT
IN WHICH THE POLITICS OF SEDUCTION GIVE WAY TO THE POLITICS OF CONFRONTATION

THE BOY KING'S ENDLESS SUMMER
IN WHICH THE FAULT IS IN THEIR STAR WARS AND IN THEMSELVES

TRANSFUSING THE BLUE BLOOD WITH RED TO PUMP UP THE RED STATES

SURRENDERING TO VICE
THE BOY KING SUBMITS TO THE DARK FATHER

SLEEPING WITH THE ENEMY
IN WHICH THE SAUDIS FLY AWAY FROM 9/11 BLAME IN THEIR PRIVATE JETS

AS THE WORLD TURNS ON US
IN WHICH FURIOUS GEORGE UPENDS HIS SIRE'S FRIENDLY DIPLOMACY

A CYNICAL CHAPTER
FEEDING THE FEAR AND STOKING THE HOMELAND INSECURITY

ON PIETY AND PETTIFOGGERY

IN WHICH CHENEY, RUMMY, WOLFIE, CONDI, CHALABI AND THE NEOCON GANG HIJACK THE WAR ON TERROR

IN WHICH THE READER ROOTS FOR THE GALLANT COLIN POWELL TO PREVAIL AGAINST THE PENTAGON VISIGOTHS

HEY DUDE, WHERE'S MY COVERT ACTION?
IN WHICH TOP GUN IS TOPPLED BY SPUTTERING SPOOKS

UNCLE DICK OF THE UNDERWORLD
IN WHICH THE DARK FATHER SHOWS HIMSELF IN THE LEAST AMIABLE LIGHT

DRUNK ON RUMMY
IN WHICH THE BOY EMPEROR HAS NO CLOTHES (OR WEAPONS)

IN WHICH THE SKULL AND BONES SCIONS, ONE WHO SAUCILY SLOUGHED OFF AND ONE WHO POMPOUSLY STRIVED UP, FACE OFF

IN MEMORIAM

Acknowledgments

■

I'm not well suited to being a polemicist and certainly never could have survived the *Times* op-ed world without the infinitely patient and unstintingly generous help of my dazzling, loyal, wise and witty friends: Leon Wieseltier, Michi Kakutani, Carl Hulse, Jill Abramson, Alessandra Stanley, Aaron Sorkin, Steve Weisman, Bill Carter, Jane Mayer, Don Van Natta, Adam Nagourney and Frank Bruni, as well as the guidance of my effervescent and elegant mentor, Arthur Gelb, and his sage wife, Barbara.

Peggy Dowd dwells happily in Bushworld, but she is the most loyal sister on the planet, so she is always there for me even when I tweak a president she passionately admires; ditto, my niece Jen.

One of the best parts of the job is sitting in Murderers' Row, where my neighbors in nattering and some negativism, Tom Friedman, Bill Safire and Johnny Apple, are always available for kvetching and counseling.

My thanks to the Arthur Sulzbergers, father and son, who have always been wonderful to me; to Howell Raines for giving me the White House beat to cover the first President Bush and an op-ed column to cover the second; to Joe Lelyveld and Anna Quindlen for

Acknowledgments

decades of support; and to Gail Collins and Andy Rosenthal, who graciously reign over our op-ed kingdom now.

I never could have ventured into the wilds of Bushworld without my very cool assistant, Julie Bosman, and my former assistant, Marc Santora.

Or without my sherpas in Bookworld, my friend Alex Ward of Times Books, the estimable Esther Newberg, and Putnam's indefatigable Neil Nyren and masterly Marilyn Ducksworth.

This book was buoyed by all my talented and giving colleagues in Washington, starting with Phil Taubman and Rick Berke; special thanks to Michael Gordon, David Johnston, Dough Jehl, David Sanger, Jeff Gerth, Neil Lewis, Rich Oppel, Phil Shenon, Todd Purdum, Kit Seelye, Robin Toner, Elizabeth Becker, Sheryl Stolberg, Eric Schmitt, Thom Shanker, Dick Stevenson, Robert Pear, Steve Labaton, John Tierney, Felicity Barringer, Jim Risen, Monica Borkowski, Jim Ruttenberg, and Adam Clymer, who rules as Bushworld's "major-league" you-know-what; my pals throughout the paper, like Frank Clines, Steve Lohr, Frank Rich, Elaine Sciolino, Linda Lake, Bernie Weinraub and Bill Keller; and elsewhere—Michael Beschloss, Gerry and Eden Rafshoon, Michael Specter, Evan Thomas, Michael Isikoff, John Broder, Michael Kinsley, Michael Duffy and Paul Costello. Thanks to Pat Tyler and Hassan Yassim for the assist on deciphering the Saudi culture.

I'm grateful for the first-rate copy editors I've been lucky enough to have at the *Times*: Sue Kirby, Linda Cohn, Steve Pickering, Karen Freeman, Bob Rudinger and Toby Harshaw.

And finally, thanks to that genius of political cartoons, Pat Oliphant, my old colleague from *The Washington Star*, who agreed to work weekends so I could have a fantastic cover—in every sense of the word.

· B U S H W O R L D ·

Introduction

■

In March 2001, I went to flat and dusty Aggieland, Texas A&M at College Station, to speak at the Bush presidential library. "We had to wait until the Silver Fox left the country to ask you," George Herbert Walker Bush told me, only half teasing, since Barbara Bush was abroad. He lured me there by promising to show me an eleven-page comic screed against *The New York Times* and a few other media miscreants that he'd typed on his computer in the Arthurian style of a column I had written portraying him as the Old King and W. as the Boy King. Like me, 41 has an easier time unfurling his feelings writing than talking, so I especially appreciated his wacky satire about a royal court, sprinkled with words like *verily, forsooth* and *liege*, and characters such as King Prescott of Greenwich, George of Crawford, Queen Bar, King Bill, Maid Monica, Hillary the Would-Be Monarch, Knight Algore, Earl Jeb of Tallahassee, Duke Cheney, Warrior Sulzberger, Knight Howell Raines, Knight Ashcroft and Lady Maureen, "charming princess" of the *Times* op-ed world. The delicious frolicking, falconing and scheming at the "moatless" court of the old warrior king, however, will have to forever remain our secret.

I was a *Times* White House reporter for the first Bush administration. Though 41 was always gracious, I know he was disappointed at first to have drawn an irreverent, newfangled "reporterette," as Rush Limbaugh would say, who wanted to focus as much on the personalities of leaders as on their policies. But I always figured it this way: Politicians can tell you they won't ever raise taxes—read their lips—or won't ever nation-build, but sometimes, because of their basic natures, needy egos and whispering Iagos, they find their way to believing or acting in glaring contradiction to their original promises. When the nation has been scarred by crises like Watergate and Vietnam, it has been because presidents have let their demons overcome experience and common sense.

Poppy Bush had been expecting a traditional pin-striped *Times* correspondent, one with a name like Chatsworth Farnsworth III, who would scribble about 41's role leading the Atlantic alliance. The son of Prescott Bush and Dorothy Walker is a modest man, whose mother warned him so often against focusing on what he called "the big I" that he would cut the personal pronoun off the start of his sentences and just plunge into the verb, as in "Not going to do it," or "Nah-ga-da-it," as Dana Carvey would say on *Saturday Night Live.* (41 joked that he was "a Dana Carvey soundalike.") Or use staccato Bushspeak, as in his encomium to his coffee warmer: "Mug warmer. Electric. 93-point-25-dash-1, it says." It made him squirm to be inspected by the press closely or saucily. One New Year's Eve, over dinner in Houston, Brent Scowcroft, 41's national security adviser, formally requested that I stop referring to Mr. Bush in stories as acting "goofy." And the president himself complained in amused chagrin to his press secretary, Marlin Fitzwater, in one of the little "blue notes" he sent out to his staff, that I had been sitting cross-legged and arms crossed, "like some Hinnianistic Buddhist" pose at a golf course in Kennebunkport, staring at him in a "Gail Sheehy" manner as he was teeing off. Actually, I was just trying to muster some interest in golf. But I guess it's hard to tee off when you're teed off. Another time, on Air Force One, when he came back to talk to a bunch of reporters, he ordered me to "stop staring" at him; I lowered my eyes.

But over the years, 41 tried to adapt. He has often kidded me about "our love-hate relationship," dubbing me his "favorite-unfavorite big foot columnist" and chastising me about being a "limo-lib" who cast him unfairly as an "elitist." He loved it when I wrote columns tweaking the Clintons and hated it when I wrote columns tweaking the Bushes, the two rival political dynasties of meritocracy and aristocracy—both driven by feelings of entitlement—that I seem destined to cover in endless succession. Poppy Bush sometimes threatens to seek psychiatric counseling to cure himself of this "love-hate" syndrome, knowing that will make me laugh. Both Bush *père* and *fils* are notoriously allergic to introspection and analysis, considering even questions about TV and movie tastes a dread attempt to put them "on the couch" and plumb the unconscious depths.

After moderating the panel on "The Media and the White House" at his library, the former president took me, along with a bunch of his former officials, to a red-meat feast at a local barbecue joint. He was charming, and glowing with pride at being only the second man in history to have his son follow him into the Oval Office.

But in hushed voices, out in the parking lot, some of his former aides, men who had worked for the pragmatic, realpolitik team of "the Velvet Hammer" James Baker and "H.W.," as 41 sometimes differentiates himself from his presidential namesake, confided that they were already anxious and mystified about the chest-thumping, ideological foreign-policy tone of Bush II.

In its first two months, the new administration had gotten into tussles with Russia and China, blowing off treaties and making the rest of the world jittery. After running against the hormonal irresponsibility of the Clinton era, could W. be indulging in an even more destructive teenage rebellion against his family? Prodded by the "forward-leaning," my-way-or-the-highway twins, Dick Cheney and Donald Rumsfeld, Bush the younger was doing an Oedipal loop-de-loop, intemperately shredding the internationalism and traditional alliances so cherished by his father and grandfather, a Wall Street banker and Connecticut senator. (My two older brothers were Senate pages in the early fifties for JFK, LBJ, Richard Nixon and Prescott Bush, whom they described as a central casting senator, tall and craggy, favoring gray worsted suits even in warm weather.) W. was replacing the old family motto of noblesse oblige with a new one: Oblige *this*. It seemed odd that Mr. Popularity at Yale, the gregarious frat president who gave everyone cute nicknames and led pranks like scalding DKE pledges with hot wire hangers, was suddenly scalding the world and not leaving them laughing.

At the barbecue dinner, a top official of Bush I fretted that the Bush II foreign-policy team—the seasoned hands who were supposed to be the adults taking over from those Clinton adolescents who seemed to make it up as they went along—was too belligerent, too conservative, too blunt, too negative and too improvisational in dealing with the globe on everything from missile defense to Kyoto. (W. mocked enviros as "green, green lima beans.") "These guys are linear," the official said. "They have to have black and white. They have to have bogeymen."

Bush 43 exhibited a weird combination of arrogance and tentativeness. "You're never quite sure," another Bush I official observed, "if those papers in front of W. blew away in the wind, if he would know what to say."

The old man, as his admiring former officials called him, reflected only paternal pride in W.'s fledgling presidency, even though his son was consciously patterning himself not on his own father but on Ronald Reagan. The Great Communicator so overshadowed his vice president that the syntax-mangling Poppy seemed to droop a bit in the Gipper's presence, managing to look shorter even though he was taller. One of 41's speechwriters called it his "deferential Episcopalian tilt."

Bush 43 certainly wasn't following in the diplomatic footsteps of his father, who practiced an intensely personal, folksy, feet-up style of diplomacy. I spent half of 41's presidency watching him aggressively charming world leaders—sometimes too aggressively. He loved demonically driving visiting heads of state on his cigarette boat around the Kennebunkport bays—except François Mitterrand, who begged off, saying he got mal de mer. Continuing a social diplomacy tradition he'd practiced as ambassador to the UN and liaison to Beijing, he dragged Prime Minister Yitzhak Shamir of Israel to the Air and Space Museum to see the movie *To Fly*, King Hussein down the river from Mount Vernon on a boat, and Egyptian president Hosni Mubarak to his first baseball game to see the Orioles play the Red Sox, complete with hot dogs and horseradish. When the announcer gave the names of the celebrities in attendance at Memorial Stadium, the name Ted Williams got a roar from the crowd, while the name Mubarak provoked only silent wonderment. ("Who did he play for? The Indians?") Bush 41 loved Saudi Prince Bandar so much, pheasant hunting at his British estate and allowing Bandar alone to smoke cigars at Kennebunkport, that the Saudi ambassador became known as "Bandar Bush."

41's still at it. He invited Mikhail Gorbachev to come to College Station for his eightieth birthday parachute jump and tried to persuade the former Head of the Evil Empire to jump with him. "Afraid," Gorbachev demurred. W. attended his dad's birthday party but did not stay to watch him fall 5,000 feet, returning to the White House for a T-ball game.

For Poppy, who belonged to three men's clubs in Washington and the all-male Bohemian Grove in California, the global stage was the ultimate exclusive men's club—Margaret Thatcher, "the Iron Lady," who ordered Bush Senior not to "go wobbly" on Saddam, included.

Before 41's 1990 summit with Gorbachev, Richard Perle, the cold war arms expert who would one day be a leading Bush hawk on Iraq, pooh-poohed such personal diplomacy. "It's very easy to get caught up in personal relationships and fail thereby to analyze the situation accurately," Perle sniffed.

H.W. and his pal Baker had an ad hoc, practical, and sometimes disturbingly unsentimental "we know best" foreign policy, with none of the moral umbrage of Jimmy Carter or soaring dreams of Ronald Reagan. As Tom Friedman and I wrote in a *Times* magazine piece in 1990: "They regard themselves as good people who will do the correct thing and, if circumstances permit, the right thing. The approach is: split the difference. Keep things stable. Democracy where possible. Free markets where possible. Apple pie where possible. . . . If what seems reasonable at the moment is to side with the Chinese power elite rather than the students in Tiananmen Square, then you side with those in power. If what seems reasonable is to split the difference between the aspirations of Lithuanians and the interests of Gorbachev, then you split the difference. . . . Bush and Baker failed to convey passion on issues, and that can be a real liability."

Long before his son strutted as "Top Gun," *Time* magazine had hailed the elder Bush and Baker as "Top Guns on Top of the World" on their Febuary 13, 1989, cover.

It became clear during W.'s 2000 campaign that the one-term Texas governor, who got sober and serious late in life, had not studied up on foreign policy at his father's knee. In his time around the White House, when he was still known as "Junior," he had hung out with Lee Atwater, the Machiavellian wunderkind of the revived Republican Party, in the political chop shop. Junior was the loyalty enforcer, making sure that Bush staffers were vetted as true-blue. He was a good-time guy with a quick temper, not considered by the Bush family and staff as presidential material, or even gubernatorial material.

I came a cropper of him once, back in those days, when I was on summer duty at Kennebunkport as the *Times* White House reporter. Wanting some playful payback against his dad for making reporters awake at dawn to watch him tee off for one of his breathless games of "aerobic golf" or "golf polo," as we called it, I rummaged around in my suitcase and came up with a "Bob Dole for President in '88" T-shirt and a "Jesse Jackson for President in '88" hat. I knew 41 would get the joke, but when father and son swung by me in their golf cart, Poppy wasn't looking and Junior gave me a scary glare. Later he sent back word that he was not amused. I comforted myself with the knowledge that Junior, a Midland businessman, would never be in a position to wreak revenge on me. After all, Jeb was the family comer.

W.'s quick turnaround from black sheep to boy king took a large measure of grit and discipline. When I ran into him covering his

Texas state house and White House races, he was genial, appreciatively noting my green cowboy boots or bantering about his parents. On the day he announced he would run for president, we reminisced about the golf course contretemps, sitting on the back porch of the Bush estate in Kennebunkport, overlooking the sparkling Atlantic, as his parents perched nearby. Grinning disarmingly, W. asked, "Are you still holding that against me?"

One of Barbara Bush's White House aides had predicted that W. would never make it through a presidential run because he was too much like his mother, prickly, tart-tongued, an injustice collector. But he surprised everyone—including his parents—and got his Roman candle side under control. His father had helped to swaddle him with a foreign-policy "dream team" that would give voters confidence—even if there were a few slips along the way, like the pop quiz that had W. sputtering "General" when asked who the head of Pakistan was. The patrician bequeathed to the prodigal son his own foreign-policy war council—Cheney, Colin Powell, Condoleezza Rice and Paul Wolfowitz—to tutor him and confer gravitas upon him.

Dick Cheney was just the sort of family retainer and consigliere the Bushes loved—deferential, loyal, leakproof, not competitive. So when, as head of the vice-presidential search committee, Cheney chose himself, both father and son were well pleased.

But it soon became clear that this wasn't the cautious, modulated Dick Cheney of Bush I, such an invisible staff man that the Secret Service gave him the code name "Backseat" when he was in the Ford White House. This Dick Cheney was quietly but firmly running the show, and the show was swaggering and ideological. He brought in his mentor from the Nixon and Ford years, the charismatically cranky Donald Rumsfeld, the famous infighter who had been a sharp-elbowed rival to Bush Senior in the old days, rooting for Bush for CIA director because he thought it would hurt 41's chances to be president. Rummy, of course, thought he would make a stronger president than H.W., whom he considered flighty and insubstantial, pulled up the ladder by his pedigree and given appointed jobs by his friends.

Cheney brought in a neocon chief of staff, Scooter Libby, a protégé of Wolfowitz, and Rummy swept into the Pentagon the neocon gang of Wolfowitz, Doug Feith, William Luti, Stephen Cambone and, as Pentagon advisers, Richard Perle and Newt Gingrich. Condi Rice was the tyro president's remedial foreign-policy governess and workout partner, which left her little time to do her real job, sorting through and brokering national security information on things like Al Qaeda terrorist threats. Terrorism was considered a leftover Clinton problem and this White House disdained everything Clinton. Their concerns were more retro; Rummy was fixated on getting a missile defense shield and developing laser weapons in space; Cheney was turning back the clock on environmental progress with secret energy meetings paying off all their oil cronies who had fed the fundraising engine.

The new Bushies wanted to be feared, as Reagan was in the world, and brought an intensely moralistic component to their foreign policy. But they didn't seem to care about the flip side as the sunny Reagan did—being revered. Or even about being collegial, as 41 did.

With each passing day of the Bush restoration, it became clearer that we were entering the primal territory of ancient myth, in which the son must define himself by vanquishing the father. While W. loved his dad and was close to him, he wanted out of his shadow. Even as he acted out with alcohol and pranks and a lackadaisical record at school and the National Guard, W. was also emulating his dad's stuffed résumé—Yale, Skull and Bones, fighter pilot, Midland oilman, politics—and usually falling short. Where his dad was captain of Andover's soccer and baseball teams and Yale's '48 baseball team, W. had to settle for head cheerleader and self-appointed role of "Stickball Commissioner" at Andover. While his dad was a fighter pilot who got shot down in World War II, W. avoided Vietnam and settled for flying jets in the National Guard, "defending Texas against Oklahoma," as one Bush I official sardonically noted.

Marlin Fitzwater once mused to me that the first President Bush would have been better off if he were all preppy or all Texan, that the strain of trying to be striped watchband and pork rinds, blue blood and red meat, tripped him up.

The second President Bush had found the experience of watching his dad fail to get a second term very painful. He was going to make sure that when he said "fixin'" and "bidness," it rang true; that he was a real conservative, not a moderate, like his grandfather, and not a moderate pretending to be a conservative, like his father. He was going to be a Southern born-again evangelical Christian, not an Episcopalian like his father and grandfather. More than anything, he was going to make sure he was never called a wimp, as his father had been on the "Wimp Factor" cover of *Newsweek* during his first presidential campaign—an incident so traumatic for 41 that he counted the number of times the word had been used in the story and demanded a meeting with Kay Graham, the publisher of *Newsweek*.

From the start, W. and Karl Rove used Bush *père* as a reverse playbook; if they avoided the father's missteps with the right, they could keep their base happy. It informed everything, including Middle East policy. Daddy Bush loved the Arabs, especially the Saudis (the ultimate elite men's club), and he could be tough and impatient with Israel, sending his support among American Jews plummeting.

Rove and W. believed that winning a larger share of the Jewish vote would be key to getting that second term his dad missed out on. W. preferred to go easy on Israel, even when Ariel Sharon took advantage and reneged on his own promises to 43 to ease his harsh rule over the Palestinians.

I often wonder what Bush the elder must have been thinking after 9/11 as the neocons started their drumbeat about the need to rectify the huge mistake of not getting rid of Saddam in '91; and watching, from the sidelines, as his son reached back in time to fix the ending of a war that 41 felt he'd ended as well as he could. And what did 41 make of the biggest mystery of all, even among some conservatives—why had Cheney and Scowcroft protégé Condi gone so haywire?

It's easy for me to believe that the manners-obsessed and gallant 41 would not want to tread on 43's presidency by offering a lot of unsolicited advice. But it's hard for me to believe the son wouldn't take advantage of his dad's counsel on diplomacy and Saddam. He was, as he told Bob Woodward, relying on two other fathers. Pressed by Woodward on why he did not consult the only other president to go to war with Iraq before he himself went to war with Iraq, 43 said: "He is the wrong father to appeal to in terms of strength; there is a Higher Father that I appealed to."

In addition to his relationship with Jesus, W. felt he could especially trust Cheney because Cheney didn't want to run for president. 43 seemed totally under the sway of this Darth Vader Dark Father who was steering him back in time, with fixations on Star Wars and rewriting the end of Desert Storm. Cheney, who was burrowed down in his secret undisclosed locations after 9/11 reading worst-case scenarios on terrorism and lugubrious tomes contending that war is the natural state of mankind, yanked the formerly sunny sonny into a neo-Hobbesian world where, as neocon guru Robert Kagan put it, "Americans are from Mars and Europeans are from Venus," a gloomy universe where America must throw off weak international institutions and prevail with a muscular unilateralism.

All presidents are in a bubble, but the boy king was so insulated he was in a thermos. He said he did not read newspapers. His dad read everything about himself—even reporter's pool reports for other reporters. W. preferred to get his information directly from his advisers. His regents put their own spin and filter on the information they fed him, creating an alternative universe where they were never wrong because they never let in any information showing they were wrong and because they conjured up information to prove they were right. They transmit; they don't receive. They didn't listen to Congress or to allies or to Bush *père* or his friends, like Baker and Scowcroft.

I went on W's first foreign trip in May 2002 and he wore his chip on his shoulder, proudly. Sometimes the little-traveled 43 seemed like an accidental tourist. As a British reporter wrote, he did not always seem sure what country he was in. He was bristly at the anti-American demonstrations and the politely condescending attitude of the French and Germans. When the president got irritated at Élysée Palace and called NBC's David Gregory a pretentious "intercontinental" for playfully asking Jacques Chirac a question in French, it puzzled the French reporters I was sitting with. How could it be rude to speak French to a Frenchman in France?

Everything had been transformed by September 11, 2001. You could see in President Bush's eyes, darting and daunted, as he stayed frozen in his seat after learning about the second plane going into the World Trade tower, reading with second-graders, that the bill for his lifelong lack of seriousness had come due. (Maybe that's why he sat so long, when he should have been scrambling jets.) Bush and Cheney were frightened for America and wanted to protect the country; but they also began wielding fear as a political weapon.

The wave of positive feeling and sympathy for America after 9/11 dissipated quickly, as the emboldened Bush crew continued to strong-arm the world. For them, 9/11 represented an opportunity beyond the war on terror. It was a chance to pool their various grandiose dreams for transforming American psychology, Arab political culture, the American military, the security of Israel and the strategic direction of the Middle East. They were conservatives, but their audacious and profligate schemes for social and political engineering at home and abroad made Hillary Clinton's unwieldly health care plan look piddling.

Cheney and Rummy wanted to toughen up the American character, to exorcise sixties moral relativism, the Clintonesque if-it-feels-good-do-it ethos, the post-Vietnam focus on America's imperfections and limitations, and the ambivalence about using force. Dick and Lynne Cheney had long been critics of multiculturalism and the blame-America-first attitude. The vice president had wanted to establish America's primacy as the sole superpower for a decade. And the neocons had long had utopian dreams about making the world over in their own image of America's image. Though most had managed to avoid military service, they subscribed to the theory that war is too important to be left to the generals; they wanted to reduce the rest of the world to subservience and spread democracy through coercion.

Back in 1992, when W. was still just the cocky, hot-tempered scion whose political judgment was considered dubious, hanging around on the edge of his dad's reelection campaign, Cheney, then the Bush I defense secretary, and his aides Libby and Wolfowitz were already preparing what would someday be known as the Bush doctrine, an aggressive, unilateral policy that told the world to get back, Jack.

That '92 "Defense Planning Guidance" draft, a big swinging-stick "Empire Strikes First" manifesto, called for unapologetic world domination, asserting that America's mission after the cold war would be to intervene to thwart any countries, allied or hostile, from becoming a rival to America's superpower stature. Western Europe, Asia and the former Soviet Union, the document declared, could not be allowed to challenge U.S. supremacy.

It stirred outrage among some senior Bush I officials and members of Congress who got wind of it. Senator Robert Byrd of West Virginia denounced the draft as "myopic," and warned, "In the long run, it will be counterproductive to the very goal of world leadership that it cherishes."

The first President Bush cringed at such solipsistic grandiosity, and Colin Powell considered it voodoo foreign policy. They squelched it, but it rose up from the dead like a blood-starved vampire, when Cheney, Scooter and Wolfie found a younger, more malleable President Bush, who was drawn to the notion of letting the world know in no uncertain terms who the sheriff was.

Two other steroid-infused manifestos would find a host body in W. years after they were written. In 1996, three men who would become Bush national security advisers and leading hawks in the whack-Iraq group—Richard Perle, Douglas Feith and David Wurmser—helped write a report about how Israel could transcend the problems with the Palestinians by changing the "balance of power" in the Middle East and replacing Saddam; they had prepared the report for then–Israeli prime minister Benjamin Netanyahu. Even the hard-line Bibi found the plan too far-out and rejected it. And in 1997, while W. was worrying about changing the

Texas taxes and execution controversies, Bill Kristol, now of the *Weekly Standard* and Fox News, and other conservatives formed a nonprofit group called "Project for the New American Century." They published a "statement of principles" signed by Jeb Bush and future Bush officials Rummy, Cheney, Wolfie, Scooter Libby and Elliott Abrams. It rejected 41's realpolitik, called for a return to "a Reaganite policy of military strength and moral clarity," foreshadowing what five years later would become 43's preemption strategy.

"America has a vital role in maintaining peace and security in Europe, Asia, and the Middle East," they wrote. "If we shirk our responsibilities, we invite challenges to our fundamental interests. The history of the 20th century should have taught us that it is important to shape circumstances before crises emerge, and to meet threats before they become dire." It was a kick-the-door-in policy straight out of Philip K. Dick's science fiction *Minority Report:* Identify the future bad guys and arrest them before they commit the crime.

America, the signers of this barrel-chested declaration wrote, should "challenge regimes hostile to our interests and values."

Just as Cheney, Scooter and Wolfie wanted to correct what they saw as errors in their previous life in government, so did Rummy. As he told Bob Woodward, he had had a hard time getting control over the Pentagon the first time he was secretary of defense in the Ford White House. Now he wanted to make his mark with a transformation of the military, showing that smaller, more agile forces could be sent to dispatch more villains; he would stubbornly cling to his theories, even when experts like General Eric Shinseki and Senator John McCain warned him he could not achieve security or troop safety in an Iraqi occupation with such a reduced force.

In addition to the neocons wanting to transform the Middle East and Rummy wanting to transform the military and Cheney wanting to transform the American psyche, this was a chance for W. to complete his transformation from the screwup son to the son who fixed his father's screwups, from a man favored by history into a man who changed history. Indeed, W. wanted to change the end of the very war his father wrote about proudly in his book *A World Transformed.*

Perle was no Pitt and Wolfowitz was no Clooney, but they pulled off an "Ocean's 9/11" heist of the war on terror, slick and over budget. The hawks knew it would be too hard to sell an eschatological scheme to stomp out Islamic terrorism by giving the Arab world an extreme makeover. They needed a smoke screen, and why not the smoke of a mushroom cloud? Saddam was the perfect villain, and the perfect lab monkey to test all their bold theories on. The neocons had always been burned up that they didn't get to see Saddam, running like a rat across the sands, at the end of Desert Storm. They felt passionately that the first President Bush had betrayed the Shiites and Kurds by letting Saddam slaughter them after 41 had urged them to "take matters into their own hands and force Saddam Hussein, the dictator, to step aside." Despite pushing the first Iraq war as a moral obligation, the pragmatic Desert Storm team was reluctant to interfere when Saddam sent out his helicopters to kill the resistance because it feared radical Islamic factions might take over if Saddam was sacked.

Back in 1991, as Bush I defense secretary Dick Cheney defended the decision not to go into Baghdad, saying that America would simply have installed a "puppet regime." "How long would we have to stay there to keep this regime in power?" he said. "How effective would it be if it were perceived as the puppet regime of the United States military? It gets to be a very difficult, a very nebulous, a very long, drawn-out kind of commitment, what I would describe as a quagmire. We have absolutely no interest in getting U.S. military forces involved inside Iraq."

In *A World Transformed*, Bush *père* and Scowcroft write that it was Cheney who helped make the decision that Saddam could keep using his helicopters as gunships to put down the uprisings, a decision that in retrospect 41 seems to have regretted. But Bush Senior defended his decision not to sack Saddam then, saying he had no "exit strategy," something he also intensely worried about when his son went to war with Iraq. "Going in and occupying Iraq, thus unilaterally exceeding the United Nations' mandate, would have destroyed the precedent of international response to aggression that we hoped to establish," he wrote. "Had we gone the invasion route, the United States could conceivably still be an occupying power in a bitterly hostile land. It would have been a dramatically different— and perhaps barren—outcome."

The neocon heist, a decade in the making, nurtured in the Clinton years in the offices of the American Enterprise Institute, a conservative think tank where Cheney mingled with Perle, Feith and Wolfowitz, went quickly and smoothly. Cheney lurked over at Langley, breathing down CIA analysts' necks. And Feith developed his own CIA in the Pentagon to forge the link between Saddam and Al Qaeda that the CIA couldn't turn up.

Ahmad Chalabi also helped gin up the "evidence" they needed. He provided defectors to link Saddam and Al Qaeda, and to inflate Saddam's nonexistent arsenal into a threat to U.S. security, even reportedly getting an aide's relative, code-named "Curveball," to become a key source on WMD, a charge Chalabi denied. They successfully persuaded many Americans of a lie—that Saddam was behind 9/11. A study released last year showed that of three misconceptions about Iraq—that Al Qaeda and Iraq were connected, that

WMD had been found, and that the world approved of the U.S. invasion of Iraq—80 percent of Fox viewers believed at least one of them. On the flip side, only 23 percent of PBS viewers believed at least one misconception.

In a plot twist worthy of Evelyn Waugh, the neocons conning America got conned by a con man. The Bush administration pals of Chalabi, convicted embezzler in Jordan and alleged Iranian spy, paid him $39 million (the U.S. government paid him at least a hundred million from '92 until his Baghdad house was raided in May) to feed them the empire cakewalk fantasies they wanted to hear, and to help build the trompe l'oeil case against Saddam that would end up costing America a billion a week.

As Vincent Cannistraro, a former CIA counterterrorism specialist who now consults for the government, told *The New Yorker*'s Jane Mayer, "With Chalabi, we paid to fool ourselves. It's horrible. In other times, it might be funny. But a lot of people are dead as a result of this. It's reprehensible." (Chalabi, too, wanted to topple Saddam to avenge his powerful father, who had been thrown out of Iraq decades ago.)

In what Senator Bob Graham called "incestuous amplification," the bogus stories of Chalabi and his friends on WMD ricocheted through an echo chamber of government and media, making it sound as though multiple, reliable sources were corroborating the same story, when it was the same unreliable source.

Colin Powell knew that Cheney had an unhealthy "fever" about Saddam, as he told Woodward, and he knew Feith's Pentagon "Gestapo office," as he contemptuously dubbed it, was hyping evidence. He holed up with George Tenet to try to weed out some of the bogus Cheney & Co. stuff from his UN speech making the case for war, but, in the end, he did not have the gumption to fend off the hawks or sound the alarm loudly with the president. Rummy and Cheney moved the war plan along so quickly that by the time W. had to decide, it was easy for the regents to suggest it would be wimpish to turn back at that point. W., or "The Man," as Cheney liked to call him, certainly could not abide the "W"-word.

Wolfowitz of Arabia and his aides grabbed control of the occupation from the State Department, rejecting the diplomats' postwar plans even as they failed to prepare adequate ones of their own, and State sulked.

W. had gambled huge, risking his own legacy while undercutting his dad's. It was an intense and historic family drama, all the more remarkable because the father and son who hate being put "on the couch" were now involved in a Freudian tango that was rocking the world.

In an interview in May with *The Washington Times*, W. said he was determined not to repeat what he thinks were the two big mistakes of his father's one-term presidency: abandoning Iraq and not beating the Democrats. He vowed never to do what his father did— "cut and run early" from Iraq, saying: "Freedom will prevail, so long as the United States and allies don't give the people of Iraq mixed signals, so long as we don't cower in the face of suiciders, or do what many Iraqis still suspect might happen, and that is cut and run early, like what happened in '91." Of course, some would say that cutting and running is exactly what the Bush team did, first in Afghanistan to hurry on to Iraq. And again when Chalabi led America into what General Anthony Zinni in 2001 predicted would be a "Bay of Goats" in Iraq, and the administration wanted to hurry out before W.'s reelection campaign began.

The president's chief of staff, Andy Card, who was deputy chief of staff in the Bush I White House, said the difference in the two presidents was Texas, implying the second Bush was the real Texas, as in, tougher. W., he said, "came from West Texas. And West Texas was his home for a lot longer than it was for the former president. He was the governor of Texas. He wasn't the first envoy to China or the UN ambassador or the CIA director. His training was dealing with problems on the streets of Laredo or Dallas or Houston or Midland or Austin. This president came with a kind of street smarts and recognition of the importance of the resolve of America."

Even for a president who favors Western bumper sticker talk, the "cut and run early" crack directed toward his own father seemed so harsh, it made you wince and wonder: Is this what happens when international strategy is reduced to a psychodrama of family competition?

W. avenged his dad, replaced his dad, made his dad proud and rebelled against his dad, all with the same war.

I have covered other feverish bouts where Washington was overtaken by the convoluted psychologies of people in power: the Iran-contra hearings, the Clarence Thomas–Anita Hill sexual harassment hearings, the Clinton impeachment hearings, the 2000 election stalemate (the heist before the heist). But this is the most astonishing and dangerous subordination of American history to particular psyches I've seen. It is bad enough that two presidents have been trapped in Bushworld, the perverse theme park created by W.'s posse. But now all of America, and most of the planet, find themselves trapped in Bushworld with them.

Adventures in an
Alternate Reality

■

I t's their reality. We just live and die in it.

In Bushworld, our troops go to war and get killed, but you never see the bodies coming home.

In Bushworld, flag-draped remains of the fallen are important to revere and show the nation, but only in political ads hawking the president's leadership against terror.

In Bushworld, we can create an exciting Iraqi democracy as long as it doesn't control its own military, pass any laws or have any power.

In Bushworld, we can win over Falluja by bulldozing it.

In Bushworld, it was worth going to war so Iraqis can express their feelings ("Down With America!") without having their tongues cut out, although we cannot yet allow them to express intemperate feelings in newspapers ("Down With America!") without shutting them down.

In Bushworld, it's fine to take $700 million that Congress provided for the war in Afghanistan and 9/11 recovery and divert it to the war in Iraq that you're insisting you're not planning.

In Bushworld, you don't consult your father, the expert in being president during a war with Iraq, but you do talk to your Higher Father, who can't talk back to warn you to get an exit strategy or chide you for using Him for political purposes.

In Bushworld, it's O.K. to run for reelection as the avenger of 9/11, even as you make secret deals with the Arab kingdom where most of the 9/11 hijackers came from.

In Bushworld, you get to strut around like a tough military guy and paint your rival as a chicken hawk, even though he's the one who won medals in combat and was praised by his superior officers for fulfilling all his obligations.

In Bushworld, it makes sense to press for transparency in Mr. and Mrs. Rival while cultivating your own opacity.

In Bushworld, you can reign as the antiterror president even after hearing an intelligence report about Al Qaeda's plans to attack America and then stepping outside to clear brush.

In Bushworld, those who dissemble about the troops and money it will take to get Iraq on its feet are patriots, while those who are honest are patronizingly marginalized.

In Bushworld, they struggle to keep church and state separate in Iraq, even as they increasingly merge the two in America.

In Bushworld, you can claim to be the environmental president on Earth Day while being the industry president every other day.

In Bushworld, you brag about how well Afghanistan is going, even though soldiers like Pat Tillman are still dying and the Taliban are running freely around the border areas, hiding Osama and delaying elections.

In Bushworld, imperfect intelligence is good enough to knock over Iraq. But even better evidence that North Korea is building the weapons that Saddam could only dream about is hidden away.

In Bushworld, the CIA says it can't find out whether there are WMD in Iraq unless we invade on the grounds that there are WMD.

In Bushworld, there's no irony that so many who did so much to avoid the Vietnam draft have now strained the military so much that lawmakers are talking about bringing back the draft.

In Bushworld, we're making progress in the war on terror by fighting a war that creates terrorists.

In Bushworld, you don't need to bother asking your vice president and top Defense Department officials whether you should go to war in Iraq, because they've already maneuvered you into going to war.

In Bushworld, it's perfectly natural for the president and vice president to appear before the 9/11 commission like the Olsen twins.

In Bushworld, you expound on remaking the Middle East and spreading pro-American sentiments even as you expand anti-American sentiments by ineptly occupying Iraq and unstintingly backing Ariel Sharon on West Bank settlements.

In Bushworld, we went to war to give Iraq a democratic process, yet we disdain the democratic process that causes allies to pull out troops.

In Bushworld, you pride yourself on the fact that your administration does not leak to the press, while you flood the best-known journalist in Washington with inside information.

In Bushworld, you list Bob Woodward's *Plan of Attack* as recommended reading on your campaign Web site, even though it makes you seem divorced from reality. That is, unless you live in Bushworld.

■

The
Old King
Is Deposed

■

In Which the Black Sheep

Usurps the Dutiful

Brother

■

November 5, 1992

Poppy Packs Up

◼

It was beginning to sink in, very painfully, that he had been fired and now he was expected to go back to Washington and take all his stuff out of the Oval Office, the worn Yale baseball mitt, the drawers full of tennis balls, the family pictures, the black and white horseshoes, his black Swiss Army knife with "President Bush" engraved in silver.

As George Bush got ready to leave Houston yesterday morning and fly back to the capital, he took a call from one of the few senior administration officials who had remained loyal to the end. Could he have been better served by the people in charge of his campaign? the official asked, in an account of the conversation.

Frustration and Anger

"Don't get me started on that," the president snapped, his voice raw with anger, frustration and blame.

On his flight back to Washington from Indianapolis, Vice President Dan Quayle was openly critical of the campaign management, telling reporters that their defeat was less a result of the depressed economy than of the failure of the campaign to articulate its own domestic agenda. They never had a message, he said scathingly, because "that takes a strategy."

A Republican electoral debacle is not a pretty thing. The finger-pointing and back-stabbing that had consumed the White House and the party for months got even worse yesterday, with everyone blaming everyone else for "the worst campaign ever seen," in the words of Ed Rollins, the Republican strategist who presided over Ronald Reagan's 1984 landslide, and defected this year to briefly help run Ross Perot's campaign.

End of Cold War

Trapped in an atmosphere described by one White House official as "a little surreal," Republicans offered dozens of reasons for the humiliating rejection of the man who had been wildly popular only a year and a half ago, reasons stretching back to the beginning of the Bush administration and going right up to the last weekend of the campaign.

"Look, we ran out of steam in the second half of the second Reagan administration," said William J. Bennett, a former official of the Reagan and Bush administrations. "We've been in office for 12 years. We got tired. We forgot why we came."

And in a poignant echo of the Democratic message that the sixty-eight-year-old president's time had passed, he added: "It's generational. George Bush genuinely believed that the major job he had was to win the peace and end the cold war."

While there were acres of criticism about the dispirited leadership of James A. Baker III, the maladroit management of Robert M. Teeter and Frederic V. Malek, the politically disastrous economic advice of Richard G. Darman and Nicholas F. Brady, there was also a sense that George Bush was responsible for his own failure in the end, because he was unable to read or give voice to the public's mood and imbue his presidency with passion, poetry and a plan.

"It's him," Mr. Rollins said of Mr. Bush. "He's a guy who thought he was a great politician because he had been the national party chairman and because he knew the name of every national committeeman and state party chairman. But he never understood what was going on in the country. Ronald Reagan was never a state party chairman and he didn't know the names of any committeemen, but he always knew where the country was."

Alarms Sound But Go Unheeded

Although his manner was modest, Mr. Bush is a politician, with a politician's ego, and he grew complacent, freezing out old friends and advisers who long ago tried to sound the alarm, and surrounding himself with politically tone-deaf economic advisers who were reviled by the conservatives who helped elect the president.

"As down home as he and Barbara were," an old friend of Mr. Bush said, "after a while they got used to the idea that they were in the White House and that's the way it ought to be."

It was a measure of Mr. Bush's alienation that as late as Saturday, Mr. Teeter was telling reporters on the president's final campaign train trip through Wisconsin that they were still working on consolidating the Republicans' base. And it was not until Saturday morning that Mr. Bush began to realize that he might have underestimated Bill Clinton, when the president saw that he had dropped 10 points after Thursday night's internal tracking polls showed the election in a dead heat at 39 to 39, and many of the respondents on Friday night had mentioned the day's news reports suggesting there was more to his role in the Iran-contra scandal than he had admitted.

"Our numbers just went in the tank after that," said a senior campaign adviser, who believed the Iran-contra report was the most damaging thing that happened in the stretch, along with the bite that Ross Perot took out of Mr. Bush's support in Louisiana, Ohio, Michigan and New Jersey.

There were sharp paradoxes here. George Bush had made a point of distinguishing himself from the Reagan style as soon as he was elected, implying that his predecessor was too packaged, too handled and too out of touch.

"Wake me, shake me," Mr. Bush said at his first postelection news conference, responding to a question that recalled the time that Mr. Reagan was not awakened to deal with the Soviet Union's downing of a South Korean airliner.

Missing Ingredient: A Lee Atwater

"The joke is he speaks of himself as a hands-on person when he's as hands-off as Reagan in his own way," said one Bush intimate outside the administration, who could talk for an hour straight at the top of his lungs about the way Mr. Bush had surrounded himself with second-rate talent and clones. "He was only comfortable with a damn white-bread crowd, a bunch of white male Protestant number-crunchers and bean-counters. He lacked a Lee Atwater."

He also lacked any women in his governing inner circle, and today top campaign officials were mourning that lack of diversity in the mix of advice the president received. "The place where we really got killed was in the suburbs, where Republican women left us," said one Bush campaign official, who believes it was a mistake, given the party's unyielding antiabortion stance, to veto the family leave bill.

There was a debate within the campaign in September about whether the president should reverse his position and sign the bill, which would have required employers to give leaves to workers for medical and family emergencies. Margaret Tutwiler, Mr. Baker's chief aide, argued in favor of a reversal and Mr. Darman, Boyden Gray and Mr. Quayle argued against the idea because it would give Mr. Bush an appearance of waffling. Mr. Baker was uncharacteristically undecided.

Everything about the Republican campaign seemed three beats behind, a strange phenomenon given the fact that Mr. Baker was considered "the gold standard for running Presidential campaigns in this era," as James Carville, the Clinton strategist, said yesterday.

Mr. Baker, who deeply resented the move and loathed the prospect of being a handler once more, waited until the last minute to move to the White House from the State Department. When many Republicans urged the president to fight back against the pounding he was getting from Democrats and Patrick J. Buchanan in the primaries, he insisted he would stick to his habit of starting the campaign as late as possible, after Labor Day.

Many of Baker's own aides agreed with Mr. Carville's assessment that the Republican convention was "idiotic," and many high-level Republicans privately pronounced themselves ashamed of the strident tone. Mary Matalin, the deputy campaign manager, went to the president to complain that the party was getting an image of being "intolerant" and "homophobic," but Mr. Bush seemed surprised that she could say that.

He had handed off responsibility for the tone of the convention to his former aide, Craig Fuller, who felt that a dramatic play was needed to consolidate the disenchanted conservative base. Mr. Baker refused to become engaged in the convention planning, only reviewing Mr. Bush's speech, because he took a brief vacation in Wyoming after his efforts in the Middle East.

After the convention, Mr. Baker was never able to focus Mr. Bush as tightly as he had in 1988. Even campaign officials who admired Mr. Baker said it was clear to everyone inside that he "had lost his edge, and was much more indecisive and not sure of his own judgment."

Mr. Baker, who had spent much of the last four years out of the country, was ambivalent about the campaign and relying on old instincts that were now out of sync, his campaign staffers said, adding that he was slow to pick up on the Perot-inspired revolution in media. Mr. Bush "waited way too long to go the Larry King route," one senior campaign official said.

Mr. Baker decided to hide in the White House, avoid the press that he had once courted so brilliantly. "He wasn't sharp, he wasn't boning up every day by dealing with press questions," said one campaign official.

With Mr. Baker working hard but in a slump, fearing he would end up on the cover of a magazine with James Carville, as though he had never been a statesman, Mr. Bush was left more to his own devices.

The president did not keep pounding away on the economic message he had presented in a speech in Detroit at the beginning of the fall campaign and, in the end, was reduced to an almost completely negative message bashing Clinton on trust and character.

"At the end of the day, Bush was always more comfortable attacking Clinton and tearing him down than he was articulating his own vision," said one campaign official. "He never convinced voters he was going to do something here at home. He never offered a compelling picture of what he would do or how he would do it."

A year ago, when the country was growing anxious about the economy and the conservatives were demanding that Mr. Bush adopt an aggressive economic agenda and a confrontational stance toward Congress, Mr. Bush decided to go by his own internal clock and the official Washington political calendar. At Mr. Darman's urging, he waited more than a month for the State of the Union address and repackaged his familiar, tepid agenda.

As long ago as September of 1991, when Mr. Bush's popularity was still topping 70 percent, Bill Kristol, Mr. Quayle's chief of staff, and others in the White House were alarmed at the polling numbers showing that more than 75 percent of the respondents thought the country was on "the wrong track."

Flurry of Motion But Lack of Agenda

Mr. Bush did not care. From the beginning of his administration, it was clear that he had no ideas or programs he wanted to enact, that his greatest pleasure came from simply being president. After his first hundred days in office, it was clear that he was practicing the politics of minimalism. Although Mr. Bush came to be a man in constant motion—always on the road, especially as the threat from Mr. Clinton grew—pundits were charging that the president had no agenda, no money, no strategy, no message, no ideology, no worldview. They also accused him of having no explanation of his mysterious role in the Iran-contra scandal.

Unlike Mr. Reagan, Mr. Bush had no fixed principles to fall back on, because his ideology was friendship. So he was only as good or as bad as the advisers he relied on, and many of his advisers in the last four years were remarkably inept and unpopular.

His advisers' plan from the beginning was to maintain the status quo on domestic affairs and only to do enough to have something to run on in 1992. The plan for foreign affairs was not much more ambitious before war in the Persian Gulf intervened, and Mr. Bush's advisers dubbed his initial policy toward the Soviet Union "status quo plus."

In the fall of 1990, after Congress had passed the Americans with Disabilities Act and amendments to the Clean Air Act, John H. Sununu, Mr. Bush's abrasive chief of staff, said that as far as the Bush administration was concerned, Congress could take the rest of the president's term off because "there's not a single piece of legislation that needs to be passed in the two years" remaining.

After the Los Angeles riots, when Mr. Bush did not seem to be able to react in any substantive way and had rejected White House officials' suggestions that he create a sort of civilian conservation corps that would help rebuild the inner cities, one administration official sighed, "He can't even fake it."

As he has often done in his career, Mr. Bush thought he could throw red meat to the conservatives and reassure the moderates, without either group's catching on. Just so, he would sometimes wear a red AIDS ribbon that would appear on his lapel for the politically correct photograph opportunity and then disappear when he spoke to more conservative audiences.

As he demonstrated again and again, with his tepid responses to the horror of the slaughters in Tiananmen Square and to the excitement of the historic moments when the Berlin Wall came down and Communism collapsed in the Soviet Union, Mr. Bush had no feel for capturing and projecting the fears, angers and delights of the American public.

Words meant little to him. The first act of his White House was to downgrade the speechwriters and take away their White House mess privileges. On the campaign, Mr. Baker no longer reviewed all of Mr. Bush's stump speeches and they were written by Steven Provost, a former public relations officer for Kentucky Fried Chicken who was reviled by Mr. Baker's aides as "the chicken salesman writing Bush's speeches."

When Mr. Bush broke the "Read My Lips" pledge about not raising taxes, and made the joke "Read My Hips," he truly believed that Americans did not expect politicians to keep such pledges.

"When he rescinded read my lips, he asked people to read his mind," said Peggy Noonan, who wrote the "Read My Lips" line into Mr. Bush's speech.

"He was a doomed President because he simply misunderstood,

as a pol with an ego, what had happened to him in 1988," she said. "He thought that the American people elected him resoundingly in a landslide because of his own charming, gallant, ambivalent self. They elected him because of what he said he was, a continuance of Reaganism."

November 30, 1993

Jeb and Junior:
Sibling Smashdown

■

At a campaign stop at Olin Ordnance, a weapons factory in St. Petersburg, Florida, Jeb Bush talked to the employees about how he would like to abolish the Florida Department of Education and impose tougher penalties on teenagers caught with guns.

Then the Republican candidate for governor asked if there were any questions.

"You're familiar with the Skull and Crossbones Society?" Jackie Miller, a secretary, asked. "I mean, Skull and Bones."

"Yeah, I've heard about it," he replied dryly, about the Yale secret society to which both his father and grandfather belonged.

"And you're familiar with the Trilateral Commission and the Council on Foreign Relations?" she asked.

"Yeah," the candidate said, in a weary voice.

"Well, can you tell the people here what your family membership in that is?" she demanded. "Isn't your aim to take control of the United States?"

In its own surreal way, the moment perfectly captured the difficulties faced by Jeb Bush, who is seeking the Republican nomination for governor in Florida, and his older brother, George, who is involved in the same pursuit in Texas, as they try to step out of the shadow of their famous father, George Bush.

The former president had been hit with the same wacky accusation about being "a One World tool of the Communist–Wall Street internationalist conspiracy" in his Texas Senate bid in 1964. In his autobiography, the senior Mr. Bush wryly noted that one John Birch Society pamphlet went so far as to suggest that Barbara Bush's father, the president of McCall publishing, was putting out a Communist manifesto called *Redbook Magazine.*

Jeb Bush told Ms. Miller politely that any implication that his family wanted to undermine America's sovereignty was insulting. "There are very few people who have served this country with the honor and distinction of my Dad," he said.

As he rode to another event afterward, the slender six-foot-four candidate observed, "As the son of a famous person, I carry the pluses and minuses of past wars."

Unlike the forty-year-old John Ellis Bush (known as "Jeb"), who faces some stiff primary competition, the forty-six-year-old George Walker Bush (known as "George W." or "Junior"), a managing partner in the Texas Rangers baseball team, seems to have an easy road to the Republican nomination. But once each is past the primaries, Governor Lawton Chiles of Florida is considered more vulnerable than his counterpart in Texas, Ann W. Richards.

Darts Already Flying

If the tart-tongued oldest Bush son wins, he will have the satisfaction of running against the tart-tongued woman who mocked his father at the 1988 Democratic National Convention as a preppy with a silver foot in his mouth.

Ms. Richards has already been diminishing her potential rival by referring to him as "Shrub," as in a small bush, and Junior. He is not technically a junior because he has only three of his father's four names. As Ms. Richards dryly observed to advisers, "He's missing his Herbert."

In Texas, where they like a little barbed wire in their political rassles, everyone is looking forward to 1994. "This is going to be a fun year, that's all," said State Senator David Sibley, who introduced George W. Bush at a Waco rally.

The older brother's advisers predict that Bill Clinton, who took the White House with the support of Ms. Richards, will be an albatross for the governor. George W. denies there is any motivation of avenging the family name. "I bear no ill will personally toward the current Governor," he says, but he adds that there is more to running the state than "funny sound bites."

"I'm a proud child," he said at a rally in College Station, the home of his father's presidential library, at Texas A&M University. "Being George Bush's son—they say, is it a plus or a negative? It's a huge plus as far as I'm concerned, and by the time the campaign is over, people are going to know that, in this George Bush, they've got someone to be the governor who knows what it means to fight for values."

Benefits in Curiosity

Although the Bushes also allude to the minuses of being related to a president who was decisively rejected by the public last year, many strategists consider their name their main selling points. It provides instant recognition and access to political and fund-raising networks, and allows them to finesse the fact that neither has held elective office. George lost a bid for Congress in 1978.

When a recent Texas poll showed that George W. Bush was within eight percentage points of Ms. Richards, the governor's supporters suggested that this was probably because many respondents mistook the son for the father.

Jeb Bush acknowledges that his "semi-celebrity" status helps. "It almost embarrasses me to say it, because I don't think I'm a celebrity by any stretch of the imagination, but I think I do get bigger crowds," he said. "There's more curiosity."

The younger brother said he drew his lessons in the '92 race from the Democrats. "My father served with distinction in a different time," he said. "But it's 1993, and the country has changed dramatically. The way the Clinton campaign used alternative means of communication—it was about breaking the mold of how you campaign."

Imbued with the Bush creed of competition, the two brothers have been eager to run for years. As Jeb has noted, "We were taught never to sit on the sidelines."

When George W. Bush considered running for governor in 1990, his mother urged him against it while his father was still in the White House. And Jeb Bush likes to tell the story about how, when he was head of the Dade County Republican Party in 1986, he called his father to discuss a possible run for Congress.

The father rattled off points to consider: Would it be too much of a sacrifice for his wife and three children? Could he afford to keep two houses in Miami and Washington? Jeb decided to wait.

Drawbacks in a Double Race

The novelty of two Bushes running for governor has spurred commentary about "Rockefeller-style dynasties," and memories of other presidential offspring who tried the political route successfully (John Quincy Adams and Robert Taft) and unsuccessfully (Robert Todd Lincoln and Maureen Reagan).

Some strategists say it will be harder for Jeb Bush, who announced first and who has more political experience, including a stint as Florida secretary of commerce, now that his brother has entered the race.

"It hurts because it makes it seem more like a political grab by Tweedledee and Tweedledum, a matter of family obligation, rather than that they really want to do something for the people," said Ray Strother, a Democratic consultant.

Jeb Bush worries that, with George running, too, "it turns it into a *People* magazine story," but shrugs that he has "no control" over his brother.

Jeb's advisers said privately that he was annoyed at the way some of his campaign lines had been co-opted by George.

After Jeb Bush said, "I am running for governor not because I am George and Barbara Bush's son; I am running because I am George P. and Noelle and Jeb's father," George W. began saying: "I am not running for governor because I am George Bush's son. I am running because I am Jenna and Barbara's father."

Karl Rove, an Austin consultant working for George, laughingly acknowledges: "George heard Jeb use the line and thought it was so good, he stole it. He admits it."

Unlike the Kennedy clan, which has offered the same brand of liberal Democratic politics through several generations, the Bushes span the trajectory of Republican politics. Grandfather Prescott Bush, a Connecticut senator, was an Eisenhower Republican. George Bush started as a hybrid of moderate Republicanism and the more conservative politics of his adopted state, and then leaped to the right as Ronald Reagan's vice president.

The sons do not display their father's flexibility, sticking instead to the strict conservative line, which they attribute to their years in Texas. Like their father, they are fervent believers in a market economy. They oppose abortion, and they believe in strengthening local control over education and in boot camps for juvenile offenders.

As for adult sexual offenders, George W. Bush says, "I believe most are beyond rehabilitation. I wish they'd put them away and make them stay there."

It is odd to watch the brothers on the trail, reflecting bits and pieces of their parents. Unlike their father, they used subjects and verbs in their sentences.

George W. Bush is introduced as "a Yale graduate, a fighter pilot, a man who worked in the oil business in Midland." (His duty as a fighter pilot was in the National Guard.) Like Dad before him, he boasts that he "knows what it means to meet a payroll." But when the Texas-reared George W. talks with a twang about "fixin' guvment" and "eatin' barbecue," it does not seem the stretch it did for his Greenwich-bred father.

Jeb Bush attended the University of Texas, not Yale, but, like his father, he graduated in two and a half years and with a Phi Beta

Kappa key, too. In an act that was a surprise to his patrician family, Jeb told his parents in 1974 he was marrying a Mexican named Columba Garnica whom he had met as an Andover student on a work-study program in Mexico. In addition, he converted from his family's Episcopalianism to Roman Catholicism. The couple settled happily in Miami, where Jeb became a partner in a commercial real estate business.

He is the image of his mother, especially when he smiles, but in political temperament, he is more like his father. (While George W. looks like his father, Barbara Bush has said the oldest boy gets his acerbic streak from her.)

Although there are Bushian flashes of impatience, Jeb Bush also has his father's congeniality and desire to charm. Asked about a bunch of thank-you notes he had been writing on monogrammed stationery, he grinned and said, "It's genetic, I guess."

For his part, George W. is not working hard to curb his spiteful side. He is still scorning the national political press that he claims treated his father unfairly, refusing to give a plane seat or an interview to a Washington-based reporter during a five-day opening campaign swing.

There are occasional flashes of cockiness and temper. At a rally in Waco, Jack Golden, a college student wearing a "Bush for Governor" sticker, tried to talk to the candidate, after he had finished a press conference, about prison sentences for drug users.

"You don't need to hold a press conference," Mr. Bush snapped at the student. "I'm the guy who holds a press conference."

His father's former political advisers give George W. mixed grades for his role in the Bush campaigns. They said he was loyal and worked hard, and they gave him points for being the one to dismiss John H. Sununu, the autocratic chief of staff. But they fault him for advising the president to put his 1992 campaign in the hands of a phlegmatic troika: Robert M. Teeter, Frederic V. Malek and Robert A. Mosbacher.

But George W. does have a short, snappy campaign speech, while his more earnest brother tends to get a bit bogged down in Al Gore–style talk about "visioning," "prioritizing," "empowering" and "sharing a good exchange of ideas."

An End to Retirement?

As soon as they have had a chance to build up independent images, both men want their parents to campaign for them. Their father carried both Florida and Texas in the 1992 race, and the former first lady is popular in each state.

Although it might seem soon for George and Barbara Bush to plunge back into the political fray, Jeb Bush said, "I called my Dad up last January and told him I was doing it, and he said, 'Go for it.'"

Writing to a reporter, the former president described his bittersweet feelings about passing the political torch. "There is no way I can possibly describe the feeling of pride that I have in my boys," he said. "Last year was not pleasant for any of us; and now, knowing what lies ahead, they are both willing to try. I am very proud of them both."

Although Mrs. Bush has said she found it painful to see her family exposed to press dissection during the White House years, she is showing her trouper side. "You bet I am going to campaign," she said recently.

Asked if his mother had given him any advice, Jeb Bush smiled her smile and replied: "She just said, 'Be plainspoken and speak your mind.'"

Takin' Up for Daddy

■

The Bushes were supposed to be celebrating. But they were too busy vindicating.

The Yalie was too a Texan. George Bush did too make the right decision when he took his foot off Saddam's neck. Dan Quayle was not a mistake. George Bush should too have raised taxes. George Bush was too a better man than Bill Clinton.

Two-term presidents have the luxury of obsessing about their legacy. One-term presidents are left rationalizing their rejection.

That may be why Bush *fils* the Texas governor played cactus at the august tableau of the Bush presidential library at Texas A&M. Stepping up to the microphone with his mother and father, Bill and Hillary Clinton and all the other White House alumni decorously arranged behind him, George W. praised his father as "a man who entered the political arena and left with his integrity intact." Get it?

As President Clinton looked down intently at his speech, Governor Bush spit out an anathema against the man who had beat his fa-

ther. George Bush, his eldest son said, was a "war hero, loving husband . . . and a President who brought dignity and character and
honor to the White House."

He talked about the judgment of "objective historians." Subtext:
The Bushes still loathe Peter Jennings, Dan Rather and Ted Koppel.
(One of the governor's strategists drolly told me I was O.K., for a
Commie.)

The Aggie cadets in brown shirts sitting near me whooped at the
governor's brazenness.

The Clintonites grumbled that as George W. sneered at Mr. Clinton's ethics, Neil Bush, who barely survived his brush with the S and
L scandal, was in the front row, and that the Bushies, so scornful of
Clinton-Gore fund-raising escapades in the White House and on Air
Force One, had pressured the White House into giving one of their
rich friends, the Aga Khan, a ride back from the dedication to Washington on Air Force One.

George Stephanopoulos found George W.'s edgy speech not only
bad manners but bad politics. "Get over it," he said. "They keep believing they can exalt themselves by running down Clinton's character. But Clinton keeps winning."

George W. was serving notice on that stage that he would be the instrument of vindicating his father's loss to Bill Clinton, by whupping
Al Gore's Ellen DeGeneres–lovin', no-controlling-legal-authority-
excusin', tree-huggin' self. At the luncheon the governor hosted afterward, one Aggie big shot speculated about the land the university
could use for the George W. Bush Presidential Library, so that it
could be adjacent to his dad's.

Bush *père* must have feared they were on the brink of a horrify-
ing etiquette breach, because he made a point of saying in his
speech that Bill had beat him "fair and square."

George W. does not have the exquisite manners or clubby discretion of his father. He brags that he went to Sam Houston Elementary School in Midland, not Greenwich Day School, and he speaks with a twang that makes you believe this George Bush really does like beef jerky. Like his mother, he can bristle, and blow—and he never forgets a slight, much less a rout.

After his father's defeat, the hotheaded Junior transformed himself into an engaging, disciplined politician, a presidential contender. (He and rival Dan Quayle greeted each other warily at the dedication.)

"George W. is more like Reagan than like Bush," said a former Bush official who thinks George W. will be the next president. "He knows what he believes in."

George Senior, who hates reflection, self-aggrandizement and assessing blame, insists he will not write his presidential memoirs.

His ambivalence about attention was on poignant display at the dedication. He bit the inside of his cheek and squirmed and looked sheepish, at times almost scowling, at all the lavish praise from his predecessors. (Nancy Reagan, who never invited the Bushes to dinner at the White House residence in eight years, couldn't resist a bit of condescension, calling Mr. Bush Ronald Reagan's "other loyal partner." Barbara listened, all Greenwich granite.)

Since Mr. Bush will not sit still to write about "the big I," he must find other ways to make sure his administration gets credit for starting some of the economic and foreign policies that have contributed to peace and prosperity—not to mention a second term for Mr. Clinton.

Why write a memoir when you can run a son?

April 7, 1999

President Frat Boy?

■

Wˣe've all been exhausted by the faux culture wars of the
Clinton era.

Ever since Bill Clinton was elected, conservatives have been acting as though the Oval Office had been festooned with macramé
and bongs, as if there were some crazy free love, war-protesting, pig-
hating, Bobby Seale–supporting, Carlos Castaneda–reading, Bob
Dylan–grooving hippie running the country.

Ken Starr, Newt Gingrich, Bob Barr, Pat Buchanan and a flock of
other Republicans who look like FBI agents have all tried, without
success, to turn back the clock. But their notion of a big McGover-
nick revival was always hallucinatory. The day-trippers have all become day traders. Dylan is singing in Vegas.

The phony struggle between the black-and-white fifties and psychedelic sixties may be coming to an end. Bill and Hillary may be
the last of the hippie-yuppies.

As I scan the Republican horizon for 2000, all I see are frat boys—

jocks and reformed party animals such as George W. Bush, Dan Quayle and John McCain, plus Elizabeth Dole, a Southern deb, who definitely looks like a throwback to the days of unassailable girdles and unmussable hairdos.

It's easier to picture Al Gore in a Canadian Mountie uniform than a fringed jacket. He's Dudley Do-Right, with a wholesome blond wife named Tipper who hates dirty rock lyrics and an all-American brood right out of a *Pleasantville* Formica kitchen, smiling serenely behind a stack of golden pancakes. Tipper has already signaled that she will not be a libber like Hillary; she will spend her time mothering, not horning in on policy. "I spend a lot of time," she said, "on keeping the family together."

The leader of the frat pack is Mr. Bush, who made his debut in *The New York Times* in 1967 in a story about "frat-branding" at Delta Kappa Epsilon, the Yale fraternity of which he was once president.

Steve Weisman, a Yale student then stringing for *The New York Times* (who is now a member of the *Times*'s editorial board) reported on a *Yale Daily News* article accusing campus fraternities of carrying on "sadistic and obscene" initiation procedures.

"The charge that has caused the most controversy on the Yale campus," Mr. Weisman wrote, "is that Delta Kappa Epsilon applied a 'hot branding iron' to the small of the back of its 40 new members in ceremonies two weeks ago. A photograph showing a scab in the shape of the Greek letter delta, approximately a half inch wide, appeared with the article. A former president of Delta said that the branding is done with a hot coat hanger. But the former president, George Bush, a Yale senior, said that the resulting wound is 'only a cigarette burn.'" The fraternities were fined by the Yale Interfraternity Council.

Frat prankster George told Mr. Weisman that he was amazed that anyone was making a fuss about the branding, that at colleges in Texas they used cattle prods on pledges. There's something that doesn't compute about branding irons and Yale. If there did have to be branding, shouldn't it have been less *Animal House* and something more discreetly WASPy, like the logos for J. Press or Top-Siders?

Later, in a newspaper interview, W. explained away the incident, saying, "There's no scarring mark physically or mentally."

Interest in the Republican front-runner's younger, wilder years has been building and the pressure is on for him to provide details of just how wild he got. Asked by a reporter recently about whether he had ever used marijuana or cocaine, Mr. Bush replied: "I'm not going to talk about what I did as a child. It is irrelevant what I did 20 to 30 years ago."

Mr. Bush's spokeswoman, Karen Hughes, dismissed a report in the *Star* tabloid suggesting that there exists a photo of the young Mr. Bush nude and drunk and dancing on a bar. "Yeah," she said, "and green aliens have landed on the lawn of the governor's mansion."

At the thirtieth reunion of the Yale class of '68 last year, there was disappointment that Mr. Bush did not show up and excitement about his plans to run for president. But his buddies were quick to assure everyone, "George has really changed a lot since Yale."

Presumably, if frat branding becomes an issue in his campaign, Mr. Bush will be able to spin the incident by saying that it proves, even better than pork rinds, that he is a true Texan.

■

The Regents Enter

In Which the Old King

Encircles the Dauphin

with His Trusted

Counselors

■

Freudian Face-Off

■

A l Gore is the Tin Man: immobile, rusting, decent, badly in need of that oil can.

George W. Bush is the Scarecrow: charming, limber, cocky, fidgety, seeking to stuff his head with a few more weighty thoughts. (Dan Quayle and Gary Bauer are, of course, the Flying Monkeys.)

Al Gore is so feminized and diversified and ecologically correct, he's practically lactating.

George Bush is all swagger, with macho campaign accessories of custom-made ostrich-leather black cowboy boots emblazoned with "G.W.B." and a huge belt buckle with "Gov. George W. Bush," as well as baseball statistics, pork and beans and a Betty Crocker wife.

Now comes the "I am worthy, Daddy" Freudian face-off of dauphins named after famous fathers and shaped by strong mothers.

Al is the Good Son, the early achieving scion from Harvard and Tennessee who always thought he would be president. (So did his parents.) George is the Prodigal Son, the late-blooming scion from

Yale and Texas who never thought he would be president. (Neither did his parents.)

As the robotic, plodding Mr. Gore tries to loosen up, the loose, quicksilver Mr. Bush tries to stay robotically on message.

The subtext of the Bush campaign is: What Bill Clinton did with Monica stinks; I was raised right and you can count on me to behave with more dignity. The subtext of the Gore campaign is the same.

You don't often get to see a presidential candidate bloom right before your eyes. But as W. debuted in Iowa and New Hampshire, Republicans, Democrats and journalists realized that he might just pull it off, at the same time he realized it, at the same time his parents, who had long assumed it would be Jeb, realized it.

As late as Christmas, W. said, he was fifty-fifty about running. As late as last week, he was nervous. On Sunday, when we talked by the sparkling Atlantic on the back porch of the family home in Kennebunkport, W. wore an Astros T-shirt and a big grin.

"All I can tell you," he said, "is I was fairly anxious for the week leading up to this, but when I got up there in Cedar Rapids, it felt good. I think that's an interesting measurement.

"I'm telling you, people out there, they're looking for something—dignity, integrity, optimism, big themes. I know what I believe in. I believe the big issues are going to be China and Russia. There will be moments when situations, incidents will flare up. It's important for the President to think globally. But in the long run, security in the world is going to be how do we deal with China and how do we deal with Russia. People think the Russian situation, or used to think, Russia was not an issue. It's a huge issue. But if the East Timorians decide to revolt, I'm sure I'll have a statement."

The statement, one hopes, will call them the East Timorese.

"I think what's important for you to know is that I feel I know what to do," he continued. "I really do. I may not be able to tell you exactly the nuance of the East Timorian situation but I'll ask Condi Rice or I'll ask Paul Wolfowitz or I'll ask Dick Cheney. I'll ask the people who've had experience.

"I'm smart enough to know what I don't know and I have good judgment about who will either be telling me the truth or has got some agenda that is not a right agenda. And I'm tough enough to tell somebody to kiss off if they're trying to put one over on me or on the country."

In a few short years, the Prodigal Son has become a popular politician, deft at working a room and skilled at domestic politics. But all those years that his father was so deeply engaged in world affairs, W. was still finding himself. So now he's starting from scratch, getting coached on foreign affairs.

W.'s father tried to reassure reporters on this matter by saying that his son has a good issues team. But you kind of want the president to be past the point of tutorials.

The Good Son, who was applying himself while his rival was finding himself, is not green. But he is beige, and so puckered in his pronouncements that his Hollywood pals want to coach him on how to talk to people.

One knows his subjects cold but can't heat up an audience. The other promises the global vision thing as soon as he gets his geography down.

It's going to be an interesting year, Toto.

June 23, 1999

Bushfellas

■

T here's a story out of Hollywood that Francis Ford Coppola is wooing Leonardo DiCaprio to play the young Sonny Corleone in *The Godfather, Part IV.*

It is hard to picture the girlish Leo as the supermacho gangster depicted with memorable volatility and virility by James Caan in the original *Godfather.* And after *Godfather III* soiled the legacy of the first two Oscar-winning films, is it really necessary to beat a dead horse's head?

Besides, the 2000 political race is already a sequel, with a cast of familiar names—Bush, Gore, Clinton, Dole—and its own version of the *Godfather* saga.

The Bush family has been dubbed the "WASP Corleones" by Howard Fineman of *Newsweek.* Like his mother and father, George W. lives by a simple code: Either you're with us or you're not.

Even some of W.'s friends have compared him to Sonny Corleone, the hotheaded, cocky heir to the family business. Despite being the oldest, Sonny, like W., was not the one his father thought had the temperament to follow in his footsteps.

You get the feeling with W., as with Sonny, that he's one insult away from blowing up and losing his chance at succession. It's there, bristling right beneath the surface, that unforgiving, unforgetting, sharp-tongued nature he inherited from his mother.

With Sonny, it was his brother-in-law Carlo who beat up his sister, Connie, and provoked him into falling into the trap at the tollbooth.

With W., it might be one too many questions from the huge press pack trailing him about ethanol, gun control or his youthful libertinism.

It is entertaining to imagine the former President Bush as a preppy Don Corleone, sitting up at Kennebunkport overseeing the family councils, with Jeb as Michael, Neil as Fredo and Doro as Connie. Don Georgio would receive political supplicants, dispense favors and ask for services from the vast group of politicos and policy hands under Bush family protection.

Instead of cannoli, there are tuna sandwiches on white bread with Tabasco sauce. Instead of red wine and Strega, there are martinis. Instead of hugging each other, they give Skull and Bones secret handshakes. Instead of the crooner Johnny "I Want a Horse's Head in That Studio Executive's Bed" Fontane, there is Lee "I'm Proud to Be an American" Greenwood. Instead of a cement-shoe thing, it's a white-shoe thing.

The WASPy Godfather is looking for a splash of revenge by taking the White House back from the rival family now occupying the sacred turf. The Bushes feel about the Clintons the way Don Corleone felt about Don Tattaglia, who insisted on bringing darker elements into the business.

You can imagine Don Georgio in a darkened room—with Brent

Scowcroft as consigliere and Bar as Luca Brasi—doing his own Bushspeak version of Mafiaspeak: "Message: The family cares. This race is about the honor thing. We shall have our justice. An eye for an eye. They're out to get my boy. They're out to get me. Before we're finished, our enemies will summer with the fishes. They won't be able to keep their snorkels above the water level. The bluefish rots from the head down.

"We'll try to persuade Forbes and McCain and Quayle to get out of the race. We'll make them an offer they can't refuse. Forbes will wake up screaming in the night when he finds bloodied flat-tax plans under his silk sheets. Dan Quayle will perish in a hailstorm of potatoes. We can kick McCain right into the end zone by letting the word out to the other families that he's really serious about this campaign finance reform nonsense. It's bad for everybody's business.

"Let us be frank. If W. blows up, we've always got Jeb waiting in the wings. I always thought he would be the one to take over the family business anyway. But we've got to keep an eye on Jeb's wife. Why did Columba embarrass the family by trying to save a few hundred dollars in duties on $19,000 in clothing and jewelry she got in Paris? If she had come to me, my purse would have been hers. What have I ever done to make her treat me so disrespectfully?"

Don Georgio noted that the restless W. was not paying attention to the family council. He was playing video golf and avoiding his foreign affairs coaches. If he refused to be instructed, Junior could never become the Don.

September 15, 1999

Trust But Verify

■

After W. dropped his handkerchief in June, he sat on the porch by the ocean in Kennebunkport. I asked him if it was scary to run for president, when he knew so little about foreign affairs.

"There will be moments when situations, incidents will flare up," he replied. "It's important for the President to think globally." He said the crucial thing was how a chief executive dealt with Russia and China, and whether he knew which foreign-policy advisers to trust and which to "kiss off," as he put it.

"But," he added, picking a regional hot spot out of a hat, "if the East Timorians decide to revolt, I'm sure I'll have a statement."

He talked about the murderous state of the Indonesian territory with that W. touch of flipness and swagger we have come to know. He was so unfamiliar with the tensions there that he called the citizens East Timorians rather than East Timorese. His implicit point was that there was still plenty of time for lessons from his foreign-policy tutors, Poppy's crowd—George Shultz, Condoleezza Rice and Dick Cheney.

But we're in a fast, mercurial universe. One minute we're scarcely paying attention to some roiling conflict on the other side of the world, and the next we're debating whether to send American troops over there, wherever there is, and whatever it is they're killing each other about.

Less than three months after talking about that Timor statement, the Texas governor had to actually put it out. Or more likely, his tutors did.

W. sensed the irony of this. After visiting a Bedford, New Hampshire, elementary school last week—where he drolly told the kids, "Some people say that I proved that if you get a C average, you can end up being successful in life"—he answered reporters' questions about his position on East Timor. Before and after he spoke the words "East Timorese," he paused pregnantly.

Then the candidate who had recently learned the correct term himself asked the press, with a sly smile, "Everybody knew that?"

It's a weird reversal of his father's '92 campaign. Bush Senior fumbled because he seemed too obsessed with foreign policy at a time when the economy was tanking. "In my life," W. told me dryly that day in Maine, "I never tried to rush the natural progression of growing up."

And that is the issue that gnaws. Has he grown up? Can we trust him? He wants us to believe that his gut instincts and moral framework can carry him over the lacunae in his knowledge of geopolitics. He wants us to believe that his transformation from rowdy late bloomer to mature statesman is complete and nonreversible.

"A lot of people around the world would find it rather frightening to envision a President of the United States, at the moment of probably America's greatest power in history, who seems completely uninformed on the state of the world," says Alan Brinkley, a history professor at Columbia University. "It's one thing to rely on the advice of aides because you have respect for their judgment. It's another to do it because you don't know enough to distinguish good advice from bad advice."

But Michael Beschloss, another historian, says that, post–cold war, "we have a lot of local and regional threats that are probably indecipherable even to a Presidential candidate who has had a lot of history in foreign policy. So we might be better with a President who is a quick study, who chooses good people, and who knows how to use them."

He notes that Ronald Reagan had no foreign-affairs experience when he was elected, yet he had a lot to do with ending the cold war. (Although he did know what he thought of pinkos.)

And, Mr. Beschloss says, we might have avoided Vietnam if Lyndon Johnson had been as secure on foreign policy as he was on domestic policy. He might not have been so easily swayed by misguided Kennedy holdovers like Robert McNamara.

Bill Clinton did a lot of reading about the history of the Balkan conflict. But he still miscalculated the determination of Slobodan Milosevic when he developed the plan to bomb Serbia. And even if we did not worry about Mr. Clinton's grasp of the issues, we had to worry about whether there was any post-Monica "Wag the Dog" syndrome involved in his bombing decisions about Iraq and Sudan.

W.'s father greatly admired Henry Stimson, the diplomat and soldier, whose credo was: "The only way to make a man trustworthy is to trust him."

That's true—occasionally.

Here Comes the Son

■

If Al Gore is stiff because his father always expected him to be president, perhaps W. is loose because his father never expected him to be president.

In the years his dad ran the country, W. was never considered a contender, or even a consigliere. He came in occasionally, playing the bouncer, strutting his family ties, barking at reporters and conducting loyalty tests for Poppy. He was, as Richard Ben Cramer wrote, "the Roman candle of the family."

His mother was afraid to sit him next to the queen of England at a White House dinner. The only big thing he did was deliver the news to the arrogant chief of staff, John Sununu, that he was through.

The Bushes assumed Jeb would follow in his father's Top-Siders (the ones with the flag of Texas painted on them). Everybody deemed Junior too much like his blunt and prickly mom to be a good pol.

So how did the flower bloom from the cactus?

"You're so much more mature now," I remarked to the Texas governor.

"So are you," he replied saucily.

In an interview last Friday, he recalled that his temperament had been questioned when he ran against Ann Richards. "There was a lot in the '94 spin about losing my temper," he said. "I think people remembered in '92 how fierce a defender I was of George Bush. I told some people that I didn't like what they wrote about him. I plead guilty for defending his honor. I thought that was my role, to go to Washington and be a loyalty enforcer within the ranks but also somebody who just defended his dad.

"Sometimes I maybe stepped over the line in terms of civility," he continued. "People shouldn't have taken that personally. And I evidently developed a reputation as somebody who was quick with the quip. Maybe the Barbara Bush in me was coming out. But there is a difference between being the loyal defender of one's dad and being a person who has a responsibility to lead."

I asked him how much of his astonishing poll numbers and campaign windfall could be attributed to his father. Are people just melding the two Bushes? Do a lot of voters have buyer's remorse about Bill Clinton, wanting to support the son to make up for ousting the father?

"It's hard for me to tell," says the son who would clearly like to avenge his father's loss. "Sure, I think a lot of people respect Dad, and '92 was a moment in time, and then later people sat back and reflected and realized what a good fella he is. But, man, I don't know. I hope people are making their minds up based upon what I'm saying and what the other candidates are saying."

W. has no problem with "the big I," as his father used to call the dread personal pronoun. Former President Bush was Phi Beta Kappa at Yale, but he followed his mother's advice not to brag, and usually skipped straight to the verb.

"That's the difference between a Phi Beta Kappa and a gentleman's C," W. jokes self-deprecatingly about his own comfort with the "I" word.

He says he would rather be unfavorably compared with his father than have his father unfavorably compared with him. "There's gonna be bad comparisons, and it does hurt. Because one of the great true things about the Bush family is that love and loyalty for our dad and mom.

"It's much easier this time around for me than in the '92 campaign. And I've realized, it's harder to see someone you love hurt, for people to say ugly things about someone you care about, than it is when somebody says something ugly about yourself.

"When they say 'His Dad was a sound thinker, he may not be,' that doesn't bother me in the least. It's the other way around that bothers me. He's a good man, George Bush. He's a really, really good guy."

W., in his upcoming memoir, *A Charge to Keep*, and his father, in a new book of letters, both print a letter from Poppy to George and Jeb in August 1998. It reads in part:

"Do not worry when you see the stories that compare you favorably to a Dad for whom English was a second language and for whom the word destiny meant nothing. . . . At some point both of you may want to say, 'Well, I don't agree with my Dad on that point' or 'Frankly I think Dad was wrong on that.' Do it. Chart your own course, not just on the issues but on defining yourself. . . . Nothing can ever be written that will drive a wedge between us—nothing at all. . . . So read my lips, no more worrying . . . your proud and devoted, Dad."

Name That General!

■

T here's a wonderful old Calvin Trillin essay about how he and his wife, Alice, would give each other global hot spots for Christmas.

If Calvin unwrapped a map of Iran, with the message "Leave It to Me," he was free not to keep up with news on Iran, or figure how to pronounce the names of Iranian dictators and generals. Alice would read everything and inform her husband only if Iran was about to start a Worldwide Nuclear Conflagration.

A global hot spot, the writer observed, was like "some dreadful old uncle who is always alarming the family with emergencies that are invariably described as beyond solution."

I want the same deal with the president. If I'm not up to the daily strain of distinguishing between General Muzaffar Usmani and General Khwaja Ziauddin, the guy elected to be better be.

Once again, W. has given an interview on foreign affairs that seems willfully clueless. Although the coup in Pakistan had been front-page news for weeks, he drew a blank on the name of its leader, outrageously declaring: "The new Pakistani general, he's just been elected—not elected, this guy took over office. It appears this guy is going to bring stability to the country and I think that's good news for the subcontinent."

As W. painfully reached to retrieve the name of the Pakistani leader, General Pervez Musharraf, you could almost hear the music swelling from the Regis Philbin quiz show, *Who Wants to Be a Millionaire*. But unlike the stumped contestants on that show, Mr. Bush was not allowed to call a friend for help. ("Yo, Condi!")

"I can't name the general," he stammered on, before going generic with a final try: "General."

Mr. Bush has tried to blame "gotcha" journalism rather than his failure to do his homework. But the Boston TV reporter did not ask trick questions about obscure spots like Burkina Faso, or try to trip up W. on the difference between Iran and Irian. ("Yo, Condi!")

If W. had been reading the newspaper closely the last few weeks, he could have aced his quiz. India and Pakistan were central to the recent debate on the nuclear test ban treaty, and India's prime minister—whose name also escaped Mr. Bush—has been in office a year and a half. Mr. Bush was also unable to name the leader of Chechnya, long one of the diciest pieces of the crumbling Soviet empire. He correctly provided part of the name of the president of Taiwan, "Lee," but it sounded suspiciously like a lucky guess.

The encounter was reminiscent of that famous Roger Mudd interview with an utterly inarticulate Teddy Kennedy. Men who are running largely because of their last name sometimes trip over their entitlement.

The Texas governor had the cornered look of a man who has been winging it too long, and hiding behind his advisers' skirts too long.

He let himself be rolled on an interview he should have seen coming. The question has been hanging out there for months about whether Bush the Younger knows enough about the world to deal with all the loons, coups and wars that spring up like twisters across the post–cold war plains.

His intensive foreign affairs coaching (which must have included Global Hot Spots 101) supposedly began last winter, yet the gaffes keep coming. So it was natural to try to ascertain whether he was studying or slacking. Has his huge advantage in money and family made him so cocky he doesn't care about the gaps in his knowledge?

His interview smirk—that anti-intellectual bravado—was jarring. Has he grown so accustomed to getting things easily—Yale, the National Guard, lucrative business deals—that he expects family connections to carry him through here?

Former President Bush had a passion for foreign policy. "You couldn't get him to go to an education briefing with Lamar Alexander, but he'd spend three days with some two-bit dictator from Sri Lanka," recalled an official in the Bush White House.

But when the ex-president was accused of knowing heaps more about Berlin, Germany, than Berlin, New Hampshire, his press secretary, Marlin Fitzwater, began carrying around an index card with the price of eggs and milk and gas.

W. can try an index card with names of mutinous generals, or scrawl them on his shirt cuff. But he should remember that by the time his father got his index cards, it was already too late.

McCain Picks Up the Mo in Motown

■

It is a campaign straight out of Capra.

A decent guy takes on the System, and the brutes who run the System move in to destroy the upstart. They paint the populist hero as crazy or deceitful. After a bout of self-pity, when he hates the whole rotten show, he rallies with some sentimental hooey about American ideals and routs the ruling-class bullies.

"Why, your type's as old as history," John Doe tells his tormentors. "If you can't lay your dirty fingers on a decent idea and twist it and squeeze it and stuff it into your own pockets, you slap it down. Like dogs, if you can't eat something, you bury it!"

Of course, like John McCain, the Capra heroes battling Big Money could often get a little insufferable. They could be sanctimonious and overemotional and flaky. The idea of virtue triumphing over greed was always a celluloid dream. But it seems even more far-fetched now, in a society where greed is a virtue.

Mike Murphy, Mr. McCain's strategist, says he doesn't think the

Republican Establishment "is a bunch of guys in straw boaters on telephones yelling 'Get McCain!' It's more like 100 lobbyists in Washington scared that their contracts won't be renewed."

With the help of moderates and without the religious right smothering him, Mr. McCain won in Michigan, so he can continue to dog the son of the Establishment.

Mr. Bush's greatest appeal was to conservatives. Many others here were less impressed. "I've done a lot of research on Bush—the man's done nothing," said George Thomas, thirty, who works in computers, as he voted for Mr. McCain in Royal Oak.

What's remarkable about the Republican race is that the arcs of the two campaigns mirror the arcs of the candidates' life stories.

Mr. Bush started in New Hampshire as a slacker. As in his life, he relied on his name and powerful friends to keep him afloat in his campaign until he decided to apply himself late in the game.

"This is a process of steeling me to become your president," he told *Newsweek* on the eve of the South Carolina primary.

Usually, people get their steel before they run for president. Anyhow, Mr. Bush probably should have spelled it "steal." He purloined everything he could lay his hands on from the McCain campaign— the populist bus, the reformer message, the one-on-one town halls, even the design of the Web site.

Mr. McCain, who spent his life getting in trouble for his impulsiveness and thin skin, let his emotions get away from him in the last couple of weeks. If there was one thing that was obvious, it was that the Bush team, humiliated in New Hampshire, was going to be ruthless and vicious in that most conservative and wired state for the Bushes, South Carolina. It was clearly going to use all the tricks from the Atwater playbook—nasty push polls, racial wedge issues, let-a-third-party-do-the-dirty-work flyers and e-mails. The candidate would smile and call himself a uniter, not a divider, while his team madly divided.

But when it began to happen, Mr. McCain reacted viscerally rather than cerebrally. He was furious about Mr. Bush trotting out a discredited veteran to trash him for "forgetting" veterans; he was enraged that a Boy Scout got a push-polling call branding him "a liar"; and he overreached in a television commercial, comparing Mr. Bush to Bill Clinton, then pulled back too far, adopting an absurdly broad definition of negative advertising that tied his hands on pointing out unfair Bush tactics. He capped a bad week by using a self-defeating caustic tone in his South Carolina concession speech, and began intemperately railing about "jerks" and "idiots."

People said from the start that it was too easy to get under Mr. McCain's skin, and that his judgment was questionable at moments of maximum pressure. He also has a tendency to fall in love with an idea, harping so much on busting Washington's iron triangle that he never set out any other issues.

Not only did he not fight back strongly enough and quickly enough in South Carolina, but his Michigan campaign degenerated into a wish that voters would get huffy over Mr. Bush's brutal tactics. But Mr. McCain does have incredible tenacity, and he hung on until he got to an electorate more suited to him.

So far, we've learned that one candidate drifts and the other gets wound up. So now we know what we already knew.

A Babysitter for Junior

■

In Bushworld, it's always Day 41 of Desert Storm, that glorious day the president's approval ratings soared toward 91.

The head-scratching choice of Dick Cheney is explained by the fact that he was in the bunker during the family's finest hour. They would have preferred Colin Powell, who was also in the bunker during their finest hour. But they let Brent Scowcroft, who was also in the bunker during their finest hour, help seal the deal for Mr. Cheney.

It's impossible to work up even a solitary goose bump for a former staff member in the Ford White House. A prosperous, well-fed, balding, bland, male Republican Washington insider and former House leader who voted to the right of the NRA and Newt Gingrich.

In Congress, Mr. Cheney was way, way out there, always willing to pony up money to guerrillas in Nicaragua and Angola but not to poor women whose lives were endangered by their pregnancies.

When Trent Lott starts gushing about somebody, Katie bar the door.

The Texas governor who promised to be a "different kind of Republican," the candidate who used words like "inclusive" and "compassionate" and "heart," is now running with a guy who defended cop-killer bullets and plastic guns that could slip through airport metal detectors.

The million moms marching will love that.

The Bush convention in Philadelphia will be gauzy, trying to appeal to women, moderates and minorities, showcasing Elizabeth Dole, Condoleezza Rice (also in the bunker at the finest hour), John McCain, General Powell and Laura Bush. The opening theme is "Leave no child behind." It will be delicious to see how the Republicans deal with those Cheney votes against Head Start.

"Inclusive" loses a little punch when you are running with someone who in 1986 opposed a call to release Nelson Mandela after twenty-three years in prison, and often voted against the economic sanctions that helped crush apartheid.

The Cheney choice is about the past. But then, W.'s campaign has always been less about vision than vindication. The dauphin must reclaim the throne because the Bushes must restore the halcyon days of the ruling-class court that thrived before that dissolute commoner Bill Clinton usurped it.

The family yearns to go back to the "honorable" days, the golden era of Establishment reign—before the decision not to go into Baghdad began to fester, before Bill Clinton stole credit for the thrumming economy, before first ladies went all weird on us.

Mr. Cheney was picked because he is the anti-Quayle. George I was determined that George II not repeat his mistake, choosing someone young and callow. The ticket already had that covered.

Back in 1988 Mr. Cheney, then a House luminary, would have been a good choice for George I. For George II, he comes across as the babysitter.

Mr. Cheney has been minding Junior all year—first coaching him in foreign affairs, then helping him sort through his VP picks, and now stepping in to provide a steady hand on the tiller.

The past dictated the choice in this way as well: W., who had loafed through long years when he could have been prepping for the presidency, felt he needed some heaviness on the ticket.

The Bushes hate being "psychoanalyzed," as they call it. They don't like personal questions. And yet they make many crucial decisions based on personality.

The father chose Dan Quayle and the son chose Dick Cheney for the same reason: They wanted men who liked them, men with whom they had "a comfort level."

And while Mr. Cheney might have voted like Tom DeLay, he has a calm and avuncular air. He vetted the other candidates, but he himself was vetted by W. and Poppy, who, as usual, trusted their instincts.

I doubt either Bush would have felt comfortable running with a woman. Or with anyone who challenged their egos or made waves, like John McCain. They need a history of loyalty, and they have a preference for deference. Dick Cheney is one of their guys, in the Club. And they know best.

Before the Bushes mess up any more vice-presidential picks, for Jeb or George P., they might want to stop checking their gut and start checking the voting record.

A ticket with two rich white Texas oilmen who went to Yale, avoided Vietnam and act more moderate than they are? For the Bushes, that's a perfect fit.

August 2, 2000

New Century, Old Grudges

■

O.K. Now we're in business.

After an icky evening of Republican kissy-face and blaxploitation (*Affirmative Action, the Musical*), Poppy unleashed Chiang!

Unleashing Chiang, in the loopy Bush family patois used in golf and tennis, means giving the ball a good whack.

After a week of President Clinton taunting W., saying that the Republican candidate's message was merely "My daddy was president," Daddy lost it.

"And if he continues that, then I'm going to tell the nation what I think about him as a human being and a person," the former president threatened on NBC's *Today.*

Our summer of torpid politics suddenly came alive with the freaky spectacle of two presidents trash-talking. The race turns out to be what we thought it was all along: President Bush vs. President Clinton.

George Senior is determined to prove once and for all that Bill

Clinton is a tacky hick who defiled the presidency. Bill Clinton is determined to prove once and for all that George Senior is an irrelevant aristocrat who thinks the presidency is a family heirloom.

Two intensely competitive chief executives, who had been trying not to meddle too much in the campaigns of their protégés, bolting off the reservation in a bid for vindication.

George Senior is fighting for the second term he feels he was gypped out of by Bill Clinton. And Bill Clinton is fighting for the third term he needs to launder his legacy.

W. and Al are alternately bystanders and stand-ins in the big rematch.

It is as though the tape of the '92 election, on pause all these years, has started rolling again.

The presidential hissy fit is driven by class rage. Edith Wharton would have savored this drama of manners.

The Bushes have been privately steaming that Gore/Clinton have not abided by Marquis of Queensberry Rules, allowing the Republicans to enjoy their nomination party without any Democrats throwing a punch.

Bush *père* believes his manners toward his successor have been impeccable, and that he has been discreet out of loyalty to the office.

"Who's been more gracious and charitable to Bill Clinton, even during Lewinsky?" asked the former president's old friend Alan Simpson, the former Wyoming senator.

So the Bushes felt the gentlemanly rules of order were broken over the last week when the Democrats put out an ad attacking Dick Cheney's conservative record and two more attacking W. on health care and the environment, and when Bill Clinton repeatedly mocked W. as a coddled daddy's boy at fund-raisers.

"The country was in the ditch," Mr. Clinton said in Boston last

Friday, talking about '92, comparing the Bush White House to a ditzy *Wayne's World.*

Nobody gave Mr. Clinton, who never knew his own father and who had to stand up to an abusive, alcoholic stepfather, a solid gold key to success. And he clearly thinks Al Gore, another princeling raised to be president by a famous political father, is not up to the challenge of gutting the Bushes on the entitlement issue.

It has to be galling to Mr. Clinton that Americans don't seem inclined to reward his vice president for the purring economy. And he is surely fed up with the Republicans acting as if his two terms were merely *Bushus interruptus.*

The remarkable thing is that this class war has caused everyone to reverse roles. In '92, W. was the vindictive one who lashed out when his father was criticized. Now Dad has taken Junior's role. And while it is usually vice presidents who serve as hatchet men, now Bill Clinton does that for his vice president.

Even though Mr. Simpson says that the Bushes avoided publicly criticizing Mr. Clinton about Monica Lewinsky, that is in fact the subtext of W.'s campaign—restoring "honor and dignity" to the White House. Mr. Clinton thinks a rejection of Mr. Gore would be a ratification of the Bushes' contention that he sullied the White House. The president can also see that it is hard for Al Gore to attack, because even people who agree with Mr. Gore find him insufferable on the attack. W. and Mr. Gore will probably keep campaigning, but we all know it's not about them anymore. Maybe it never was.

September 13, 2000

Grilled Over Rats

■

I t's the year of the rat.

On CBS's *Survivor*, rats were a leitmotif. The contestants ate grilled rat while competing to see who was the biggest rat.

In our political reality drama, rats have also scurried center stage. The presidential race, which seems doomed to stay on a tatty, ratty low road, has fallen into another kerfuffle over a sneaky epithet.

Gore campaign aides went nuts when they figured out that a Republican ad lacing into the vice president on prescription drugs had one frame that flashed the word "RATS" in big white letters, as a Cubist fragment of the word "bueaucrats."

W. dismissed the charge, saying "conspiracy theories abound. . . ." Just as his father used to parrot the tactical talk of his handlers, W. spouted insider jargon. "This ad is coming out of rotation" anyway, he said.

He denied over and over that there was any subliminal intent.

Well, actually, he denied over and over that there was any "subliminable" intent.

The reporters pounced on that superfluous syllable, taking off after the Republican for not being able to pronounce the crime he was
accused of. Soon we had an abominable subliminable flapdoodle.

The hullabaloo, I think, is preposterous. One RATS, and Bush is a
SNAKE?

Experts tell me that animation and graphics are done by computer,
frame by frame. So if the word "RATS" appeared on the screen, even
for a thirtieth of a second, it could only happen if somebody told a
computer he wanted the word "RATS" to appear in a frame. Poppycock. When it comes to **Republicans**, reporters **are** just too fin**icky.**

Whiny and baby**i**sh Gore aides are **blowing it** out of proportion.

All those **Big** Feet at **Time** and other publications who keep saying that W. is too jejune to run for president have **goof**ed!

The **N**otion that W. is so **add**led by Al Gore that he has resorted
to being crypto**graphic** in going after h**is** critics is utterly **without**
merit. It was surely un**intent**ional.

A **GOP**her couldn't dig a bigger hole than Al Gore does when he
makes these **ad** hominem **attacks** with his supercilious sound **bites**
about how he's "never seen anything like" the RATS. Autumn
should be **big** picture **time.**

Why **is** everyone piling on poor Governor Bush, never than**king** him
for bringing a new tone to politics, always treating him as a **frat** boy?

To suggest **That man**iacal desperation drove those fine Bush professionals in Austin to **has**tily approve a brainwashing ad is a c**an**ard
out of control—be**go**ne, pundits!

This was just more evidence that the Gore camp is packed with
re**now**ned **slip**pery strategists who will get their come**upp**ance in
November.

Before Gore Officials continue this misguided **course** of railing against the **Republicans**, they should remember that most TV viewers are not **replay**ing the ad in slow motion, frame by frame, in some Paul-McCartney-is-dead moment. So why go **ball**istic at **that** one little **way**ward word fragment?

The truth is, it's **Bush** league that the Gore **team turns** to demeaning its rival **when it falls back** on snitching and peddling gaffes to reporters.

Remember that Al Gore may be leading now, but he is still struggling to claim any votes in the **South**, from the mountains of North **Carolina** to the beaches of Dade Country.

What about the real issues Americans care about, like your drug pr**I**ces and **your** pressing questions about school **staffi**ng? The Gore cabal should stop be**rat**ing the Bushies because, **boy**, do they look silly.

Wouldn't it be better to **Talk about** the merits of the Bush plan to secure **lower**-cost drugs for our aging **parents**?

Should a man like George W. **Bush** suffer such in**dignity** at the **hand**s of dis**honor**able Democrats and biased, liberal journalists? Hardly. **H**ands off, you vultures.

It's simply a Gore c**Al**umny. The Democrats should learn to stop tattling and play by the **rules.**

W., don't pay any heed to the media sharks circling, to the frenzy of bluefish. As your dad always liked to say before he cast his line, "Those bluefish are dead meat." I be**lie**ve there was no subliminal or subliminable message in your ad.

Remember, it's only **the** middle of September. It's not too late to re**cover** your lead. Chin **up**, Mr. Bush, your critics are just **stupid!**

West Wing Chaperone

■

The Bushies kept telling me that, eventually, I would feel the Cheney magic. They said it would tingle "like champagne," as one member of the clan put it.

In the debate on Thursday night, Big Time finally got to me—big-time. I was swept up in a vanilla gust of Cheney chic.

Let Al Gore sigh and roll his eyes and do his smarmy Eddie Haskell. ("With all due respect, Mrs. Cleaver, for a mom you're quite a babe.") Let W. snort and sniffle and get that look of thinly veiled terror when he hears a three-syllable name with too many consonants in it. Let Holy Joe Lieberman gush about his personal odyssey of ethnic acceptance. Bring me the bald, pasty head of Big Time Cheney.

In a race where every gesture is contrived, every event is stage managed, and all the phrases, comebacks and footwear are focus-grouped, Big Time never stoops to conquer.

It was fifty minutes into the vice-presidential debate before the

Republican even bothered to look at the camera and address the viewers at home, rather than Bernard Shaw.

It's curiously refreshing to see a candidate act so aloof, and even vaguely put out, as though the campaign were taking precious time away from his golden-years fishing.

The other guys are always cuddling, kissing, misting, sharing family stories and trying to Feel Deeply all the injustices of the world.

Big Time is an unrepentant old-school guy, an insider's insider who blanches at glad-handing and gauzy handling. He does Feel Deeply, but he Feels Deeply that it was wrong for the press to hound him into giving up his stock options. He Feels Deeply, as he showed when he tried to restrict the press during Desert Storm, that he much prefers the Second Amendment to the First.

He may be politically atavistic and autistic, but at least he's authentic.

It's bracing to see a candidate who doesn't even bother to pretend that he's having a good time reading to schoolchildren or letting babies drool on him or hearing sob stories from the downtrodden. He is here as a Bush family retainer, after all. He prefers to pander up.

He is a Republican who got rich buoyed by government connections and contracts, even though he protested in the debate that "the government had absolutely nothing to do" with his success. He shares with W. the rugged pretense that he is an utterly self-made man.

When Mr. Shaw told the two running mates that they should pretend to be black for a question on racial profiling, Holy Joe was happy to get jiggy with it. Big Time, however, had the honesty to look at Mr. Shaw as though he were whack.

"Well, Bernie," he began, "I, I'd like to answer your question to the best of my ability but I—I don't think I can understand fully what it would be like."

In the debate, it became clear that Mr. Cheney is not so much running for vice president as chief of staff, or Chaperone. He will be the smart disciplinarian who, with that phlegmatic baritone monotone, will tether the squirmy, squeaky W. He will keep an eye on the nuclear codes while Junior sits in the Oval, playing video golf.

Mr. Cheney provided the heft for the intellectually unburdened Gerald Ford. He can do it again for W.

He is preternaturally placid. The excitable Bushes, who hate being upstaged and who hate disloyalty, find that reassuring.

But they sell Big Time short. In the debate, he was so smooth that he inadvertently made W. look as if he were still in political diapers.

In Washington, you always have to be very suspicious of anyone who is not fairly panting with ambition, anyone who seems self-effacing.

If Dick Cheney were in a Tom Clancy–style thriller, he'd be the White House official who blends into the woodwork in the first act, only to quietly usurp the president in the second—the bespectacled puppet master who blackmails uncooperative congressmen, fakes authorizations for CIA covert operations and makes deals with cartels.

Think Gene Hackman as a conniving Cheney turning on Keanu Reeves as a hapless President W. (And, of course, Angela Lansbury, circa *The Manchurian Candidate*, as Lynne.)

What if Big Time's thin lips hide a crocodile's grin?

Be afraid, Bushes. Be very afraid.

War of the Chads

In Which the High Court Purloins the Throne for the Bush Dynasty

November 5, 2000

I Feel Pretty (The View from Inside Al Gore's Head)

■

I feel stunning
   And entrancing,
Feel like running and dancing for joy . . .

O.K., enough gloating. Behave, Albert. Just look in the mirror now and put on your serious I-only-care-about-the-issues face.

If I rub in a tad more of this mahogany-colored industrial mousse, the Spot will disappear under my Reagan pompadour.

Whew! Now that W. has slipped on a mud pie at the finish line, I can admit I was scared, just like all the other Democrats. Things were stickier than a barrel of Goo Goo Clusters.

It would be awful to blow it just because no one can stand the sight of me. Or to win the Electoral College but not the popular vote. Ouch!

How could I lose to a guy who promises to fix Social Security without knowing it's a federal program? He probably thought it was a dating service.

But my inner teleprompter tells me I've got a much better shot now. Goody-goody for the goody-goody!

Only forty-eight more hours and I am Martin Sheen. I can upgrade to Air Force One. Only seventy-six days, eight hours and fifteen minutes and I will never, ever have to lay eyes on that megalomaniac Bill Clinton again! *Ding-dong!*

I know I haven't been the best candidate. But you try running with Clinton Past while Clinton Present is hanging on for dear life, trying to polish Clinton Future. It's like climbing Mount Rainier with ankle weights and sandbags on your back.

I couldn't believe how everyone in my camp was doubting me, from the president (even though we tried to confine him to Black Entertainment Television and keep him off CNN) to my overpaid Washington hacks to all those Democrats who wanted me to brag on our economy and campaign with Bill, because people like him.

It seemed as if the only people who still believed in me were Tipper, Karenna and my pal Marty Peretz. Which was fortunate, since they were the only three I ever talked to.

Even Tipper was getting fed up with me kissing and hugging her a hundred times a day. She actually pushed me away at one point when I was going in for a big one. That hurt.

But no matter how dark things got, I reckoned that in the end, Boy Scout would trump Frat Boy, especially if somebody could find something better to pin on him than the Case of the Purloined Debate Prep Video.

For some reason, voters never get excited about me. That's why I had to hook up with Clinton in the first place. But now people have no other choice—unless they want President Adam Sandler.

No way will Americans go for toga state dinners and a leader who might steal the White House Christmas wreath as a hazing prank.

Once the Maine Democrats ratted out Bush on that embarrassing little tipsy-driving incident up in Kennebunkport (it was great that the news broke on conservative Fox!), everyone realized that W. had even less controlling legal authority than I did. Buddhists vs. Budweisers.

That's what W. gets for hanging out at the family estate, chugging beers with Australian tennis players, while I worked like a dog campaigning for my first congressional seat, so I could spend twelve hours a day grinding away on the House Subcommittee on Oversight and Investigations of the Resource Conservation and Recovery Act.

W. should never have run against me in the first place. The only rationale for his campaign was avenging his father's loss. And revenge is not a healthy reason to seek the highest office in the land. A president must not be filled with bile. A president must bring everyone together.

Where's my PalmPilot? I need to do a couple e-mails to kick off the Gore era starting Tuesday night.

Note to self: Clinton said I would be "the next best thing" to having him for another four years. He can next-best this: The new site for our radioactive dump is on the Arkansas River, next to the Clinton library.

Note to congressional liaison: Whenever we announce highway money for New York, give Chuck Schumer forty-eight hours' notice so he can get full credit (and Senator Hillary can get lost).

Note to Karenna: Anything those Maine Democrats in the wacky hats want from us—yea-a-a-ah!—give it to them.

Deadlock: Which Will It Be?

■

The president-elect is surrounded by manic-depressive aides who are pumped and then slumped, doing high fives one moment and singing the blues the next.

It is the biggest, most terrifying moment of his life. He is struggling to stay cool, and not sink under the pounding pressure and begin bawling or swatting the dog. As the world watches his capital, he tries to act as though he is the One. But inside, he rages at the thief trying to snatch the election, and is tormented by a dripping acid of what-ifs and what-nexts.

He can't believe that his fate hangs on slivers of punched paper and postmarks on overseas ballots.

He has been diligent about getting in his runs and weight training. And for the benefit of the press vultures, he has had jolly-looking double dates with his running mate and the wives.

The president-elect wants to seem statesmanlike. He would like to put the country's needs ahead of his own, not only because it's right, but because it's smart politics.

But he just can't. He has to win this puppy. Those lamebrained talking heads keep saying, "The loser will be the winner." But he knows that the loser will be the loser.

The winner gets to live in the White House and take his friends on Air Force One and run the world. The loser has to start begging for donations again, and kissing up to all those bozos in New Hampshire—day after day, year after year.

He frets whether the septuagenarian secretary of state protecting his interests down in Tallahassee is up to the job. But he's comforted in the knowledge that the oppo-research guys are digging up dirt, trying to figure out, if worst comes to worst, how to swing the electors his way.

It's great, after a grueling year on the road, to be back in his own bed. But it's not easy being cooped up with his jittery wife. She was never sure she wanted to be First Lady, but she doesn't want to be Loser Lady either.

Once in a while, he ventures out to the microphones to seize the upper hand. But it is beginning to dawn on him that Americans prefer him when he's out of sight and they don't have to listen to his annoying speech patterns.

To unwind, he fantasizes about how much fun it will be to kick Bill Clinton out of the White House. He's so happy he got more votes than that egomaniac. The president-elect relishes the thought of making the Oval Office dignified again.

But he reserves his true loathing for the smug phony who is trying to steal the election. The thief wants to count only the votes where he's ahead and he's willing to twist any law or argument or principle to serve his partisan purposes.

Americans believe in fairness, and they'll see right through that scam.

On the *Saturday Night Live* skits, the governor and the vice president have to share the Oval Office, yuking it up and acting like a cuddly Odd Couple. But the president-elect doesn't even want to be in the same room with that lowlife—much less share the West Wing.

That spoiled Southern preppy from the fancy Beltway family keeps saying that the president-elect is the one who has gotten ahead just on his inherited glory. It's so unfair. There's only one candidate who has worked his way up, paid his dues, taken his hits, learned his lessons, worked his heart out in this race.

The president-elect doesn't even believe his opponent really wants the job. Once the pretender stops embarrassing the country with his whining and admits defeat, he should move on to another line of work. He's just desperately trying to live up to his daddy's dreams—and impress that strong mother of his.

The president-elect knows he can kiss good-bye most of his campaign promises. The tax cut. Bold Social Security and Medicare reforms.

He is keeping close tabs on who's sticking by him and who's sticking in the knife. He knows that his top congressional allies are 1,000 percent behind him—as long as public opinion is behind him. But he also suspects that those allies secretly hope he'll concede so that they can make big off-year gains in the congressional elections and torment a weak president from the other party.

And that Katherine Harris. For as long as he lives, he will never forget how she brazenly tried to grab the election and declare the winner. Astonishing!

The president-elect is already thinking about how he can repay her.

Oyez! Oyez! Oy Vey!
This Is One Nutty Election!

■

T he old Don had helped the humiliated man in the black robe get justice. He had treated the judge's enemies as his own enemies.

He had caused those who tried to ruin the judge to weep bitter tears. He made sure the nominee under his protection got justice and became a justice.

"Someday, and that day may never come, I will call upon you to do me a service in return," the old Don, the head of the WASP Corleones, whispered to the younger man.

For Clarence Thomas, that day has arrived. Don Georgio of Kennebunkport needs a splash of service in connection with the hotheaded Sonny, who has gotten himself into his biggest scrape yet. Nearly a decade has passed, and now it's time for Clarence to repay his political godfather.

Imagine what might have secretly transpired between the two:

"Look how the Democrats massacred my boy with dimpled ballots and endless hand recounts," an emotional Don Georgio confides in Justice Thomas. "It's a low-tech lynching. I want you to use all your powers and all your skills. I don't want his mother to see him this way."

Just when you thought our electoral spectacle could not get more surreal, labyrinthine, incestuous and conspiratorial, we now have Jeb's legislature joining W.'s lawsuit before Daddy's old Supreme Court.

"It's just a family affair," laughed a Bush aide in Tallahassee.

If the Bush forces angrily discounted a decision of the Florida Supreme Court that went against them, because all the justices were appointed by Democratic governors, then why would the Gore forces trust a decision of the U.S. Supreme Court if it went against them, when seven of nine justices were appointed by Republican presidents, including two by W.'s dad?

The highest court in the land is supposed to be above politics. But nothing has been above politics so far in this presidential mud wrestle.

And the two candidates whose marathon donnybrook has now spilled into the Supreme Court made that body a major campaign issue.

W. expressed the highest respect for Clarence Thomas and Antonin Scalia. Al Gore seized on this to scare women voters: "When the names of Scalia and Thomas are used as benchmarks for who would be appointed, those are code words, and nobody should mistake this, for saying that the governor would appoint people who would overturn *Roe v. Wade*."

How rich to see W., whose campaign was steeped in skepticism about Washington, the federal government and trial lawyers, send his lawyers to Washington to petition a states' rights Supreme Court to overturn a state decision.

The theme of revenge, so prominent in the race, is continuing in the coda. Cuban Americans in Florida, still angry at the Clinton administration over the seizure of Elian González, threatened to go back to the streets, which helped stop the Miami-Dade hand count that Al was hoping would put him over the top.

The Bush team filed suit with the Supreme Court in Washington knowing that the Supreme Court in Florida would "always be a problem and that there had to be recourse," as one Bushie put it.

But the legal tactics of the two camps are running ahead of their political strategies.

Bush advisers were riding the tiger this weekend, unsure if the high court would prolong the wrangling rather than head it off. Their hope had been that W. would eke out an edge in votes by the 5 P.M. Sunday deadline, and Katherine Harris would hold a press conference certifying W. the winner.

Then he could have emerged and declared himself the president-elect—as Napoleon once took the crown from the pope and proclaimed himself emperor.

"We were counting on Katherine 'Where is my ambassadorship? I held up my end of the deal' Harris to complete her duty," a Bush adviser in Florida said mordantly.

But now they are not sure what to do. If Al Gore "steals enough votes to win" on Sunday, in the Bush argot, at least the W. camp will have the U.S. Supreme Court to keep hopes alive. But what if W. gets his votes, and then the justices validate the Gore hand recounts— hoisting W. with his own legal petard?

Will W. get Jebby's legislature to come to his rescue? Will Al keep counting and counting and counting . . .

Ahab vs. the Waco Whale

■

President-elect Mini-Me has not yet started gnawing on his cat, as the *Austin Powers* Mini-Me did to the hairless Mr. Bigglesworth.

But W. is starting to weird me out.

Why is our kinda-sorta chief executive the low man on his own totem pole?

We knew that his political nannies told him stuff only on a need-to-know basis. But now that the guy is seconds away from the White House, we learn that his handlers deal with him on a needs-not-to-know basis.

Last week in Austin, our wannabe president George Bush, miniature clone of President George Bush, happily told reporters that Dick Cheney had "had no heart attack."

The hospital, the Cheney family and Mr. Bush's press aide, Karen Hughes, knew that Mr. Cheney had, that morning, undergone a heart procedure. But Ms. Hughes did not tell that to her boss before he spoke so rosily and ignorantly about Mr. Cheney's condition.

When the election ended, Mini-Me was shocked that he had not won in a landslide. His strategists had apparently failed to inform him that things were getting tight, just as they hadn't alerted him that he was cratering in New Hampshire. Did they not trust him with the information, fearing he might get cranky?

Presidents get dangerously insulated in the White House. But this boy's in a bubble before he even gets to the Oval bubble.

Sure, Al Gore, aka Monsieur Tussaud, is an insufferable maniac for detail who hates delegating and is engineering every move in Florida. Like Ahab, he's so consumed with absurd attempts to prove he actually won Florida by nine votes that one friend described him to the A.P.'s Sandra Sobieraj as a "lost soul."

But Mini-Me also seems lost, because he isn't consumed enough with nailing down and planning his presidency. The grown-ups keep sending him off to play. They know he doesn't like messes, he doesn't do serious well and he can't do follow-up answers except to refer reporters to James Baker, his Manchurian operator.

So it's best to let him go fool around at the ranch or go to the gym for three-hour workouts while they take care of complicated stuff like the Supreme Court and the trompe l'oeil transition, and while they try to restore Poppy's White House to its original glory, as lovingly as though it were da Vinci's *Last Supper.*

"The usual case would have been for Dick Cheney to go to all the funerals and George Bush to do all the work," says Rahm Emanuel, a former Clinton adviser. "But it's turning out the other way around. Cheney needs a patients' bill of rights."

Mr. Cheney was the most reluctant of campaigners. But now we are in the Cheney ascendancy. The Bush team hurried him out of his hospital bed to the microphones because they know he sounds reassuring, mature.

During the campaign, W. had a swagger, a John Wayne gunslinger pose. But now when he comes out to face the cameras he blinks and shrinks, looking tremulous and frightened, dwarfed by American flags.

He struggles to exude authority. He furrows his brow, trying to look more sagacious, but he ends up looking as if he has indigestion. Appearing confused at his own speech, he seems like a first-grade actor in a production of *James and the Giant Peach*. Are his blinks Morse code for "Oh, man, don't let that teleprompter break"?

Republicans sanguinely compare him to Ronald Reagan, but at least President Reagan had the gift of reassurance before the camera.

It's telling that CNN's Candy Crowley, who covers the Texas governor, is not only better on TV, but much harder working and better informed than her subject.

Karen Hughes tried to make Mini-Me appear statesmanlike by saying that, while no foreign leaders had called to congratulate W., he had placed a call to congratulate Vicente Fox on his upcoming unclouded inauguration as president of Mexico. Whenever he seems callow, W. cleaves to his friendly neighbor to the south to show international flair.

Asked yesterday why Mini-Me had retreated yet again to the Waco ranch, Ms. Hughes said it was "a tranquil place where it's easy to do some thinking and reflecting."

Nice try. Mini-Me is not Proust in the Brambles.

W. does not seem to grasp that the president can't delegate the presidency itself. Of course, his aides might not have told him that yet.

High and Low

■

Everyone is counting on the Supreme Court to bring civility, integrity and sanity to our election collision.

Unfortunately, in the immortal words of the old Don, "Nah-ga-da-it." (The court is not going to do it.)

For the Kennebunkport Corleones, the Supreme Court deliberation serves the same function as the dazzling crosscut scene in *The Godfather*, when Michael attends his godchild's christening while his capos fan out to ice his rivals.

The movie church and the real court offer pious recitations and reverent ceremony that distract from the less savory stuff being done to secure the Family's interests.

The WASP Corleones think it would be nice if the highest court helped them rub out Al Gore. But should the justices fail them—and the Bushes know where they live—they are pursuing other angles, some in sunlight and some in shadow, to grind Gore into little bits of chad and sprinkle him in the Everglades.

The Supreme Court may know a lot. But the Family knows best.

Sonny dissolves on contact. But he will be president. Of course, the dream could quickly corrode. Bush II may suffer the same painful fate as Bush I, economic slump leading to one term. And what if in 2004 we have another Bush-Clinton race? Hilllary may want to avenge Bill, just as W. avenged his dad's loss to Bill.

The Family has already paid a high price. Jeb's future is jeopardized. Sonny's future is jeopardized. Dick Cheney's health is jeopardized.

But, with its back against the wall, the Family drops the New England niceties. Consider Willie Horton, Anita Hill and John McCain in South Carolina. It was only business.

The Bushes sense trouble in Florida's Seminole and Martin counties with those GOP-doctored absentee ballot applications and the chance that thousands of Sonny's votes might be thrown out. They despise Al Gore as a weasel, agitating for those votes to be thrown out (just like the military ballots) after all his talk about counting every vote.

Let the Supreme Court palaver with Bush lawyers about the statutory use of the words "shall," "may" and "must," in determining whether Katherine Harris had to consider hand counts before certification.

Crosscut: The Bushes "shall" demand help from Ms. Harris, they "may" have sent a mob of khaki-clad Hill aides to intimidate the Miami-Dade canvassing board, and they "must" hang on to the count favoring W., as opposed to risking a true count.

Let the Supreme Court dissect Article II, Section 1, Clause 2 about the State Legislature's authority to regulate electors.

Crosscut: Jeb's legislature is primed to do the wet work in a special session, guaranteeing Sonny Florida's 25 electoral votes no matter what else happens. Hired legal experts backed up plans to ram

Sonny through, putting the veneer of legitimacy on the power grab. And after all his tortured ambivalence, Jeb has come out and admitted he will do what it takes to put big brother in the White House.

"I can't recuse myself from my constitutional duties as governor of the state, and I can't recuse myself from being my brother's brother, either," Jeb says. "I know the Gore campaign would love for me to basically disown my family, but I'm going to do what's right." Right.

Let the Supreme Court examine page 37-A as it relates to Section 102.166, debating whether the manual recounts are "authorized" or "required."

Crosscut: The Bushes dumping a horse head in the bed of Alex Penelas, the Democratic mayor of Miami-Dade County. Mr. Penelas, after conferring with Republicans, mysteriously stopped supporting the vice president's effort to get a recount. The mayor's Cuban American constituents never bought Mr. Gore's pandering on Elian. Democrats charge that Mr. Penelas pulled a Tessio and cut a deal with the other family. He is considering switching parties and running for Congress. In which case, the Bushes could return the great service he did them.

Let the Supreme Court hold a disquisition over whether Title 3, U.S. Code, Chapter 1, Section 5 is, as Laurence Tribe claims, "all carrot and no stick."

Crosscut: The Bushes prepare a last line of defense with Tom De-Lay and Trent Lott, who are all stick and no carrot.

The Beginning of the End?
Or the End of the Beginning?

■

I feel positively giggly.

Not as giggly as Al Gore. But very happy indeed.

The vice president is hugely relieved at his last-minute reprieve. He invited Jesse Jackson over to pray with him on Friday evening, and the last time Reverend Jackson was pressed into service as White House spiritual adviser was when he went to pray with Hillary and Chelsea and Bill, after the president finally coughed up the truth about Monica.

After Al prayed, he partied.

Team Gore knew many thought that the vice president had gone cuckoo when he pegged his chances as fifty-fifty on Tuesday. "We were not in la-la land, we were not naive about what was going on," said Tom Nides, a campaign adviser, after the Florida Supreme Court plucked Mr. Gore from the brink. "So to say we're jubilant now is an understatement."

But I am just as relieved.

I was really dreading Mr. Gore's concession speech, the one he was working on Friday, for the second time, when the court lifted the noose from his neck, for the second time.

If there is one thing worse than watching Al Gore get his way, it would be watching Al Gore not get his way.

You know and I know that if Eddie Haskell ever does have to give that Farewell . . . and Hello Again! Address sacrificing a presidency he is sure he won and setting himself up for another run no one wants him to make, it is going to be the most self-righteous, self-aggrandizing, self-serving speech in the history of politics and literature.

" 'Tis a far, far better thing that I do than I have ever done. We few, we happy few, we band of lawyers. Yet *Bushus* says he was ambitious, and *Bushus* is an honorable man. When the calla lilies are in bloom again, once more unto the breach. We shall fight them on the beaches, we shall fight them on the landing grounds. This is not the end. It is not even the beginning of the end. But it is, perhaps, the end of the beginning."

So now these guys are either 193 or 154 votes apart. The Insufferable and the Insufficient gave America indigestion, so it was, in fact, inevitable that they would end up in this interminable intermezzo.

A sour James Baker called Friday's Florida Supreme Court ruling "sad for our democracy." Actually, O Velvet Hammer, you've got it backward.

When you try to obscure truth, as the Bush crowd has, that is sad for our democracy. When you try to reveal truth, as the Florida Supreme Court did, that is swell for our democracy.

Our unelection is superior to our election in every way. The campaign was never about anything. Lockbox, prescription drugs, blah, blah.

Now we are fighting over bedrock principles of freedom. The sanctity of the vote, the idea that every vote counts.

Although the Florida Supremes may get slapped again by the Big Supremes, at least their slim majority opinion did strike a genuine chord of principle in a mud bath where the leaders are making phony claims of principle while grabbing at the prize.

W. used family muscle to try to stop counting votes while he was ahead. Al kept saying he wanted to count all the votes, when he really just wanted to harvest more Democratic votes and suppress Republican ones.

But the Florida Supreme Court took a stab at fairness, saying: Let's count all the disputed ballots by hand in every county.

Because of the closeness of the race and the messiness of the count, and because of the different and confusing standards for manual recounting, we may never know who won.

But it's the presidency. Isn't that worth the effort to try to get it right?

The Bushes are always gracious, until they need to go ugly.

When he thought he had it in the bag, W. told Scott Pelley on *60 Minutes II* that he could appreciate the vice president's anguish.

But now that Mr. Gore has not come out to "do the right thing for the country"—Bush parlance for "give us back the White House now"—the Bush cartel will get ruthless.

If Jeb has to ruin his career ramming W. through, he will. If W. has to owe Tom DeLay the world, he will.

And, for that matter, if Al can get away with electing himself by breaking a Senate tie, he will.

December 13, 2000

The Bloom Is Off the Robe

■

CHIEF JUSTICE REHNQUIST: We'll hear argument now on No. 00-949, *President-Elect Bush and Vice President–Elect Cheney v. Albert Gore Jr. et al.*

JUSTICE SCALIA: Mr. Olson, the legal predicate that seems to have slipped your muddled mind is that recounts are only triggered if there's a problem with the machinery, not in the case of voter error. Come on, Ted, do I have to plead your case for Bush as well as hear it?

JUSTICE O'CONNOR: Well, Mr. Boies, why can't those ninnies down in Florida simply follow the instructions for voting, for goodness' sakes? At the Chevy Chase Club, my friends have been asking me why people too stupid or slack to punch a hole through a piece of paper even deserve a vote.

JUSTICE SCALIA: That's it, Sandy, baby. Suffrage, shmuffrage.

CHIEF JUSTICE REHNQUIST: Mr. Boies, you fail to grasp the concept of equal protection for the conservative justices who want to retire. I'm seventy-six. Sandy is seventy. We started out long ago, working our hearts out for Barry Goldwater, and we're pooped. My back is killing me! But we can't leave until we install a Republican president. Al Gore would replace us with that hippy-dippy Mario Cuomo or that flower child Larry Tribe, or some minority who actually cares about the rights of the dispossessed.

JUSTICE GINSBURG: Mr. Boies—may I call you David?—I love you.

JUSTICE SCALIA: Ruthie, zip it. Mr. Boies, as you surely have noticed by now, I am the Big Brain here. So I will explain what should be *res ipsa loquitor*, not to mention a priori. We stopped the vote counting because if we did not, Al Gore might have won. Then I would never have had a chance to be chief justice.

I have put up with so much hokum. When they upheld *Roe v. Wade*. When they made all-male military academies admit women. I became bitter and marginalized. Never mind Al Gore's due process. What am I due in this process?

MR. KLOCK: If I may, Justice Brandeis—

JUSTICE SCALIA: I'm Scalia, dimwit. To continue, it may look hypocritical if the court's conservatives suppress the will of the people and install a states' rights president by federal fiat. I know I have spent my career fighting against muscular assertions of judicial power. But now I see that judicial tyranny, judiciously used, can be a good thing. I don't believe in making laws from the bench. But making presidents? That's different. Hey, who ever said the Constitution is engraved in stone, anyhow? Text is important, but so is subtext. Why should I prop up a pathetic pol who vilified Clarence and me during his campaign?

This court is riddled with conflicts of interest. Clarence's wife, Ginny, is over at the Heritage Foundation gathering conservatives' résumés for possible appointments in the new administration. My son is a partner at Ted Olson's law firm. Another son just got hired by another law firm working for Bush. But if I had recused myself, there would have been a tie. And then those radicals on the Florida Supreme Court could have been affirmed. And President Gore might have made Ruthie the chief.

JUSTICE THOMAS (to himself): If this thing runs long, I'm going to miss *Trailer Park Nurses* and *Room Servicing* on the Spice channel.

JUSTICE STEVENS: De-novo, de-lightful, de-lovely. Why don't we just devise a standard to count all the votes?

JUSTICE SOUTER: I know the Bushes are furious at me. That'll teach 'em to assume that a guy living like a monk in an isolated New Hampshire farmhouse is some kind of Live Free or Die nut.

JUSTICE O'CONNOR: Mr. Boies, while we are on the subject of irreparable harm, are you aware that if I side with you, it could put in jeopardy the membership of my husband, John, in the Bohemian Grove? He does so enjoy his week of stag frolicking and drag shows in the California redwoods with President Bush, Cap Weinberger, Bill Buckley, David Rockefeller and Henry Kissinger.

CHIEF JUSTICE REHNQUIST: We're dropping in the polls on the question of our fairness, but we still need to anoint Bush president. It's best for us. We'll just have to work harder to hide the truth: that we are driven by all the same petty human emotions as everybody else in this town—ambition, partisanship, political debts and revenge.

MR. KLOCK: How true, Chief Justice Holmes.

■

Oedipus Wrecks

■

In Which

the Family Drama

Aeschylates

■

When the Boy King Ruled

■

Reign of George II. After the Hundred Chads' War, the Bush dynasty once more seized power.

The boy king, George II, ascended the throne in 2001. To safeguard the sheltered dauphin, fearing he might wander out of the palace and get lost, the royal seamstresses stitched his name and title on the lapels of all his garments and the blacksmith hammered his name onto his brass belt buckle.

George II began his reign amid anxieties about the economy, the fuel supply and royal taxation. The kingdom quivered with doubt about whether the handsome, charming youth would become an able, assured ruler or an indolent, indecisive one.

Role of the Regents. George I and Queen Mother Bar, who liked to pretend they were not running things, chose a trio of Regents: the Duke of Halliburton was first minister; Cardinal Rumsfeld was secretary for war and Colin of Arabia was secretary for foreign affairs.

Contessa Rice tutored the boy king in geography, government and history, but he was an indifferent student. Like England's Edward II, George II was bored by the duties of kingship and easily swayed by favorites.

The Regents were happy to let their charge immerse himself in sport and games while they reawakened the two eras they most admired: his father's reign, with its victorious military campaign, and the Golden Age of Dullness that came to pass during the brief dominion of Gerald the Pardoner.

Peasants and burghers resented sovereign attempts to enhance the privileges of the nobles. Opposition to George II among dissidents and malcontents crystallized around the former king, William the Smooth, living in luxurious exile in Embassy Row, a stone's throw from court, with a member of Parliament.

Court Life. George II was not sickly or dull-witted, as many of the Bourbon boy kings had been. And he was less spoiled than P'u-i, the Last Emperor of China, who was three when he first sat on the Dragon Throne. P'u-i demanded one hundred dishes at every meal and chased away bad moods by having eunuchs flogged in his presence. George II was often tempted to flog the press, but he was too well mannered to flog the servants.

He exercised admirable discipline over his hot temper, which he inherited from the Queen Mother. And he controlled his taste for grog. He had no tantrums like England's Edward VI, who took the throne at nine and once got so enraged that he tore a live falcon into four pieces.

George II was an obedient son who emulated his father, the old king, in all respects. He felt no need to put his own stamp on his monarchy. Unlike France's Sun King, America's Son King did not create a brilliant cultural and intellectual life at court. He was content merely to restore George I's royal council, horseshoe tournaments and strumming troubadours from the southern provinces.

He also renewed Bushian alliances with the princes of business and the barons of oil. George II welcomed all petitions to sink wells in pristine parts of the kingdom, and encouraged his royal grounds-keeper, Lady Gale of Colorado, to drill throughout Alaska. Unlike his Catholic predecessor, John of Camelot, George of Crawford tore down the antiquated wall between church and state and legislated against sin.

Although he never missed a beheading or a hanging, he was largely indifferent to the glittering social life at court. He preferred to take Queen Laura, a highly learned woman, and escape the pressures of constant delegation by retreating to the brambly isolation of their country seat.

Influence of Katherine de Medicis. George II issued only one official public proclamation: "The Edict of Loyalty to All the Bushes."

Unlike other monarchs, he did not exile or execute jealous and scheming family members. He had always suspected his younger brother Jeb was less than vigorous in protecting his southern flank during the Hundred Chads' War. He did not like Jeb's overreliance on the Countess of Not Counting, Katherine de Medicis. But he did not want *la guerre folle*, a silly, fratricidal War of the Rosebushes, so he did not charge Jeb with treason. He did, however, christen him the Black Prince.

War of Succession. In 2002, the kingdom entered a dark period when the regents fell into a ruthless struggle for power. George II was oblivious to the intrigues all around him and ruled serenely until 2008, when Jeb of Tallahassee arose to do battle with Hillary of Chappaqua.

Pappy and Poppy

■

Jackie Kennedy understood the power of myth. After her husband died, she planted the shimmering fable of Camelot. And she told her shattered brother-in-law Bobby to read Edith Hamilton's *The Greek Way.*

Bobby was transfixed by the great families of Greek mythology. He recognized the hubris of the House of Atreus, with doom seeping down through the generations.

As Ms. Hamilton wrote of the family of Agamemnon, Clytemnestra and Electra: "It was an ill-fated house. . . . A curse seemed to hang over the family, making men sin in spite of themselves and bringing suffering and death down upon the innocent as well as the guilty."

As Aeschylus wrote of the cursed house, "before the old wound can be healed, there is fresh blood flowing."

America broke with the Old World, but we never lost our taste for ruling families and their melodramas. Washington now is a cat's cradle of them. The Bushes. The Clintons. And our fascination with the Kennedys has survived four decades, even with all the revelations about the ugly side of the glam dynasty.

The Camelot books keep coming. And opening Friday is *13 Days*, a Kevin Costner movie about the Cuban missile crisis, in which Jack and Bobby seem very young and very scared facing down the Red Menace.

The Kennedys were the thrilling, self-destroying dynasty. The Bushes are the dull, self-preserving one.

"The Kennedys flew too close to the sun. The Bushes just ask for more pork rinds," says my friend Evan Thomas, who wrote *Robert Kennedy: His Life.*

The Bushes hate the D-word, as they call it. They think it implies easy inheritance of high offices without striving.

W.'s not into Greek mythology. Grandiose introspection wouldn't be his style. And the fact that he spoke of our NATO allies "the Grecians" during the campaign is a giveaway he's not reading Edith Hamilton.

The Bush campaign did have a subtext of revenge and sibling rivalry. But the Fates never seemed to hover ominously. "The Kennedys had demonic problems, fabulous women, deep human flaws," Evan Thomas says. "The Bushies act like they're in a frat house."

His book offers a gripping portrait of Bobby, racked by fears after JFK's death that he caused it by pursuing the mob, despite his father's warnings not to (and there was also that little matter of stalking Castro); he is also terrified about being blackmailed by J. Edgar Hoover and smeared by LBJ, and haunted about his own possible assassination.

The only torment for Jeb, when it appeared he might have failed to work through his ambivalence in time to deliver Florida to W., was whether he would get a Thanksgiving drumstick.

The dynasties have always moved in opposite directions. The Bushes were trying to de-Anglicize and lose the silver spoon while the Kennedys were trying to Anglicize and seize it. The ambitious adventurers wanted to seem like diffident WASPy aristocrats, and vice versa.

Prescott Bush, a Wall Street banker and senator from Greenwich, had the pedigreed "Tennis, anyone?" family Joe Kennedy frantically emulated. The Kennedy patriarch, a brilliantly ruthless businessman and legendarily successful bootlegger, had the buccaneering background the two white-bread Georges would frantically emulate.

Even as raffish Kennedys laundered their past, infiltrating WASP havens like Hyannis Port, marrying Miss Porter's School debutantes named Bouvier, giving white-glove teas for female voters during campaigns, effete Bushes roughened their edges, emigrating to macho West Texas as wildcatters, marrying Midland librarians and Mexican students, having barbecues for supporters.

The working-class Democrats liked leaders with pretensions to royalty. The royalist Republicans, needing to appeal to Joe Sixpack, had to trade the country club and martini image for Buds and burgers.

The Bush dynasty may be more blithe because neither Prescott nor Poppy ever pushed his sons into politics. Pappy, as JFK once jokingly referred to his stage father ("I could feel Pappy's eyes on the back of my neck," he wrote a pal), demanded his heirs go into politics, and would not take no for an answer.

It was purely Greek that, after his stroke, one of the few words that old Joe could speak in response to good news or bad was "No." As the tragedies rained down upon him, he could only moan, "No-no-no-no."

■

Washington's Transit

■

In Which the Politics of Seduction Give Way to the Politics of Confrontation

■

The Age of Mars

■

M ommy's gone.
Daddy's home.

The nurturing, sharing, empathizing, self-examining, gossiping, bumping, grinding administration is leaving.

The stern disciplinarians are on board.

The "Let's figure out how we all feel about this" White House is over.

The "We know what's best, follow our rules" White House is beginning.

The lip biting is over.

The tight lips are here.

We are losing a secretary of state who thinks flirting and dancing and strategic jewelry wearing are all valuable diplomatic skills.

Now we will have a trio of presidential counselors—including the secretary of state—who hail from the macho world of the Pentagon.

We will no longer have a president who is dying to know what we think and who is dying to tell us what he thinks, preferably at great length.

Now we will have a president who thinks introspection is for sissies and justifying your actions is a nuisance.

We are saying good-bye to a president, elected by women, who talked about What Women Want, who handed over large chunks of government to his wife, and who even read Deborah Tannen to see how to better communicate with women.

We are saying hello to a president, elected by white men and absentee military ballots, who defended executions and guns and wants to beef up the military, and who reads about hurricanes and sports figures.

We are going from Clinton Technicolor to Bush black-and-white. There is nothing about the government President-elect W. is putting together that feels the least bit modern.

"The new administration is 'Nick at Nite,'" cracked a Clinton White House official. "It feels so old, it's almost a kinescope."

W. and Colin Powell were spotted at Morton's steak house digging into juicy porterhouses. Rummy Rumsfeld wants to revive the cold war dream of a missile shield.

Where is W.'s boomerness? Why is such a young president acting so atavistic?

Our first boomer president and vice president tried so aggressively to be modern. There were gurus, facilitators, BlackBerrys.

But the second boomer president is doing everything he can to get the power out of boomers' hands and back into those of the gray generation between World War II and Vietnam.

Bill Clinton was the first Age of Aquarius chief executive. But at

Yale, W. was largely oblivious to the social upheaval of the sixties. He said he never liked the Beatles after they got into that "kind of a weird psychedelic period." W. is not a Renaissance Weekend guy. He's a Boca Grande guy.

If Bill and Al tried too hard to be trendy, W. tries too hard not to be.

He has a defiant antitrendy streak, curling his lip at fads and fashions and the Clinton-Gore style of finger-in-the-wind.

Despite the multigender, multicultural cast of some of his top appointments, and despite the relentless parade of women and ethnic entertainers at the Philadelphia convention and planned for the inaugural, his big choices—the roomful of men he will rely on to tell him what to do—reflect a bland, unadventurous adherence to tradition.

His inner circle has a very mahogany corporate suite, musty men's club feel to it, an "I Like Ike" feel.

When W. met the press with his choice for attorney general, John Ashcroft, before Christmas, he vividly showed how important it is to him that his White House be as leakproof as the Skull and Bones "tomb."

"When he gives me his legal advice," W. said of Mr. Ashcroft, "you won't know about it unless I tell you." In a little while he added: "Whatever counsel it is, I hope I don't read about it." And a little later he told his designee: "Just don't tell them what your advice is."

W. is having the same two-day economic summit that Bill Clinton had before his administration began. But unlike Mr. Clinton—who dazzled reporters and those who watched the forum on television—Mr. Bush will discuss his prepackaged recession with business and

Wall Street big shots in the privacy of the governor's mansion in Austin. The event will be closed to TV and the press.

I can already tell that W.'s vexed answer, when he is asked to justify anything, will be identical to his father's: "If you're so smart, why aren't you president?"

Just call it the drowning of the Age of Aquarius.

April 29, 2001

I Have a Nickname!

■

S o I found myself on Friday in the Cobra Reading Room on the Web.

I had discovered on the Hotline, the *Racing Form* of politics, that President Bush's nickname for me is "The Cobra."

I wasn't sure if that was an insult or a sign of respect. So I figured I'd read up on some cobra traits.

"The cobra lives near towns where mice and rats abound." Well, I thought, that fits.

"Cobras have extensive tissues that store fat." Yup.

"The venom of cobras acts powerfully on the nerves of those it attacks." Clearly.

Maybe the president had it right. I was a major-league asp.

I puzzled over whether W. fancied himself the mongoose or the snake charmer in this allegory. Either way, I knew he would expect me to hiss a bit about his first hundred days.

It has been a strange start. Al Gore jokes he should be addressed as "Your Adequacy." But W. risks being "Your Inadequacy."

Men customarily build their presidencies around their strengths. W. has built his around his weaknesses.

His White House reminds me of the 1937 movie *Damsel in Distress*, in which Fred Astaire has to frantically pirouette around Joan Fontaine to make up for the fact that she cannot dance.

Bush officials are always frantically pirouetting around W., making up for his stumbles and lacunae.

Last week, the president threw the planet into a turmoil when he went on *Good Morning America* and said he was willing to "do whatever it took to help Taiwan defend herself" against a Chinese attack, including sending American forces.

Obviously, Mr. Bush did not set out to change nearly thirty years of American policy on a morning chat show. But, sensitive about W.'s reputation as a featherweight, his aides did not want the president to have to admit he made a boo-boo and is a yo-yo who can't be trusted to carry on a brief discussion about his own policies with hard-hitting Charlie Gibson. (Hiss!)

So they tried to soften his statement while letting it stand, thereby enraging Beijing further.

On Friday night, Uncle Dick Cheney had to go on *Larry King* and explain in that reassuring basso that the Kid was not changing policy.

W.'s advisers tried to make him look more impressive in his first forays into diplomacy by keeping the big world leaders at bay and letting him hang out with lesser leaders he could talk to in Spanish.

So now we have a whole new alliance with Central and South American countries simply because W. feels more comfortable at what *USA Today* dubbed "amigo diplomacy."

The ill-prepared president doesn't seem troubled by the state of his preparedness. There's no indication he's staying up late to make up the work. He isn't even aspiring to on-the-job training. The White House simply pretends that thoughtlessness is thoughtfulness, and that the president is governing when he is gaffe-ing. (Hiss!)

His team overreacts to his father's failings. Karl Rove, aka "Boy Genius," in W.'s nickname lexicon, is so assiduous about buttering up the right, which grew disillusioned with Bush *père*, that he has alienated swing voters and Republican suburban women on the environment and abortion.

Lee Atwater, the bad-boy strategist for Bush Senior who was a mentor to Mr. Rove, aimed to keep the right happy, but he never bowed and scraped to "extra-chromosome conservatives," as he and his boss called them.

It is ironic, given how intently they are shaping Bush II to avoid the errors of Bush I, that W.'s weakness in polls at the start is the same one that sunk his dad in the end.

In last week's ABC News/*Washington Post* poll, 51 percent said the president does not "understand the problems of people like you."

When the father got tarred for being out of touch, it was because of his patrician ways and because he was absorbed in his avocation, international affairs, while this country was hurting economically.

The son has a plainspoken, colloquial style and homespun tastes. He runs from his gilded cradle, avoiding Yale and refusing to acknowledge Connecticut as his birthplace on a recent trip there. But he is not seen as a populist, either. He, too, is surrounded by wealthy older men. And they have given his economic and environmental policies a strong corporate aroma.

Air Force One is beginning to look like the company plane. (Hiss!)

Space Cowboys, Inc.

■

W henever I read *Variety*, I start having fantasies of inking a movie deal in the high six figures against the low seven figures.

Whatever that means.

I have an idea for a futuristic political thriller science fiction space Western black comedy with a stylish film noir mood. Shades of *Blade Runner, Galaxy Quest, Fail-Safe, On the Beach* and the *Exxon Valdez* oil spill.

Since it's inspired by the Bush administration, there isn't any sex. But the laser beam shoot-outs will make Jerry Bruckheimer drool.

The year is 2007. *Bush Runner, or How I Learned to Stop Worrying and Love the Shield* opens with an evocative, derivative shot of Oil Rig Earth, an industrial wasteland where the sun no longer shines, a bleak postapocalyptic world filled with oil refinery towers belching fire, Reagan replicants and animoids (genetically engineered animals eating bioengineered food based on petroleum by-products).

Because of the president's stunning success in enacting his first-term agenda—unbreathable air, undrinkable water, uneatable food, unaffordable gas—Earth is inhabited only by drilling, logging and mining personnel, androids and criminal dregs (aka pro-choice women and anyone who tried drugs but failed to get elected to high public office afterward).

The Democrats fled the planet before the last election when they realized, to their horror, that Al Gore had been right: Earth (and not just Florida) really was In the Balance.

The White House has had to move Off-World, to a hermetically sealed oval capsule, the USS *Robert Bork*. Right now, the *Bork* is orbiting Io, the third moon of Jupiter, checking out Io's Intergalactic National Wildlife Refuge for drilling possibilities.

With all the antimissile missiles, offensive weapons, satellite-attacking satellites and spy rockets (none of which work) that Dr. Strangerum, the defense secretary, has tossed into the sky, space is just as trashed as Earth.

Interior shot of Oval space lounge/war room. Captain Dick and Dr. Strangerum are sitting in Jetsons spun-aluminum chairs, drinking Johnnie Walker Red and trying to keep their glasses from flying away as they determine the fate of the universe.

The Kid, bundled in a spacesuit, is outside playing catch with an asteroid.

Dr. Strangerum: "Look at Mars and tell me that there are no Reds! We picked up a secret transmission today from the Chinese space station on the Red Planet, Dick. The Chinese were bragging about how they tricked us into spending our economy dry on Star Wars by getting their Commie friends in North Korea to pretend they had a nuclear missile. The fools! It was we who tricked the North Koreans into deceiving the Chinese into believing that we believed the North Koreans had a missile when in fact it was the Russians who duped the Chinese and the North Koreans into thinking we believed that the North Koreans had a nuclear missile, which of course—heh, heh!—allowed us to trick Congress into giving $600 billion trillion more to our pals to make weapons."

Captain Dick: "Yup."

Dr. Strangerum sips Scotch. "Remember that report we commissioned from the Bland Corporation? Those Commies want our essence, Dick. They're plotting to drain us of our precious bodily fluids."

Junior chases his asteroid inside. "Is the Texas spaceball team here yet? I have to hand out the trophies!"

Dr. Strangerum continues: "It's time to start thinking big, Dick. I've got the blueprint for a galactic missile defense shield. We'll just say we need to protect ourselves from a sneak attack by a rogue galaxy. We can get our friends at TRW, Lockheed and General Dynamics, who have a joint headquarters on Uranus, to ring really big lasers around the Milky Way."

Junior's face lights up. "Who's passing out the Milky Ways?"

Dr. Strangerum: "Can you believe the Democrats are still tree huggers, even with no trees? Gephardt's on Pluto ranting that we're the party of plutocrats just because we pipelined all our tax cuts right to the oil companies. And how about those beatnik Europeans on Neptune trying to rope us into another sissy treaty on galaxy warming? Those hootenanny, free love hippies are still trying to ban land mines—in space!"

Junior, squinting through a big telescope at a faraway planet, asks his elders: "What is that black spot on top of the gray marble?"

Captain Dick: "Alaska."

Drill, Grill and Chill

■

We want big. We want fast. We want far. We want now. We want 345 horsepower in a V-8 engine and 15 miles per gallon on the highway.

We drive behemoths. We drive them alone. This country was not built on HOV lanes.

We don't have limits. We have liberties.

If we don't wear our seat belts, it doesn't matter, because we have air bags. If the air bags don't deploy, it doesn't matter, because our cars are so beefy, we'll never get bruised. If we need to widen the streets for our all-wheel drives, we will. If we need to reinforce all the bridges in the country, so that they don't buckle and collapse under our 5,800-pound SUVs, our engineers will do that.

We'll bake the earth. We'll brown and serve it, sauté it, simmer it, sear it, fondue it, George Foreman grill it. (We invented the Foreman grill.) We might one day bring the earth to a boil and pull it like taffy. (We invented taffy.)

If rising seas obliterate the coasts, our marine geologists will sculpt new ones and Hollywood will get bright new ideas for disaster movies. If we get charred by the sun, our dermatologists will replace our skin.

If the globe gets warmer, we'll turn up the air-conditioning. (We invented air-conditioning.) We'll drive faster in our gigantic, air-conditioned cars to the new beaches that our marine geologists create.

We will let our power plants spew any chemicals we deem necessary to fire up our Interplaks, our Krups, our Black & Deckers and our Fujitsu Plasmavisions.

We will drill for oil whenever and wherever we please. If tourists don't like rigs off the coast of Florida, they can go fly-fishing in Wyoming. We won't be deterred by a few Arctic terns. We don't care about caribou. We don't care for cardigans. Give us our 69 degrees, winter and summer. Let there be light—no timers, no freaky-shaped long-life bulbs. (We invented the lightbulb.)

We want our refrigerators cold and our freezers colder. Bring on the freon. Banish those irritating toilets that restrict flow. When we flush, we flush all the way.

We will perfect the dream of nuclear power. We will put our toxic waste wherever we want, whenever we waste it. We have whole states with nothing better to do than serve as ancestral burial grounds for our effluvium. It can fester in those wide-open spaces for thousands of years.

We will have the biggest, baddest missiles, and we will point them in any direction we like, across the galaxies, through eternity, forever and ever.

We will thrust as many satellites as we want into outer space, and we will surround them with a firewall of weapons for their protection.

We will guarantee broadband and fast connections to the Internet. We will not permit anybody, anywhere, at any time to threaten the delivery of all the necessities to computers, PalmPilots and Black-Berrys: stock quotes, sports scores, real estate listings, epicurean.com recipes, porn. (O.K., so we didn't invent porn.)

By arming space, and protecting satellites, we ensure life, liberty and the pursuit of happiness—our five hundred TV channels drawn from the ether.

We will secure the inalienable right of every citizen driving by himself in his big car to be guided by a Global Positioning System. Nobody should have to call in advance for directions to a party when the satellite can show the way.

We will modify food in any way we want and send it to any country we see fit at prices that we and we alone determine in the cargo ships we choose at the time we set.

Our international banking arm—the World Bank and the IMF—will support whatever dictatorships suit us best.

We will fly up any coast of any nation on earth with any plane filled with any surveillance equipment and Top Guns that we possess.

We will build super-duper jumbo jets so Brobdingnagian that runways will be crushed under their weight at the most congested airports in the history of aviation. (We invented aviation.)

We will buy, carry, conceal and shoot firearms whenever and wherever we want, as is our constitutionally guaranteed right. (We invented the Constitution.) We will kill any criminal we want, by lethal injection or electrocution. (We invented electricity.)

We are America.

The Asbestos President

■

B eing witty about poisoned drinking water isn't easy. It requires a certain obtuse savoir faire.

Our president gave it a go Thursday night at a press dinner here.

"As you know, we're studying safe levels for arsenic in drinking water," he told the crowd of radio and TV correspondents at the Washington Hilton. "To base our decision on sound science, the scientists told us we needed to test the water glasses of about 3,000 people. Thank you for participating."

I guess a guy who can yuk it up about a woman he has executed in Texas can yuk it up about anything.

But it was a creepy moment.

It worked for Erin Brockovich to joke about the carcinogens in the water enviro-villains were sipping because she wanted to get the poison out. W. wants to keep the poison in—to help the enviro-villains who contributed to his campaign.

Forgive me, Al Gore.

I used to think you were striving too geekily to be Millennial Man. The PalmPilot on your belt. The BlackBerry. The Earth-cam you dreamed of. Citing *Futurama* as your favorite show. The obsessions about global warming and the information highway. Boldly choosing the first Jewish running mate.

But now I'm going hungry for a shred of modernity. Bush II has reeled backward so fast, economically, environmentally, globally, culturally, it's redolent of Dorothy clicking her way from the shimmering spires of Oz to a depressed black-and-white Kansas.

With the guidance of his regents, the Duke of Halliburton and Cardinal Rumsfeld, W. has set off the specter of a mushroom cloud of carcinogens and carbon dioxide emissions, nuclear power and *China Syndrome* fears, rapacious drilling and retrenchment on women's rights, the missile shield, spy tensions and the cold war.

The son has become what the father used to privately deride as an "extra chromosome" conservative.

W.'s press conference on Thursday boiled down to one exhortation: "Let's hear it for corporations!"

This administration is so hawkish that Colin Powell is cast as a sandals-and-beads peacenik. And John Ashcroft threatens to fry the FBI spy.

The Clinton team wrestled with the messy grays of a post–cold war world. The Bush team decided it was easier to bring back the cold war.

"These guys are linear," says a top official from Bush I. "They have to have black and white. They have to have bogeymen."

One veteran cold warrior who served under several presidents told me he was shocked that Bush II had refrozen the cold war.

"They've turned the clock back to 1983," he said. "It doesn't make any sense to slap the Russians around. They're already on their knees. We don't have to humiliate them. We need to use some finesse, to allow them some dignity.

"The thing I always hated about Clinton foreign policy was they seemed to be making it up as they went along. But these guys seem to be doing that, too. They are negative toward old policies, without coming up with anything positive."

The regents moved quickly to cast the administration in the gray flannel image of their salad days. (One Republican says that Henry Kissinger once called Mr. Rumsfeld the most ruthless man he knew, all global despots included.)

Not satisfied with smacking around the Russians, humiliating Christie Whitman, downsizing Condi Rice and brushing back Colin Powell, the Cheney-Rumsfeld axis has no patience for the plaints of health-conscious yuppies, either.

You can just hear Rummy, slugging back a Scotch with Cheney in the Oval after they've put the Kid to bed, grousing about the gazillion dollars' worth of investments he has to sell to avoid a conflict, and growling: "Real men can drink twice that much arsenic. And how soon can we get some lead back in the lousy paint?"

What's next? Asbestos, DDT, bomb shelters, filterless cigarettes? Patti Page? Rummy griping that Laura Bush is too assertive?

W. never seemed happier than he did on Friday at the White House, surrounded by the old-timers from the Baseball Hall of Fame, basking in memories of his beloved fifties.

He is only our second boomer president, but his White House needs Geritol. He seems older than his sprite of a father. He goes to bed early and, except for sports, is oddly disconnected from the culture. He seems to have no engagement with contemporary America, except by virtue of being the president of the United States.

How Green Is Their Valley

■

D ick and Rummy are in the lemon-and-raspberry-striped wing chairs in the Oval Office.

They like to kick back at the end of the day, down a Johnnie Walker Red and kick around how they will organize the country and the world to their liking.

Junior is out on the South Lawn, practicing placing the ball on the batting tee for the opening day of White House T-ball on Sunday.

The president is very, very excited because the San Diego Chicken is coming.

He is also puffed up because he has learned a new word: "counter-pro-lif-er-A-tion."

At one point, W. runs up to the French doors to pester the two older men: "Is it up yet? Can I see it?"

"No, son," Dick says in that slow, deliberate voice. "We're still working on it."

W. grins and races back to the diamond.

"He thinks the missile shield really exists?" Rummy smirks, sipping his Scotch. "So did Reagan. Probably better that way. Keeps the Commies guessing when the president sounds so sincere."

"Yup."

"We can stick it to the Russians, the Chinese and the North Koreans—to say nothing of Daschle, Biden and Kerry. And think of all our buddies at Boeing! Think of the billions that will go to Lockheed, TRW, General Dynamics! Can you believe those pointy heads on the ethics board want us to divest our portfolios?

"Missile defense may be pie in the sky, but our defense budget pie is, as the Kid likes to say, growing taller. Here's to the private sector—we'll be back there someday. O'Neill wants us to make sure a lot of aluminum goes into the Emperor's New Shield."

"Yup."

"It's just a matter of months before we have the arms race seething again, no matter what that flower child at the State Department thinks. Nothing like a race with only one runner. No fun being a sole superpower if you can't blow up the other guys' arsenals with imaginary airborne lasers.

"Dick, did you listen to that speech Junior gave at Fort McNair today? We've got to teach him how to pronounce 'nuclear.' Tell him it rhymes with 'avuncular.' On second thought, maybe not. And keep the details on the shield out of his speeches. It will only confuse him and enrage Chirac, Blair and Koizumi. The boy is still lost in space on who's a 'strategic competitor,' who's a 'strategic partner' and who's a 'strategic adversary.' "

"Yup."

"How's Project Blackened Skies going?" Rummy asks. "Baby, the acid rain must fall. The canary in the coal mine must croak. It's payback time for West Virginia and our brothers in oil, gas, nuclear power, mining and chemicals. By the time we're through ramming coal down the public's throats, that grimy Welsh town in *How Green Was My Valley* will look like Aspen. We'll probably have to add gas masks to the prescription drug benefit. Soot, smog, tobacco smoke, arsenic, carbon dioxide, toxic garbage from nuclear power plants, vertical drilling, horizontal drilling and loop-de-loop drilling. It's a good start, Dick, a very good start. Is that muzzle tight on Christie Whitman?"

"Yup."

"I can't believe all that whining about arsenic hasn't died down. Those babies who think we're uncaring and we base too many of our policies on cost-benefit analysis. Let's just hope the public doesn't realize the true beauty of this formula. They bear the cost; we and our cronies get the benefit."

"Yup."

John Ashcroft pops his head in. "Is this a prayer meeting? Over at Justice, we have ours in the morning. You guys aren't drinking, are you?"

Dick's mouth curls down on one side and the attorney general scurries away. He almost bumps into W., who is scampering back, out of breath.

"Hey, Uncle Dick, is it launched yet? Does it really look like a bunch of little colored paper umbrellas in the sky?"

"Bedtime, big-time, son."

"I talked to Ostrich Legs Putin on the hotline today," W. proudly tells Rummy as he leaves. "I told him we shouldn't counter-pro-lif-er-ATE each other!"

There is silence for many minutes. Finally, Rummy barks: "Dick, speak up! What are you thinking about?"

"Steak."

Mexico Likes Us!

■

W. was hanging out at the White House with the Yankees on Friday, his face aglow as he was presented with a team ball and a signed pin-striped jersey by Roger Clemens, Paul O'Neill and Mariano Rivera.

"¡Mucho gusto!" he told Mariano.

The president also gave a trophy to the Air Force Academy football team, prepared for the debut of his T-ball league and hosted a Cinco de Mayo festival on the South Lawn.

"Mi Casa Blanca es su Casa Blanca," El Presidente Jorge told the crowd, before flying off to Camp David at 3:30 P.M.

Some days, it's fun to be the boy toy of the military-industrial complex.

As the president fiddled, I burned.

Doesn't W. realize that EVERYBODY in the world HATES us?

Not Mexico. Maybe not Monaco. But EVERYBODY ELSE! Even the Swedes can't stand us, for Pete's sake.

Gerhard Schroder thinks that he and W. had no communication when they met, and that W. had trouble remembering his name. Tony Blair has to call Bill Clinton to find a sympathetic ear. And how many times can President Bush trot out Vicente Fox?

During the campaign, W. tried to soothe public doubts about the deep dry well of his foreign-policy knowledge. He promised we would feel secure with an array of veterans—Colin, Condi and Cheney.

So why, only three months in, is America roiled by all these bristly spats around the globe? We couldn't be playing the bully boy with a heavier hand if Pat Buchanan had won.

After complaining that Clinton foreign policy was erratic and impulsive, the Bush team turned out to be erratic and impulsive. The Bushies wanted to be more muscular, but have succeeded only in being more high-handed, infuriating allies and rivals with moves both unilateral and pointless.

Fed up with America's my-way-or-the-highway attitude on global warming, the missile defense shield, AIDS medication for the poor and treaties, the Europeans gleefully went along in slapping the U.S., booting us out of the U.N. Commission on Human Rights for the first time since its inception in 1947.

The U.S. was cast out while Sudan, with its slaughtering and slavery, remains in, as well as Togo, which traffics in child slaves, and Pakistan, which has a military dictator (identified by W. only as "General . . . General" in his campaign pop quiz). France won 52 votes to our 29. When you are deemed snootier than the French, you know you're in trouble.

The Bushies were needlessly humiliated in the Kabuki theater of the UN, where the outcome of a vote should never be a surprise, because they weren't paying attention. They were too busy brandishing their trompe l'oeil missile shield to worry about shielding real people in real trouble. They were too busy trying to turn Alaska into a giant oil rig and give more riches to the rich.

At a Georgetown cocktail party last week, Robert McNamara, the mastermind behind our most despicable Asian policy, told other guests W. had botched relations with Beijing so badly we could end up at war with China in the next decade. He should know.

The Bushies try to act tough but keep slipping on banana peels. After Rummy's top aide at the Pentagon issued a cold war–like memo ordering all contacts between our military and the Chinese armed forces to stop, the White House had it revoked.

The world moved on between Bush 41 and Bush 43, but maybe they missed it in Texas. A decade after the fall of the Berlin Wall, W. is in a time warp, writing a blank check for a weapons system that Rummy says doesn't have to work.

"Everyone in Europe is rubbing their eyes as this strange laconic creature with miniaturized eyes gads about alternating strange promises with stranger threats," observed one European analyst.

We have never succeeded in shooting down an intercontinental missile. At least when Ronald Reagan pushed his faux shield, it was a way to get the Soviets to spend themselves into oblivion. But there is no Soviet Union now, and Putin is broke. The military-industrial complex cannot justify its flamboyant weapons without the existence of flamboyant enemies.

It was bad enough when President Clinton rewarded his contributors with the Lincoln Bedroom. But President Bush is rewarding his contributors with the Pentagon. (*Mi Pentagono es su Pentagono.*)

May 27, 2001

No Whiff of Poof

■

It was bedlam on the Potomac, a Babel of preening Democrats and keening Republicans. W. couldn't stand it. He covered his ears.

Four nice men and a lady had given him the White House and now one mean man had taken away the Congress.

W. fled to Camp David on Friday shortly after noon. By 1:30 P.M., he was safely tucked away in the Aspen cottage for his nap, Spot and Barney curled at his feet.

He was restless, sulking into his feather pillow. "They promised me it wouldn't be so hard, that I would look good. But Uncle Dick and Rummy are making me look small.

"Uncle Dick was the one all those $100,000 donors wanted to have dinner with. What about me? He's sent invites for a June fundraiser called the President's Dinner on Dick Cheney letterhead. Aren't I the president? He put out our Energy Report with the vice-presidential seal. What happened to self-effacing?

"Rummy didn't even show up this morning for my Naval Academy speech. He said he was too busy reorganizing the Navy. Man, that is such *el toro*."

A deep voice pierced his pout.

"George," the voice intoned, "you know I always leave the room when anyone utters a vulgarity."

W. shivered. He recognized the Brahmin tones and unmangled syntax of his late grandfather, Prescott Bush, who always made him wear a tie at dinner. The craggy six-foot-four specter was frowning at him from beneath bushy eyebrows. He looked like a Roman senator, his gray hair swept back in a pompadour style and parted in the middle. He wore a double-breasted gray suit and shoes polished to a high shine.

Prescott Bush was just as full of Episcopalian rectitude as a ghost as he had been as a Connecticut senator and Wall Street banker.

W. reflexively bolted upright, hiding his plastic cup of Cheez Doodles under the covers.

"George," Prescott said, "we need to talk about noblesse oblige."

W. got squinty. "That's near Sierra Leone, right?"

"It is a concept, George, a duty. Your White House is in a shambles because you've let the party of Lincoln become the party of Rove. I must in all candor say that Jim Jeffords is right. The Vermonter left because you're being a goose about your tax cut and the missile shield. You're fobbing off disabled children, women and the environment.

"It hurt like mad when you turned your back on Connecticut and Yale, where I proudly carried the Class of 1917 banner. When I ran for the Senate, I took a Whiffenpoof quartet with me to rallies and sang bass. I was deeply saddened not to see a whiff of the poofs in your campaign.

"It's fine to mingle with the simple folk, George, but you don't ever want to become simple. How can you summer in broiling Crawford instead of Kennebunkport or Hobe Sound?

"I played golf with Ike at Burning Tree, and we talked about our progressive moderation, or moderate progressivism. I wanted to pass civil rights legislation and courageously raise taxes because it is important for the fortunate to go all out for the less fortunate. (Except at Burning Tree.)

"You and your father say class doesn't matter, while enjoying the benefits of your class. You skittered down to Midland and donned cowboy boots and proclaimed yourselves born-again, whatever that means. You ran as red-blooded Texans rather than blue-blooded Yankees, righteous Southern conservatives rather than refined New England centrists.

"Your father shed his venerable striped watchband and ate those ghastly pork rinds. After heading the United Negro College Fund at Yale and supporting Planned Parenthood, he veered to the right for Reagan. But when he became president, he hooked back to the fairway.

"Who is Grover Norquist? I have reservations about the father figures who surround you—and usurp you. They have led you on an ill-considered march to the right, away from our roots and away from where the modern Republican Party must go. Foolish wise men.

"By George, George, there was no need to offend dear old Jeffords. You punch the bully in the face, as I did Joe McCarthy—not play the bully.

"Adieu, adieu," the ghostly Whiffenpoof intoned, as he disappeared in a poof. "Boola, boola."

■

The Boy King's Endless Summer

In Which the Fault Is in Their Star Wars and in Themselves

■

■

The Relaxation Response

■

You won't believe this: The White House is trying to get W. to relax.

Top Bush aides are working hard to chill out the president with a narcoleptic's appetite for napping, a retiree's lust for vacations and a work ethic as lolling as Oblomov, the superfluous man of Russian literature.

I first heard this ten days ago from a top Republican who said he had advised Karen Hughes that W. needed to loosen up.

"He looked so nervous and uptight in the pictures of his meetings with European leaders," the Republican said. "I told Karen he's got to relax."

Then I learned that the Bush inner circle was upset that W. was so terrible on TV, and they were trying to figure out a way to get him to stop being so rigid before the cameras and show his effervescence.

It took me a while to wrap my head around this peculiar political pickle.

George W. Bush got to be president in large part because he seemed more fun and natural than Android Al. And now presidential aides and Republican lawmakers want W. to unwind, just as Karenna Gore and Naomi Wolf did with their Beta Bore, when they swaddled him in earth-tone casuals.

Relaxing has always been a leitmotif with presidents, of course. The three great naturals of modern times were JFK, Bill Clinton and Ronald Reagan. LBJ stewed over how to be cooler on TV, and Nixon never got past those flop sweats and wingtips on the beach.

But never has a president who seemed so laid back taking office had such a hard time recapturing that mojo in office. He used to be casual in scripted settings. Now he's scripted in casual settings.

On Monday his imagists sent him out, sans coat and tie, shirtsleeves rolled above the elbow, for a gambol with Laura to the Jefferson Memorial. The man who is sliding in the polls on the issue of whether he cares about average Americans and minorities was trying to seem in touch with the hoi polloi, shaking hands and chatting up tourists, singing out: "Happy Fourth of July!"

Asked what the day meant to him, he replied: "It means what these words say, for starters. The great inalienable rights of our country. We're blessed with such values in America. And I—it's—I'm a proud man to be the nation based upon such wonderful values."

Yesterday the president took his script to another casual setting, turning a bassinet into a soapbox when he and Laura visited Desiree Sayle, one of the first lady's staff who had just had a baby, at a hospital in Virginia.

He segued quickly from newborn Vivienne to the Patients' Bill of Rights, saying, "Congress needs to bring me a bill that will help the patients who come to these hospitals maintain a reasonable insurance, and a bill that doesn't help lawyers."

Then, barely taking a breath, he moved on to use the baby to plug his faith-based initiative: "A lot of babies are born sometimes where the—some babies are born where people just don't love them like they should."

By this time, the friendly baby visit had morphed into what it truly was: a stiff news conference.

"Mr. President," asked one reporter, "do you know when you'll actually make a decision on stem-cell research funding?"

"In a while," he replied.

Afterward, the president struck a Clintonesque pose and hit the fairway midweek. "I haven't played since I've been president," he said. "I've been working too hard."

He'll continue that tradition of hard work when he leaves for a long weekend in Kennebunkport on Thursday with his tennis racquet and horseshoes, and spends much of August on the Crawford ranch.

W.'s problem is that it's impossible to seem easygoing when he's finding that all the issues he's dealing with aren't easy at all.

From Election Night on, it has been one headache after another: the Jeffords defection, peeved Europeans, Karl Rove's ethical problems, polls that alarmingly echo the fall from favor of his father when he was deemed detached from the electorate.

To make matters worse, the mythic ironclad discipline and unity of his staff is showing signs of rust.

The harder it gets, the more squarely he is confronted with his own limitations. And the more squarely W. is confronted with his own limitations, the more rattled and unrelaxed he gets. And the more rattled and unrelaxed he gets, the more rattled and unrelaxed he gets.

Rip Van Rummy Awakes

■

W hen Rip Van Rummy came down from the mountain after twenty-five years, gray and lined, the village was much changed. Strange faces everywhere and a bustling, disputatious tone about it, bilious folk haranguing about politics. The very character of the people seemed different.

Poor Rummy. First he goes to Moscow and tries to explain to Vladimir Putin why the U.S. wants to shred all its treaties and put up Star Wars Saran Wrap, and the Russians wonder if he's slept through the last decade of jabbering about globalization.

At home, Henry Kissinger and his acolytes whisper that they're worried that Rummy is too far out there, in a headlong rush straight backward that's driving Russia and China together. (You know you're in trouble when Dr. Strangelove thinks *you're* Dr. Strangelove.)

Back at the Pentagon, Rummy discovers that the military brass— as irritated by the defense secretary's high-handed ways as the rest of the world—has staged a coup. In an e-mail version of *Seven Days in May*, the Joint Chiefs have mobilized allies on the Hill and sabotaged the secretary's plan to modernize and trim the services and use the money saved for the missile shield.

The chimerical shield is being pushed by a corps of Reaganite true believers in the administration, a cadre of Richard Perle types (including Richard Perle, back at the Pentagon) for whom this is not a policy but a theology.

The Bushies gave Russia a deadline yesterday of November to make a deal on changing (read abandoning) the ABM treaty, because the missile missionaries want to start clearing ground and cutting down trees this week in Alaska for silos and a command center. They probably need to hurry up and get there before the oil drillers.

Instead of Rummy doing a hostile takeover on the military, the military took over the hostile Rummy. They plotted in the Tank, their secure conference room in the Pentagon, and outfoxholed him. Now he's saying the services can decide how to move into the future themselves.

In a startling interview with Michael Duffy in *Time*, the sixty-nine-year-old with the reputation as a master infighter admitted he had been outmaneuvered because he didn't understand how much Washington had changed since 1976.

The military is politicized and no longer subservient. The press is no longer quiescent. Congress is no longer run by a few smart old Southern guys. Secrets no longer exist.

This raises the urgent question of just how conscious of the world around him Rip Van Rummy is. What sentient CNN-watching creature on the planet does not know about these changes?

He tells Mr. Duffy that when he moved back in January, "I was not into the rhythm of the place."

"My Lord, in this place, all you have to do is think about something, and it is leaked," he says. "It's like there are eavesdropping microphones on your brain."

He ran three different companies over a quarter of a century, but he doesn't seem to know about America's merger mania. About defense contractors, he sounded surprised that "they have gone from a lot to a few, and they have activities in a very large number of Congressional districts."

He's even more clueless about the press. "It's arranged for promoting conflict, difficulty and problems," he says. And this is a news flash to him?

The traditional coziness between a Republican administration and the military is shattered. The White House is angry at Rummy for knuckling under and at the military for wanting more money and no reform. And the military, which had Bill Clinton, who was terrified of crossing it, nicely tucked in its pocket by the end of his second term, now wonders if it would have fared better with Al Gore.

Well, I guess we can close the book on W.'s contention that the best way to run government is with the wisdom of corporate chieftains.

He got a trio of CEOs in there—Rummy, Dick Cheney and Paul O'Neill—and the most striking thing is how out of touch they act. Perhaps because they have been in the rarefied atmosphere of corporate suites so long, these guys seem constantly taken aback that when you state your position in Washington, it isn't the end of an argument but the beginning.

How can the people who were supposed to know how the world works not know anything about how the world works?

His Magnificent Obsession

■

I
t is hard to fathom most obsessions from the outside.

Why did Proust's Swann swoon over the sharp-featured Odette, when he knew he was wasting years of his life longing for a woman "who didn't even appeal to me"?

What made Aschenbach follow a blond boy in *Death in Venice* in such a state of distraction that "he could no longer think of anything except this ceaseless pursuit of the object that so inflamed him"?

Why did Humbert Humbert devour himself over the sulky "Lolita, light of my life, fire of my loins. My sin, my soul"?

Why did the otherwise cool Oscar Wilde wreck his life over the callow Lord Alfred Douglas so that, as he wrote in *De Profundis*, "I became the spendthrift of my own genius"?

Why did the whale engender a "special lunacy" in Ahab that "stormed his general sanity, and carried it and turned all its concentrated cannon upon its own mad mark"?

And why can George W. Bush think of nothing but a missile

shield? Our president is caught in the grip of an obsession worthy of literature.

W. seemed like a simple man, who did not get ardently aroused over anything except Little League, clearing Texas brush and peanut butter and jelly sandwiches.

But it turns out that he is darker and more complex than we thought. He is seized by a desire that defies the laws of politics and physics, a hunger that fills him with elation and despair, a thirst for an attainment that seems so close and yet so far.

While we may not understand W.'s urgent, self-destructive craving for his ineffectual missile shield any better than we understand Scarlett's urgent, self-destructive craving for her ineffectual Ashley, we must stand in awe before the purity and grandeur of his obsession. He would rather risk the world being destroyed than slow his race to build something to protect it.

Consider the hurricane of global emotions that W. has whipped up to construct The Defense That Doesn't Work against The Threat That Doesn't Exist.

The White House has signaled China that it's O.K. to build up its nuclear arsenal if it makes China feel better about W.'s Junior Star Wars. And if this leads to China's improving its nuclear warheads and to a renewal of nuclear testing, well, the obsession can justify that. And if this leads to India's and Pakistan's accelerating an arms race, well, the obsession can justify that, too. And if American kids have to go back to duck-and-cover drills, well, same deal. And if W. squanders $60 billion that could have been spent on education on technology that doesn't work—because our sophisticated antimissile interceptors can't stop primitive, wobbly missiles from rogue nations, much less germ warfare from terrorists—ditto.

W. is now at a *Blue Angel* Lola Lola level of obsession, but instead of his blood running fast for Marlene Dietrich, it's running fast for a missile doily.

He has made the Europeans angry and alarmed. He has made Vladimir Putin and Jiang Zemin much closer, and Russia is once more playing the China card. He has driven Russia and Germany closer, a pairing that caused, as his father would say, "a splash" of trouble in the past. The Joint Chiefs of Staff are furious that W. wants to downsize the services and use that money for his missile shield. Colin Powell, who is in no rush to throw weapons into space, has been sidelined in favor of Rummy and Condi and others who feed W.'s ecstatic fantasy.

Because W. has restructured the entire international security system—reviving scary alliances and threats that had faded—we may end up needing a larger military, not a smaller one.

The last time a president became infatuated with Star Wars, the obsession was easier to understand. Ronald Reagan was by temperament a utopian. He believed that the unattainable was attainable. He confused real life with the movies.

But W.—whence his magnificent obsession?

I can only speculate that it's filial, stemming from his fear of repeating his father's fatal mistake of alienating the right wing.

As much as it is reassuring to see the usually disengaged president become so deeply engaged in an issue, the world might be a safer place if W. stuck with his other obsession: demanding that the White House mess offer up three kinds of jelly with its pbjs.

A Grave Silence

■

If you called yesterday afternoon to the White House switch-board, that famously efficient Washington institution, you would hear a brief recording saying to hold for an operator and then the line would go dead.

For many hours, the most eerie thing about the American capital, under attack for the first time since the British burned the White House in the War of 1812, was the stillness at the center of the city.

New York was a clamorous inferno of pain, confusion and fear, with Mayor Rudolph Giuliani on the scene in the rubble of the World Trade Center towers and on TV trying to reassure residents about schools and transportation and hospitals.

Manhattan had the noise of the grave. Washington had the si-lence of the grave. Downtown you could smell the smoke and see the plume rising from a Pentagon full of carnage and fire and see the flag over the emptied White House flying at half-staff.

But until the nation's leaders reappeared on television after nightfall to speak of what President Bush called their "quiet, unyielding anger," no one understood what had happened. No one knew what might happen next. Would there be a gas attack? Would the White House blow up? Would another plane crash into the Capitol?

People were so hungry for clues that they gathered, as their parents did after Pearl Harbor, around radios, huddled in small groups a block from a cordoned-off White House.

A doctor, Mark Cinnamon, fifty-four, held up a radio broadcasting Peter Jennings interviewing Governor George Pataki, while fifteen strangers leaned in to listen. "We're just sharing, with an old battery-operated radio some guy handed me," he said.

On a gorgeous blue fall day, terrorism had turned into war. The city that leads the world took on a weird neutron bomb quality. No one even tried to pretend, as we are supposed to, that no matter what, terrorists cannot disrupt our government.

For much of the day we weren't sure where the president was. There were statements floating in from him from various secure zones in the air or underground. The vice president was out of sight. We didn't know where the first lady was. The secretary of state was in the air somewhere. The Capitol had been evacuated. Congressional leaders had gone off to a bunker somewhere. The Joint Chiefs of Staff could not be immediately accounted for. The CIA and FBI were stunned. Most vividly at his post was Donald Rumsfeld, who helped rescue victims at the Pentagon and stayed all day in the smoky command center.

White House officials had fled the building five minutes after the plane crashed into the Pentagon at 9:45 A.M., streaming out with some men screaming and some women barefoot and carrying their high heels.

"That floored me," said one federal official, stranded at a bus stop.

"This is supposed to be the most secure place in the world. I said, 'Why are you running? You can leave but just slow down a little.'"

Federal buildings were evacuated, coffee shops shuttered, dress shops barred. A few tourists wandered around in shorts looking confused as military planes patrolled above. D.C. police carried rifles, and Secret Service agents in black Mustangs and green Luminas blocked off the streets adjacent to the White House.

The country cannot be completely protected from fanatics willing to die. And yet, it was chilling to see how unprepared those in charge of planning seemed, after years of warnings about just such an attack. The top congressional leaders were calling each other, unsure whether to stay or go, or where to go.

"There was some confusion; no alarm bells went off," said Mitch Daniels, the Bush budget director, about the scene in the Old Executive Office Building, adding that people had decided to go "by word of mouth."

Even the president didn't seem sure of where to go.

"He is at the very top of the United States," said Tammie Owens, a subway supervisor in a bright yellow uniform, who felt that a president, like the British royal family during the blitz, needed to reassure people with his presence. "And the White House is where he should be."

David McCullough, the historian who wrote the biographies of Harry Truman and John Adams, disagreed. Mr. McCullough happened to be in town for a Laura Bush book festival and had just volunteered to give blood at a hospital. "All presidents do what they're told on matters of security," he said. "The most important thing is that the president is alive and safe and knows what's going on. We haven't seen this level of destruction on our home ground since the Civil War. This isn't the *Titanic* movie. It's real."

Cleopatra and Osama

■

It is hard to fathom how a part of the world that produced Cleopatra—who perfumed the sails of her boat so men would know she was coming and ruled with elegant authority, signing one tax decree "Make it happen"—could two millenniums later produce societies where women are swaddled breeders under house arrest.

When civilization rose in the East, it was scientific and sensual, embracing the possibilities and pleasures of life from mathematics to literature, art and fashion.

There have been many repressive regimes throughout history. But the Taliban were obsessively focused on denying gender, sexuality and the forces at the very gut of life.

When the barbarian puritans running Afghanistan began to scurry away last week, men raced to buy pinups of beautiful girls. And, in a moving and amazing tableau, some women unwrapped themselves, letting the sun shine on their faces as they smiled shyly and delightedly. A few dared to show a little ankle or put on high heels.

"Your head hurts and your eyes hurt from the limited vision," one young woman in Kabul told a reporter, discarding her despised burka. "It was very difficult to walk without falling over." (Most have held off burning burkas because, as one woman put it, "They say the Taliban beat first and asked questions afterward. They say the Northern Alliance asks questions first and beats afterward.")

In a real version of Margaret Atwood's creepy *Handmaid's Tale*, the Taliban reduced women to vessels designed to serve the needs and bolster the status of men.

"I agree that a kind of religion motivates the Taliban, but the religion in question, I'd say, is not Islam," Robert McElvaine, a history professor, wrote in *The Washington Post*. It is "insecure masculinity. These men are terrified of women."

Afghan warlords have long used castration to torture foes. The hijackers were haywire about women. Some draped towels over the prints of twenties bathing beauties in pantaloons in a Florida motel room; others indulged in lap dances, strip clubs and prostitutes, keeping busy until they got their bounty of seventy virgins.

Mohamed Atta's will had loopy, misogynistic instructions: "I don't want a pregnant woman or a person who is not clean to come and say good-bye to me" and "I don't want any women to go to my grave."

The White House, suddenly shocked by five-year-old Taliban excesses, began a campaign against their treatment of women. "Only the terrorists and the Taliban threaten to pull out women's fingernails for wearing nail polish," Laura Bush said, taking over her husband's weekly radio address.

Bush aides say the campaign will try to influence the Northern Alliance to restore women's rights and press for women in the Afghan government. Of course, they also want to impress U.S. women, who preferred Gore to Bush by 11 points. It's a freebie, an easy way to please feminists who got mad when the administration ended financing for international family-planning groups that support abortion.

This belated promotion of women as a moderating, modernizing force in the Islamic world sounds hollow.

Bush Senior went to war to liberate Kuwait, yet America has not made a fuss over the fact that Kuwaiti women still can't vote or initiate divorce proceedings. We also turn a blind eye to Saudi Arabia's treating women like chattel. There are five thousand Saudi princes, but where are the princesses?

The Saudi religious police, the *matawain*, use sticks to make sure women hide beneath their *abayas*, the long black cloaks.

Besides having to put up with polygamy, Saudi women cannot marry outside Islam, while men can. Or divorce without cause, as men can. Women also have to use separate banks and schools and obtain written permission from a male relative before traveling alone or going to a hospital. They must sit in the backseats of the cars they are not allowed to drive. (American military women stationed there are angry that they have to wear abayas and sit in the backseat when they leave the base.)

But the Bushes love that royal family and its oil. What does it matter if Saudi women can drive, as long as American women can keep driving their SUVs?

Millions of Muslim women are still considered property. The first lady might think about extending her campaign beyond Afghanistan.

Blessings and Bombings

■

In *The Crack-Up*, F. Scott Fitzgerald wrote that "[t]he test of a first-rate intelligence is the ability to hold two opposed ideas in the mind at the same time and still retain the ability to function."

So now we know for sure that George W. Bush has a first-rate intelligence.

The president, his team and the rest of us have been juggling a lot of contradictory notions since September 11.

Many who came of age during the Vietnam war, wincing at America's overweening military stance in the world, are now surprised to find themselves lustily rooting for the overwhelming display of force against the Taliban.

Over the years the country's ethos had gone from John Wayne to Jerry Springer, from gunfighter nation to anger management nation, rugged frontier mentality to designer lifestyle mentality.

Once we prided ourselves on being strong and silent. Then we got weak and chatty. And now we seem to be evolving to strong and chatty.

We are pulverizing our enemies even as we try to show them a little compassion, crushing our foes even as we try to understand and address some of their grievances against us.

We are functioning holding opposing ideas, new ones every day.

The president invited fifty-two Muslim diplomats to a traditional lamb and rice dinner at the White House Monday to wish them "a blessed Ramadan," even as the U.S. bombed Muslims in Afghanistan over Ramadan.

The president urged Americans to travel and act normally as they celebrated the holiday season, even as the White House and the Capitol were closed to public tours, and the audience for the lighting of the national Christmas tree was limited to ticket holders for the first time.

George Bush was rooting out Osama bin Laden from underground even as Dick Cheney was burrowing underground.

The president continued to cozy up to the Saudis and protect them with American forces, even though the Saudis were educating, exporting and financing terrorists.

Administration officials made the argument that the Saudis are bad rulers but great allies, even as their bad rule threatened us more than their allied behavior helped us.

The president told aides not to press the Saudis to change the strict Islamic teaching in schools that encourages young men to die for Allah and hate Western infidels. "We didn't go to the American Methodists about Tim McVeigh," Mr. Bush said to aides. This even as the president told the Muslim diplomats dining at the White House that the holidays were "a good time for people of different faiths to learn more about each other."

Condoleezza Rice urged that women be included in the post-Taliban government in Afghanistan and have equal rights. "When women are fully incorporated, a country is better off for it," she said. This even as our allies, the Northern Alliance, did not let any women into the reopened six-hundred-seat movie theater in Kabul to see the Afghan film *Uruj*, about three mujahedeen heroes who fought the Soviet invasion of Afghanistan. (No date movies or chick flicks for these guys.)

The president christened the Justice Department building for the antiwar presidential candidate Bobby Kennedy, even as the U.S. was waging a war. John Ashcroft sought to link his assault on terrorism, with its heightened surveillance and wiretaps, with his Democratic predecessor's assault on organized crime. But Kerry Kennedy Cuomo declared publicly yesterday that her father would never have swallowed the restrictions on civil liberties that the Bush attorney general is pushing.

The president continued to espouse the conservative orthodoxy of keeping the federal government from growing, even as he breathed a sigh of relief when Congress voted to turn airport screeners into federal employees, thus saving the Republicans a political beating on the issue.

After September 11, Mr. Bush promised $20 billion to New York for reconstruction, but the White House says the city has gotten enough for now, though only about half of it may be in hand. No bailouts for big business was a Bush principle, but the White House speedily funneled money to the airlines and limited payouts for insurance companies, both politically powerful industries.

Mr. Bush definitely has a talent for holding opposed ideas in his mind. But then, he did start as a compassionate conservative.

■

Transfusing the Blue Blood with Red to Pump Up the Red States

■

Oedipal Loop-de-Loop

■

S o will the president focus more on Wall Street's lipstick index or
Teddy Roosevelt's big-stick index?

The lipstick index is a way to judge a recession. When the economy goes down, lipstick sales go up. Women indulge in smaller lux-
uries and skip bigger ones.

The big-stick index is a way conservatives judge the president.
Will W. whack Saddam with the stick, or will he fold, the way his
dad did?

Mr. Bush spent his first year using his father's failures as a reverse
playbook. Trying to dodge 41's mistakes, 43 catered to congressional
right-wingers and muscled through a mammoth tax cut.

When the economy slumped, he took great pains to tell Americans he understood their pain—so he would not seem oblivious and
wrapped up in foreign affairs like his father.

Then September 11 hit and he had to get wrapped up in foreign
affairs.

If the president uses the reverse playbook now, and continues to coddle the conservatives his father neglected, he has to go topple the wacky Iraqi, completing Poppy's unfinished business.

But if he does that, he turns his attention away from the recession, repeating Poppy's mistake after his war, when he never used his celestial approval ratings to fix the economy.

It's a surreal Oedipal loop-de-loop, made all the loopier by the spectacle of history repeating itself and putting the son at the same juncture where his father made two of the most critical and criticized decisions of his presidency.

Because 41 detached from Baghdad and detached from economic angst at home, 43 is under extra pressure to attack Iraq while attacking the recession.

The man who started out as the most disengaged president in modern history is now being pestered by his aides and his conservative base to engage, engage, engage.

His political and military advisers are competing for his attention, as he decides how hotly to pursue the war at a time when the economy is foundering and deficits are back.

It is a measure of how nervous the White House is, given Republican losses in the recent gubernatorial elections, that it dumped Governor James Gilmore of Virginia as party chief last week.

Should the president rout Osama and the Taliban and then "focus like a laser beam on this economy," as Bill Clinton said when he beat Bush Senior? Or should he go on to Phase Two, as the Get Saddam crowd calls it, now that the U.S. is "on a roll," as State Department official Richard Armitage puts it?

At the moment, Mr. Bush is juggling furiously.

In his Saturday radio address, the president concentrated on the recession and expressed concern about soaring unemployment. "It's a time to reach out to Americans who are hurting," he said, "to help them put food on the table and to keep a roof over their heads."

And, if Mr. Bush has not yet decided whether to crack Saddam with the big stick, he has been talking more loudly anyway. He said if Iraq did not allow UN inspectors into the country to check for weapons of mass destruction, it would "find out" the consequences.

It's hard to say if the swagger was meant to co-opt the string of Perles—Richard Perle and others who are in full cry to crush Saddam—or to lay a real groundwork for at least bombing Iraq.

It is curious that the president tolerates such open provocation from people in his administration and connected to it, given that the clamor sets him up to look soft on Saddam if he doesn't go after Iraq.

Paul Wolfowitz, the number two Pentagon official, has been the spark plug of the Get Saddam club. Other drumbeaters are Mr. Perle, on a Pentagon advisory board, and fellow board member James Woolsey, who went on a government plane with a team from Justice and Defense to investigate whether Iraq was involved in the 9/11 attacks.

"If we cannot drive this tyrant from office," Mr. Perle said on CNN, "then we can't do anything."

In an interview with Bob Novak and Al Hunt on CNN Saturday, Donald Rumsfeld was asked about Mr. Perle's agitations.

"Look, Richard Perle is Richard Perle," he replied, praising Mr. Perle but adding: "He does not speak for the president. He does not speak for me."

So many voices, so little time. It's enough to send a president burrowing back into his feather pillow.

Who's Joey Bishop?

■

It's endsville for that bum Osama. Time to send him to the big casino. That Clyde can't hide. When that crumb is gone, ring-a-ding.

Forget about Clooney and Pitt mimicking vintage testosterone in the new Rat Pack remake. We've got the real deal right here. Septuagenarian testosterone. The suave swagger of Rummy and Cheney, enhanced by cluster bombs and secure locations instead of martinis and broads.

Who needs the men of *Ocean's Eleven* when you've got the men of September 11?

At the start of the sixties, Frank Sinatra and Dean Martin's Rat Pack was regarded as the epitome of black-tie cool and male camaraderie and assertiveness. By the end of the decade, with the blue-jeaned social revolution, they were seen as passé figures of misogynistic brio.

This administration has reversed the arc.

President Bush's veterans from the Ford administration started out as macho dinosaurs, threatening to spike the water with arsenic, drill at will, bring back coal mines and revive Star Wars and the cold war with a cocky my-way-or-the-highway attitude toward the world.

But after the terrorist attacks, the macho dinosaurs suddenly seemed like dependable protectors. All that free-floating testosterone found a worthy cause and suited the nation's bellicose mood.

After 9/11, America's obsession with celebrities and gossip dimmed, even as real people doing tough jobs began to have star allure.

Once the Sinatra Rat Pack was regarded as the ultimate men's club, "the innest in-group," as *Playboy* decreed. Now the nation digs the Bush warriors, doing it Their Way.

Back when Sinatra was the general running the clan's Vegas summit meetings, they had their own buddy-boy lingo about chicks and Charleys, punks who were nowhere and pallies who were sharp.

The Bush Rat Pack has its own tough-guy argot: Drain the swamp they live in so you can smoke the evil ones who are wanted dead or alive out of their caves as the noose tightens.

These guys are getting swooned over even more than Steven Soderbergh's repackaged Rat Pack.

CNN declared Donald Rumsfeld "the media star of America's new war," and quoted a woman calling him "the newest sex symbol."

Rummy's gruff charm and his cuffing of the press—shades of Sinatra, who labeled reporters "finks" and "losers"—has turned him into an unlikely hipster. On Sunday on *Meet the Press*, Tim Russert quizzed the defense chief about how he used to do one-arm push-ups for money in college.

Barbara Walters, who often kills to get "gets" with movie stars, used her fearsome powers of persuasion to snag tonight's TV interview with the president and first lady, the first since September 11.

And Diane Sawyer, who once rolled on the floor with Elian González and interviewed the Pets.com sock puppet, now uses her wiles to snare Dick Cheney, whose aplomb and quiet assurance have made him the Dino of the Establishment.

Ms. Sawyer asked the underground vice president to describe his "cave," the undisclosed secure location where he spends most of his time. "I know this sounds like—like, I don't know—Robin Leach or something, or one of those magazines," she said, "but we're just trying to get a visual sense of what it's like when you're there. . . . I mean, people are imagining you in some Quonset hut someplace."

She also asked Mr. Cheney to divulge whether his wife ever gives him advice, which he refused to reveal. That's *amore!*

The symbiotic relationship between Hollywood and Washington had favored Hollywood in recent years, with President Clinton playing First Groupie. But at the Kennedy Center Honors festivities here over the weekend, the Hollywood luminaries once more orbited the Washington luminaries. Colin Powell was more sought after than the king of cool, Jack Nicholson.

Julie Andrews gawked, hoping to meet Tom Daschle. And one big movie star was starstruck by Condoleezza Rice, a pianist herself, when she honored Van Cliburn. "She's in incredible shape," he marveled.

As in the original Rat Pack, there's only one woman in a choice role, Condi as Angie. And some members are less cool than others, trying too hard to belong. In the Bush Pack, it's Tom Ridge on the Peter Lawford sideline and John Ashcroft with that wacky, too-on-the-edge quality of, yes, Shirley MacLaine.

Vain or Glorious?

■

Everywhere you look these days, you see the Bush team bathed in an Olympian glow.

Laurel City, as 41 might say.

Self-consciously posing for Annie Leibovitz as Men of Steel plus Condi, the Bushies are hailed as conquering heroes and heroic conquerors in the new *Vanity Fair*.

Mr. Bush is favorably compared to Theodore Roosevelt, Ronald Reagan and Harry Truman, and proclaimed "the president who rose to the occasion." Dick Cheney is christened "The Rock" (a refreshing change from "The Drill"). And Colin Powell, "The Conscience."

Mr. Bush's weaknesses have morphed into his strengths.

"His predecessor . . . would have happily stayed up for an all-night bull session debating the nature of evil, quoting Schopenhauer and Niebuhr until the birds started chirping," Christopher Buckley writes in the magazine. "Is such complexity of mind an asset or a liability in a commander in chief?"

Rolling out its own dramatic pictures of gray flannel grit, *Newsweek* also interviews cabinet members this week on "how they're winning the war" and on their mutual admiration society.

"If they were going to pick an all-star team," says Mr. Cheney's chief of staff, Scooter Libby, "they'd pick each other."

With burnished shots of the president and vice president—nary a killer pretzel in sight—NBC is promoting Tom Brokaw's day at the White House, airing tonight, as a thrilling glimpse "inside the real West Wing."

Last week Karl Rove was crowing to Republicans that the party could ride this war to a Senate majority. Democrats huffed and puffed about Republicans politicizing the war. But it was much like CNN hawking Paula Zahn as sexy. The only startling thing was that Mr. Rove said it publicly.

The GOP is giddy at polls showing that Americans once again see the party as the big, strong daddy, protecting the Ponderosa from wolves and poachers.

I hesitate to interrupt the victory laps, the chesty posing, the passing out of medals. But something in me really wants to know: Is the war over? Did we win it or not?

The liberation of Afghanistan is a wonderful thing, of course. Our pledge to provide nearly $300 million to rebuild the ancient tribal battlefield into something resembling a democracy is well and good.

But as the late, great Peggy Lee sang, is that all there is? Wasn't it an essential goal to bring back, Dead or Alive, the Evil One and his one-eyed landlord?

Administration officials talk out of both sides of their mouths: They tell us we haven't won yet, but they keep strutting around as if we've won. They advise us to be patient, that this is a messy fight for the long haul. But wanting instant gratification, eager to milk the war for political ads, they have declared it a big success.

Given the president's own definition of the monumental goals in September, it is way too soon for Karl Rove to be dancing in the end zone.

It suits the administration to define victory in a way that makes victory achievable. This is just what the Bush 41 team did in '91. Defining victory as expelling the Iraqis from Kuwait, they quit while they were ahead.

But history has yardsticks for success that are more stringent than the ephemeral ones used by political consultants. In the case of the gulf war, history has deemed the Bush 41 definition of success too narrow.

Can we really have victory if we let the architect of 9/11 and his protector, Mullah Muhammad Omar, slip away? We let the Pakistanis spirit out some of the top Taliban warriors on planes. That was bad enough. Who knows where they are now, and whether they're planning a new attack?

Asked by Tim Russert whither Osama, Donald Rumsfeld said he could be in Afghanistan, Sudan, Somalia, Kashmir, Chechnya, Saudi Arabia or Yemen.

Mr. Russert asked if Americans could reach "closure" without capturing him. "Oh, indeed, yes," the defense secretary replied.

Oh, indeed, no. Rummy may never get a Yemeni dagger handed to him by Osama on the deck of a U.S. warship. But maybe we should stop the premature congratulations and the Patton-like preening and try to finish the job.

Let's define our success by the standards of history, not the standards of politics.

Planet of the Privileged

■

O h, the pull of Planet Enron.

The atmosphere there was so rarefied that its inhabitants were blissfully oblivious to how privileged they were.

It was a lovely place, sort of like Aspen with oil rigs. The skiing was great because there was always a pristine powder of newly shredded financial records on the slopes.

There was offshore drilling off every shore and offshore subsidiaries on every corner.

A red flag fluttered on Planet Enron, but nobody paid attention.

Journalists in Washington were hunting for Dick Cheney for months, even as he was completely visible and accessible on Planet Enron, where he lumbered down golden boulevards.

Phil and Wendy Gramm, the king and queen of the Enron prom, cruised around in their white stretch limo, rewarded for years of service, exempting and deregulating.

Paul O'Neill was also ubiquitous there, his face emblazoned and his words enshrined on the currency, which begins with thousand-dollar bills. The motto: "Companies come and go. It's part of the genius of capitalism."

Mr. O'Neill was not Treasury secretary up there, though, merely a private citizen. Kenneth Lay, still smarting that the president decided not to name him Treasury secretary on earth, anointed himself with the title on Enron.

The Bushes summered there, and W. and Jeb dropped by when they needed campaign cash. But lately, they began putting brown paper bags over their heads when they visited so no one would notice them hobnobbing with Kenny Boy.

Everyone was upwardly mobile on Planet Enron, a world more consumed with havens than have-not's.

There were, blessedly, no lower classes or riffraff. Denizens were blue blood or blue chip but never blue. There were the born rich, and there were the new rich the born rich made rich. The congenitally rich create the crony rich by ushering them onto the boards and payrolls of oil and energy companies and defense contractors.

There was no conflict of interest on Planet Enron, only confluence of interest. No income tax, only insider tips. No SEC or GAO, just CEOs, SUVs and NOBDs (Not our bankruptcy, dear). QED.

All meetings on Planet Enron were held in secret, and everyone liked it that way. Auditing was considered rude. It was a very empathetic place.

On Planet Enron, it seemed only fair that chairman-for-life Kenneth Lay should reward himself with $51 trillion in a severance package, as opposed to the $51 million he was seeking on Planet Earth.

On Planet Enron, Secretary of the Army Thomas White could whine that he came out with only $12 million from sales of the company's stock. He bravely said he "would persevere."

On Planet Enron, Karl Rove could expect people to mist up at the poignant tale of how he made mere millions instead of more millions when government ethics rules forced him to sell all of his stocks. And he could ingratiate himself with the conservative leader Ralph Reed by offering him a piece of the Enron rock.

On Planet Enron, the president, his words muffled by the brown paper bag on his head, could strike a chord complaining that his mother-in-law had lost $8,000 on Enron stock when less connected mortals lost their entire retirements.

It was a beautifully sheltered place (and not just in the Caymans sense). A place where inhabitants deluded themselves that their accomplishments and windfalls—Ivy League degrees, energy company sinecures, lucrative consulting contracts, advisory board booty— were the result of merit and hard work.

But then turmoil struck. The planet has been overrun by the Wrong Kind: government lawyers bearing subpoenas and grand juries poking around. The thin and tony air has become noxious with the threat of litigation and incarceration.

Dick Cheney is still there, but he's hiding in a secure location. Now he has caves on two planets.

President Bush, distancing himself by light-years, has ordered the U.S. government to look into cutting off all business with the planet.

On Friday, the once-serene orb imploded with the news of the sad death of a leading citizen, who shot himself in his Mercedes after telling friends he did not want to have to turn against his own.

But Planet Enron is bigger than one company or one tragedy. It's a state of mind, a subculture, a platinum card aristocracy. Its gravitational pull has long proven irresistible.

The Class President

■

O nce when I was covering the first President Bush, I took one of
his top political strategists out to dinner.

After a couple of martinis, he blurted out that the president was
having a hard time with the idea that I was the White House reporter for *The New York Times.*

Dumbfounded, I asked why.

"We just picture you someplace else—at *The Chicago Tribune*
maybe," he said.

Growing up in a Victorian mansion in Greenwich, the son of a
Connecticut senator and Wall Street banker, the president had conjured up a certain image of what the *Times* White House reporter
would be like. Someone less ethnic and working-class, with a byline
like Chatsworth Farnsworth III.

Poppy Bush was always gracious to me, even though he hated getting tweaked about being a patrician and complained that journalists cared more about class than he did.

The Bushes see the world through the prism of class, while deny-ing that class matters. They think as long as they don't act "snotty" or swan around with a lot of fancy possessions, that class is irrelevant.

They make themselves happily oblivious to the difference between thinking you are self-made and being self-made, between liking to clear brush and having to clear brush.

In a 1986 interview with George Senior and George Junior, then still a drifting forty-year-old, *The Washington Post*'s Walt Harring-ton asked the vice president how his social class shaped his life, not-ing that families like the Bushes often send their kids to expensive private schools to ensure their leg up.

"This sounds, well, un-American to George Jr., and he rages that it is crap from the 60's. Nobody thinks that way anymore!" Mr. Har-rington wrote. "But his father cuts him off. . . . He seems genuinely interested. . . . But the amazing thing is that Bush finds these ideas so novel. . . . People who work the hardest—even though some have a head start—will usually get ahead, he says. To see it otherwise is divisive."

When journalists on W.'s campaign wrote that he had been ad-mitted to Yale as a legacy, the candidate's Texas advisers pointed out that he had also gotten into Harvard, and no Bush family members had gone there.

They seemed genuinely surprised when told that Harvard would certainly have recognized the surname and wagered on the future success of the person with it.

If you don't acknowledge that being a wealthy white man with the right ancestors blesses you with the desirable sort of inequality, how can you fix the undesirable sort of inequality?

The Bushes seem to believe that the divisive thing in American society is dwelling on social and economic inequities, rather than the inequities themselves.

When critics of W.'s tax cuts say they favor the wealthy, the president indignantly accuses them of class warfare. That's designed to intimidate critics by making them seem vaguely pinko. Besides, there's nothing more effective than deploring class warfare while ensuring that your class wins. It is the Bush tax cut that is fomenting class warfare.

When the University of Michigan tries to redress a historic racial injustice by giving some advantage based on race, Mr. Bush gets offended by arbitrarily conferred advantages, as if he himself were not an affirmative action baby.

The president's preferred way of promoting diversity in higher education is throwing money at black colleges, which is not exactly a clarion call for integration.

Back in '86, when the *Post* reporter suggested that class mattered, W. found the contention un-American.

But isn't it un-American if the University of Michigan or Yale makes special room for the descendants of alumni but not the descendants of the disadvantaged?

Surrendering to Vice

The Boy King
Submits to the
Dark Father

The Axis of No Access

■

Back in the sixties, my brother would occasionally pretend to be a spy to impress girls.

It was pretty silly.

But nothing compared with the vice president pretending to be a Secret Agent Man.

Dick Cheney has taken his cloak-and-dagger routine to absurd extremes. "There's a man who leads a life of danger. . . . To everyone he meets he stays a stranger."

We are not allowed to know where Secret Agent Man sleeps. (Sometimes he'll entertain people at his residence, and then leave for his "secure, undisclosed location" at the same time his guests leave for unsecure, disclosed locations.) We are not allowed to know whom he talks to in the White House. We are not allowed to hear how he shapes our energy policy or our war plans. We may not even be allowed to cover his trip to the Middle East to prepare our allies for a campaign against Saddam.

Mr. Cheney does pop up for Sunday shows, fund-raisers and the occasional soiree. He played host at a book party at his house Monday night for his chief of staff, Scooter Libby, who has come out with a paperback of an old novel about—what else?—shadowy political intrigue. Vice, as the president called him on Tom Brokaw's White House tour, stood under a blue painting in his red tie and gray suit, talking in a low voice out of the side of his mouth, which adds to the conspiratorial aura.

Outside, guests saw an ominous sign that read: "Threat Condition Bravo."

The vice president does give up some information. He has been happy to fill in reporters on how amazing the Bush team was on 9/11 and after. And the Bush administration authorized the release to Congress of thousands of e-mails by Clinton officials, including ones sent to Al Gore.

But he prefers to operate under deep cover. The Bushes' attitude toward disclosure is embodied in Mr. Cheney: We know best. Leave it to us. In their view, the American public has been cleared for very little information about the American government.

In a speech Monday to roofing contractors, 41 grumbled about the national press, "which I now confess I hate."

And 43 spirited his Texas gubernatorial records—which would include contacts with Enron—into his father's presidential library, where reporters will have to wait months, or years, to get at them.

Just as Mr. Cheney thinks he is entitled to cook up our energy policy behind closed doors with his oil and gas buddies and Republican donors, his office had been considering treating Air Force Two like a corporate jet. Just wave good-bye to the White House press corps at Andrews and fly off to ten Middle East countries for clandestine talks.

Should we be countering the Axis of Evil with the Axis of No Access? Should our leaders leave a free press at home when they go to talk to regimes that do not countenance a free press?

Aren't we supposed to be influencing the Saudis and other Middle Eastern countries in the direction of honesty and transparency? Instead, the vice president emulates his Saudi friends—operating with high-handed secrecy, plotting with cronies to develop a petrostate and restricting the press—just as he did during Desert Storm.

Cheney staffers came up with numerous explanations why it may be difficult to take the press—all of them silly. They're not the president: they don't have two planes. They don't have the resources. They don't have the staff. They're going to a very insecure region.

On CNN last night, the conservative Bob Novak admitted the idea was unprecedented, but explained the Cheneythink.

"You do remember the Spiro Agnew and the Dan Quayle trips were circuses," he said. "Dick Cheney is going on a 10-day trip to the Middle East and his staff is considering whether they really want to take any press along. No members of the media whatsoever, to avoid all these made-up stories. . . . They may say, 'Hey, this is a business trip.'"

But that is precisely the problem. The American government is not a business. And the vice president's diplomacy in the Middle East is not a business trip.

Dick Cheney may truly be the most powerful vice president in the history of the universe. Everything he does is the public's business.

Rub-a-Dub in the Hot Tub

■

D ick and Rummy are in the Jacuzzi at Camp David.

The two masters of the Bush universe have had a lousy week. And now, with the white cast on Rummy's hand buoyed by bubbles, they just want to sip Scotch on the rocks and review the knocks.

They are keeping one eye on the Kid, who's been jogging circles around Aspen Lodge for the past nine hours.

Junior is supposed to be inside practicing how to say "malfeasance" with an *s*. But he won't do it. He's sulking. He went to Wall Street on Tuesday to show that the hero of September 11 could retaliate against the creeps who wiped out the neighborhood and also keep CEOs from looting.

But the president who got elected on the backs of CEOs and said he wanted to run the country like a CEO was about as convincing a sheriff as Barney Fife.

Rummy's war has also run into a bad patch, bombing brides instead of bin Laden.

As the two men soak, more steam is coming from the vice president than the hot tub.

"The Kid never should have gone to Wall Street in the first place," Dick grumbles. "All those poppycock reforms he and Rove rushed into the speech. Who knew our Karl was also a Marxist? When the going gets tough, the weak go polling. Who cares what Americans think? They should care what we think."

W. jogs past with a singsong chant: "It's NOT my fault, it's NOT my fault, it's BUBBA'S fault, it's BUBBA'S fault."

Dick and Rummy laugh indulgently.

"SWAT teams swooping down on CEOs?" Dick scoffs. "What nonsense. Will government lawyers ride around in stealth golf carts and read these guys their rights on the back nine?

"We certainly don't need more transparency in this country. Transparency is just a fancy kind of indecent exposure, a sick counterculture idea, whether it's about the markets, accounting or giving up the names of our Houston buddies who dictated my energy policy. I say: Zip it.

"We don't owe anybody any explanation for any thought or action that any of us have ever had or done."

Rummy grins devilishly and skillfully balances his glass on his cast in a silent toast.

"Those lily-livered liberals in Congress are outrageous—they're criminalizing greed!" Dick says. "And the spineless Republican fellow travelers on the Hill are almost worse—they'll dry up our donor base and destroy the party before they're through. McCain is just Norman Thomas with medals.

"I have nothing against sharing, of course. As long as it's us getting the shares.

"Our strategy is to slow down the House and Senate so these stiffer accounting and corporate-greed bills never see the light of day. Maybe you guys could accelerate your war on Baghdad. A righteous distraction would come in handy."

The Pentagon boss indicates with a nod of his cast that this is possible. "Bunch of anticapitalist, world-government-loving wusses," Rummy says. "They don't understand how tough we had it as CEOs. It's lonely at the top."

Junior jogs over to the Jacuzzi and tries to get Vice's attention. "Dude?"

Dick waves him off and resumes his rant: "All that stands between America and socialism are stock options. Without options, companies can't lure great leaders who will take risks—with other people's money, of course. If Congress got its way, when the stock went down, the CEO would lose money just like everyone else. But we are not everyone else."

The president tries again to get Dick's attention: "Dude?"

Dick goes on, his dander rising. "I'm sick and tired of these Sunday morning pinkos trying to impoverish the ruling class. People should get off my back about the way I cashed out of Halliburton. What's $20 million these days?"

Rummy is astonished. For the first time in the many decades he has known Dick, his friend's face is no longer affectless. Dick gives the impression of something that can only be called emotion.

But the Kid has finally lost patience. He jumps into the Jacuzzi, barely missing Rummy's cast, and sloshes right over to Vice, leaning into his ear and wailing plaintively: "Where's Karen?"

Cheneyville Christmas

◼

On TV this weekend, George Bush tells the story of George and the bush.

"George stares down at the empty robe, then picks it up, looking puzzled," the former president says. "Mary's eyes peer out of a large, flowering bush. George starts to toss the robe, then reconsiders, eyeing the robe slyly."

It's a Wonderful Life was on NBC, and the visually impaired could tune in to a version in which Bush *père* charmingly narrated the action, including the scene where Donna Reed loses her bathrobe and jumps into a hydrangea bush so Jimmy Stewart can't see her.

Poppy Bush did the voice-over as a favor for a blind woman from California who is an advocate of TV audio description for the blind.

The Christmas classic has special resonance for the Bushes this year.

Just as George Bailey reverses his life to see how things would have been different, the younger George Bush is reversing his father's life to see how things would have been different. (Rather than Pottersville, W. goes to Cheneyville, a grim, secretive place where the poor are squeezed and the environment is scrooged.)

If 41 hadn't been president, 43 would have nothing to do, since the kid spends all his time doing U-turns on the highway of Pop's presidency.

His father let Saddam stay and raised taxes to cut the deficit; the son has to get rid of Saddam and cut taxes, raising the deficit.

The son is determined to get the second term that the father didn't; the father lost his job because he did not appear to care about Americans' economic woes, so the son will make sure that he appears to care.

Thus, the Thursday night massacre of Paul O'Neill and Larry Lindsey. As heartless as Lionel Barrymore, Dick Cheney initiated the firings, brutally axing his old pal and fellow CEO, Mr. O'Neill, after assuring him that he had the president's confidence and could stay two more years. Andy Card pushed Mr. Lindsey off the sled of state.

Signaling its approval, the stock market shot up at news that the former head of Alcoa had been canned.

Before the elections, the White House distracted us from its muddled policy on the economy by fussing about Iraq. Now it distracts us from its muddled policy on Iraq by fussing about the economy.

The CEO administration has given way to the Mayberry Machiavellis, as a former Bush official calls the politically obsessed West Wing in a Karl Rove profile in *Esquire*.

Now that the Republicans have control of Congress, the Bush team can stop pretending that it has an economic policy and can try to develop one in the twenty minutes before the 2004 campaign starts up.

Next time around, they're not going to be able to whine that the meanie Tom Daschle and his Democratic Senate were to blame.

By sending a forlorn Mr. O'Neill driving back to Pittsburgh, the White House offered only a counterfeit reckoning. In a genuine reckoning, they would have admitted the tax cuts aren't cutting it. If the Bushies want their fiscal policy, they can't have their national security policy. And if they want their national security policy, they can't have their fiscal policy.

The war on Iraq will cost up to $200 billion, as Mr. Lindsey blurted out, and there is no numerical figure to represent the cost for the war on terrorism or the Department of Homeland Security or the beefing up of the FBI and the CIA.

Just as the administration is having a hard time finding an economic strategy—beyond lifting a tax on dividends for those who play the stock market—they're having a hard time finding a casus belli.

President Bush thought he had Saddam boxed in, but he has been stymied by the Iraqi scheme of cooperating but not complying.

Dropping an 11,000-page declaration of their arms programs, Iraqis showed they had learned the art of the document dump from U.S. administrations, which have figured out that the way to confound investigators and the press is to hit them with a paper blizzard. By the time the Arabic diary of obfuscation is deciphered, it will be summer again and too hot to fight.

In a costly reversal of his father's presidency, W. will have to pay for his war against Saddam. The allies and gulf states put billions in James Baker's hat the last time. But it is unlikely that George Bush's friends, like George Bailey's, will bail him out with a shower of cash at the end.

■

Sleeping with the Enemy

In Which the Saudis Fly Away from 9/11 Blame in Their Private Jets

■

May 1, 2002

This Dynasty Stuff

■

Former president Bush swats away talk about what he dismissively calls "this dynasty stuff" or "this legacy crud."

But the Texas meeting of the two royal families, the House of Saud and the House of Bush, as *Newsweek* called it, showed the cat's cradle entwining 41 and 43, two presidents perplexed and bedeviled by the same tumultuous region.

The second President Bush neglected the Middle East for fifteen months. Then the Middle East visited him in September, and he became firm in his antiterrorist resolve. Then he started vacillating—a muddled, nerve-racking period during which he still seemed to be struggling to occupy the full space of his presidency. Finally, Poppy of Arabia swept across the Texas prairie to help out.

Until the Crawford summit, W. had been pulled by Karl Rove and the conservative right into the Israeli orbit, scolding Ariel Sharon even as he ludicrously lauded him as "a man of peace," letting him get on with his brutal campaign.

Mr. Rove, focused on keeping the conservative base that W.'s dad lost and making inroads into the Jewish vote that W.'s dad never had, even dispatched hawkish Paul Wolfowitz to address a pro-Israel rally.

But just when W. seemed to have cast his lot firmly with Mr. Sharon, undercutting his own disgruntled secretary of state, he was reminded by Dad that there is nothing thicker than blood and oil.

Bush Senior and Dick Cheney, the Texas oil men and Saudi protectors in Desert Storm (and their pals Jim Baker and Brent Scowcroft), have always had a kinship with the Arab world, especially Saudi Arabia. The strategic affinity was enhanced by oil money, politics, defense contracts and bidness.

The Persian Gulf War Boys' Club is chaired by Prince Bandar, the former fighter pilot and Saudi ambassador who was always quick to offer Bush *père* and other club members a private jet ride or a British hunting jaunt or a junket at his Aspen mansion—to which he transported a British pub he had dismantled.

The Bush presidential library was built in part with millions of dollars from Saudi Arabia and Kuwait.

At a recent party at the vice president's house in Washington, Prince Bandar seemed right at home.

The House of Saud was ecstatic when W. beat Al Gore, because its pals were back. It had considered Clinton-Gore too unreliable and too pro-Israel, not like the Bush crowd, who get their energy from energy.

But the Saudis came to rue W., once Ariel Sharon embraced him.

When the disgruntled Saudis arrived in Texas last week, Poppy and Cheney took over the show, absorbing the body blows and relaying Saudi frustration to the president.

On Tuesday, Poppy had lunch with the Saudi foreign minister,

Saud al-Faisal, and Prince Bandar in Houston. On Wednesday, Crown Prince Abdullah had lunch with Cheney.

On Thursday, W. met at the ranch with Prince Abdullah, who wanted to show the president pictures of charred and maimed Palestinian children. Mr. Bush wore a suit and tie and said "Yes, sir," "No, sir" to the seventy-seven-year-old prince, showing deference to an old family friend and not showing pictures of dead and maimed in New York and Washington.

Abdullah told W. that he relies on God when he makes tough decisions, and the president said he prays a lot to God to guide him, as well.

On Friday, Prince Abdullah went with Poppy by train to the Bush presidential library in College Station. The former president showed him the collection of photographs of 41 and 43 juxtaposed with pictures of John and John Quincy Adams.

Prince Abdullah said to Poppy and Bar that, meaning no offense, it was possible that W. would be an even greater president than his dad.

Bush *père* got misty with pride. This was the signal that the royal houses of America and Saudi Arabia had overcome the threat to their relationship.

Some in the pro-Israel camp found it disgusting that the Bush family had given the Saudis a warm Texas welcome, without even pressing them to account for the Saudi face on the attacks of 9/11. They are warily watching the new Crawford-Riyadh partnership to jointly pressure Sharon and Arafat to make peace.

One thing is clear: By working more closely with the Saudi dynasty, this president may be getting closer to his dynasty's avenging dream of toppling Saddam.

I'm with Dick! Let's Make War!

■

I was dubious at first. But now I think Dick Cheney has it right.

Making the case for going to war in the Middle East to veterans on Monday, the vice president said that "our goal would be . . . a government that is democratic and pluralistic, a nation where the human rights of every ethnic and religious group are recognized and protected."

O.K., I'm on board. Let's declare war on Saudi Arabia! Let's do "regime change" in a kingdom that gives medieval a bad name.

By overthrowing the Saudi monarchy, the Cheney-Rummy-Condi-Wolfie-Perle-W. contingent could realize its dream of redrawing the Middle East map.

Once everyone realizes that we're no longer being hypocrites, coddling a corrupt, repressive dictatorship that sponsors terrorism even as we plot to crush a corrupt, repressive dictatorship that sponsors terrorism, it will transform our relationship with the Arab world.

We won't need Charlotte Beers at the State Department, thinking up Madison Avenue slogans to make the Arab avenue love us. ("Democracy! Mm-mm, good.")

If America is going to have a policy of justified preemption, in Henry Kissinger's clinical phrase, why not start by chasing out those sorry Saudi royals? If we're willing to knock over Saddam for gassing the Kurds, we should be willing to knock over the Saudis for letting the state-supported religious police burn fifteen girls to death last March in a Mecca school, forcing them back inside a fiery building because they tried to flee without their scarves. And shouldn't we preempt them before they teach more boys to hate American infidels and before they can stunt the lives of more women?

The vice president declared on Monday, "This nation will not live at the mercy of terrorists or terror regimes." I am absolutely with him.

Why should we (and our SUVs) be at the mercy of this family that we arm and protect and go to war for? The Saudis have never formally apologized to America for the fifteen Saudi citizens who came here and killed three thousand Americans as they went to work one sun-dappled September morning. They have never even tried to rewrite their incendiary terrorist-breeding textbooks or stop their newspapers from spewing anti-American, anti-Semitic lies, like their stories accusing Jews of drinking children's blood. They brazenly held a telethon, with King Fahd and Crown Prince Abdullah giving millions, to raise money for families of Palestinian suicide bombers, or "martyrs." Last week the Saudi embassy here put out a glossy brochure hailing their "humanitarian work" at the telethon.

It was embarrassing yesterday, given President Bush's swagger on Iraq, to watch him fawn over the Saudis. At lunch at his ranch he entertained Prince Bandar, the man who got private planes to spirit Osama bin Laden's relatives out of the U.S. after the attacks. Mr.

Bush also called Crown Prince Abdullah yesterday to assure him of the "eternal friendship" between their countries and to soothe hurt Saudi feelings over a lawsuit filed by 9/11 victims charging Saudi support of terrorism.

Mr. Cheney argues that we must invade Iraq while we have a strategic window for action, while Saddam's army is still reeling.

But attacking the Saudis would be even easier. They are soft and spoiled. Only yesterday Jerome Socolovsky of the A.P. wrote about how King Fahd brought thousands of members of the House of Saud to Marbella, Spain, where they stocked up on luxury items and hired North African servants. Women in veils and waterproof robes rode Jet Skis and members of the royal family talked about the 9/11 attacks as an Israeli-CIA plot.

A Saudi invasion would be like the Panama invasion during Bush I. We already have bases to use there. And this time Mr. Cheney won't have to beg the royals to use their air space, or send American forces.

Once we make Saudi Arabia into our own self-serve gas pump, its neighbors will get the democracy bug.

The Saudis would probably use surrogates to fight anyway. They pay poor workers from other countries to do their menial labor. And they paid the Americans to fight the Iraqis in 1991. The joke among the American forces then was: "What's the Saudi national anthem? 'Onward, Christian Soldiers.'"

We haven't been hit at home by any of Saddam's Scud missiles. But the human missiles launched by Saudi Arabia have taken their toll.

Under the Ramadan Moon

■

The Saudi Arabian Airlines flight from Riyadh to Jidda began with an Islamic prayer over the intercom. Later a message flashed on the screen warning men headed for Mecca, east of Jidda, that there were only twenty minutes left, then ten, to change into the *ihram*—the traditional garment signifying the shedding of material things—before the plane crossed into the holy city's airspace.

Some men went to the bathroom to drape themselves in the two white pieces of cloth. It was a striking tableau of Saudis' split nature—a gnashing negotiation between ancient and modern—to see pilgrims in white robes carrying black laptops.

As the sliver of moon was spotted and Ramadan began, Crown Prince Abdullah urged Muslims to "follow the moderate line of Islam." He is trying to calm the turbulence buffeting his kingdom from inside and out. Two events have scalded a monarchy unaccustomed to criticism, either from its submissive subjects or its cynical oil-trading partners.

Saudis are bitter at Americans who are bitter about the Saudi hijackers, Saudi money funding Islamicist terrorism and Saudi madrasas sparking animosity toward Americans.

Before 9/11, Americans could think of this place simply as an exclusive men's club where pols in pinstripes did mutually beneficial, if corrupting, deals with princes in robes.

"Americans are partly responsible for our country's lack of democracy," one Saudi newspaper editor says contemptuously. "You've been happy to pump our gas and sell us your planes and other toys."

After 9/11, wised-up Americans started trying to figure out what toxic desert flowers were growing behind the kingdom's walls.

American critics began calling for changes in boys' schools here, just as Saudi critics began calling for changes in girls' schools here.

The tragedy that shook this country, and spurred ordinarily tame Saudi papers to run blaring headlines criticizing the government, was the fire last March in the Mecca girls' school. Started by a teenager's tossed cigarette butt, the fire killed fifteen girls after the *mutawwa*, the religious police, stopped rescue workers from saving students trying to escape without scarves and *abayas*.

Hussein Shobokshi, a thirty-eight-year-old businessman from Jidda, went to the funeral. "I watched the parents carrying the wrapped bodies of their thirteen-, fourteen- and fifteen-year-old daughters to the mosque," he recalled. "I was extremely angered."

It was, as they say here, the feather that broke the camel's back. Mr. Shobokshi was among those who wrote pieces urging that the cavalier president for girls' education be sacked. He was, and despite protests from conservative clerics enraged at the dread specter of coeducation, the royal family merged the departments for girls' and boys' education.

I went to see the minister of education at his home in Riyadh.

Mohammed Ahmed Rasheed and half a dozen deputies, men in long white robes and headdresses, arrayed themselves on chairs against the walls and worried their beads. They talked fondly about time spent at American universities—Stanford, Indiana, Oklahoma, Michigan; Khedir al-Qurashi, the vice minister for girls' education, spoke of his love of Hoosiers basketball.

They were defensive about American suspicion of the religious hard-liners' influence on boys' schooling. "Why don't you go to Israeli math textbooks and see what they're saying—'If you kill 10 Arabs one day and 12 the next day, what would be the total?'" demanded one deputy, crudely and sardonically. Agreed another: "If 5 or 8 percent of our curriculum has to be changed, then 80 to 90 percent of the content of American media has to be changed."

Mr. Rasheed reminisced about how amazed he was in America to be sitting next to girls in class. "It was really the highlight of our lives," he smiled. "Though we liked it there, I don't want to have it here."

His twenty-seven-year-old son, Osama, who also attended school in the U.S., is no more liberal. "I can't see my sister or mother or wife in a room with other guys," he said.

Mr. Rasheed said the girls' curriculum would still stress the role of women as wives and mothers. A deputy explained there would be no passages in textbooks such as "Fatima went out with her friend Mohammed," and Mr. Rasheed chimed in, "That's really forbidden."

Boys and girls are not permitted to pal around, just as men and women are not allowed to date or be alone unless they are married.

Dick and Jane would never cut it here. And the angry *mutawwa* would haul in Jack and Jill before they ever got near that hill.

Frederick's of Riyadh

■

During my week in Riyadh, I had been wanting to catch a glimpse of the *mutawwa*, the bully boys from the Commission for the Promotion of Virtue and Prevention of Vice who go around harassing and arresting Saudis in the name of Islam. But since I grew up with *I Dream of Jeannie* and tales of Aladdin's lamp, I should have known that Arabia is not the place to make wishes lightly.

The religious police were reputed to look angry and have long, scraggly beards, and to clean their teeth with a tree root called *miswak*. They had been so out of control lately that Prince Naif, the interior minister, cautioned them last week to show tolerance, respect the sanctity of private homes and stop spying on people.

This kingdom is a thicket of unfathomable extremes. Frederick's of Hollywood–style lingerie shops abound, even though female sexuality is considered so threatening that the mere sight of a woman's ankle will cause civilization to crumble. As one cleric put it, women can become "the most dangerous weapon of destruction" for Islamic nations.

Saudi Arabia has some remarkable women, but you won't find them helping to run the country; the toilet seats at the Foreign Ministry are routinely left up.

On Wednesday at 11:30 P.M., I walked to the mall connected to my hotel to verify that there is a "women only" lingerie section in Harvey Nichols. (The first wife of Muhammad, who as a young man did not seem to mind high-achieving women, was a merchant; during Ramadan, trade is encouraged and stores stay open past midnight.)

My dinner companion, Adel al-Jubeir, went with me. The smooth Georgetown-educated spokesman for the Saudis has been the kingdom's point man on the Sunday talk shows, trying to repair its friendship with America after 9/11. The three-story mall was so chockablock with designer stilettos, bondage boots, transparent blouses and glittering gowns with plunging necklines that it would have made Las Vegas blush.

I felt drab, dressed in black to suit Saudi standards with a scarf over my hair, a long skirt, a sweater over a T-shirt and flats. An earlier outing with a pink skirt had caused my Ministry of Information minder to bark: "Get your *abaya*! They'll kill you!"

I made some notes on Harvey Nichols's lingerie apartheid—racks of sheer zebra and leopard Dolce & Gabbana nighties and lacy Donna Karan items—and Mr. Jubeir and I headed back to the hotel. Suddenly, four men bore down on us, two in white robes, one in a brown policeman's uniform and one in a floor-length brown A-line skirt (not a good look). They pointed to my neck and hips, and the embarrassed diplomat explained that I had been busted by the vice squad.

"They say they can see the outline of your body," he translated.

"They say they welcome you to the mall, which is a sign of our modernity, but that we are also proud of our tradition and faith, and you must respect that." The police took my passport and began making notes about the crime, oblivious to the irony of detaining me in front of the window of another lingerie shop displaying a short lacy red slip.

I figured they'd shrink away upon learning that Mr. Jubeir's boss was Crown Prince Abdullah. But they didn't. I thought I'd catch a break because I'm an American Catholic, not a Muslim. I didn't. Apparently, the *mutawwa* are not on board with the Saudis' multimillion-dollar charm offensive to persuade America that the kingdom is not a hotbed of hostile religious zealots.

Mr. Jubeir asked whether I'd "placate" the *mutawwa* by putting on an abaya from a nearby shop. I'd had to wear one of the macabre, hot black shrouds that day to see the crown prince, and I was loath to get shrouded up again to walk a few yards.

After the men argued for fifteen minutes, I fretted that I was in one of those movies where an American makes one mistake in a repressive country and ends up rotting in a dungeon. I missed John Ashcroft desperately. The Saudis, after all, have been fighting with the U.N. Committee Against Torture so they can keep using flogging and amputation of limbs as disciplinary measures.

Finally, the *mutawwa* agreed to let me go, appeased by the promise that I would soon be leaving Saudi Arabia. A relieved scofflaw, I was left to ponder a country at a turning point, a society engaged in a momentous struggle for its future, torn between secret police and secret undergarments.

Driving While Female

■

Riyadh may be the Bible Belt of the Arab world, but some of the architecture looks very *Star Wars.*

There is a sleek new skyscraper in the Saudi capital designed with a big hole in the upper stories.

"There's a bad joke," said a Saudi architect, "that we use that building to train terrorist hijackers."

Terrorism experts have been speculating that Osama's new tape is aimed at inflaming disgruntled young men in Saudi Arabia—where everyone I met bitterly complained that America is warring against Islam and shafting the Palestinians.

It's fertile ground. Saudi Arabia is the Augusta National of Islam, a sand trap where men can hang out and be men. A suffocating, strict, monochromatic world of white-robed men and black-robed women.

After the oil boom of the late seventies, orthodox Islamic clerics got so furious at the louche behavior of the royals—jetting off to

Europe, buying bigger houses and cars, and spending less time on family—that they went "into overdrive," as one Saudi official put it.

"That's when we should have put them into a box," he sighed.

Instead, the royals tried to throw the fundamentalists sops— blocking little things like cultural freedom and women's rights.

The moment when America should have tried to use its influence to help Saudi women came on November 6, 1990, as U.S. forces gathered in the kingdom to go to war in Iraq. Inspired by the American troops—including female soldiers—forty-seven women from the intelligentsia went for a joy ride to protest Saudi Arabia's being the only place where women can't drive.

"We were very, very careful to plan it correctly not to be too antagonistic to the culture," recalled one of "the drivers," as they are still known. "We were mothers, well covered, nothing anti-Islam."

Using international licenses, the women took the wheels from their brothers and husbands and drove in a convoy until police stopped them.

At first, the drivers were exhilarated. But then the clerics pounced, blaming "secular Americanist" ideas and branding the women "whores" and "harlots." They were publicly harassed, received death threats and lost their jobs. "People would make threatening calls to our homes saying 'you bitches,'" recalled one woman. "They put out flyers all over the country saying horrible things about us." Their husbands' jobs were jeopardized; their passports were revoked; they had to sign papers agreeing not to talk about the drive.

Prince Naif, the interior minister, placated the clerics, saying the women had committed "a stupid act." Driving by women, banned by custom, was made illegal as degrading to "the sanctity of women."

America was silent: Whether they drove was less important than how much it cost us to drive.

"The aftermath was much worse than we thought it would be, even now there is some backlash," said one of the women, whose twenty-two-year-old daughter even calls it a mistake.

After twelve years, on the cusp of another gulf war, came a sign that the women's ostracism was finally ending. When I was in Riyadh recently, there was a party for the opening of a museum exhibition of photographs by one of the drivers, Madeha Alajroush, who lost her job at a photography studio after the protest. The host was Princess Adelah, the daughter of Crown Prince Abdullah, and it was attended by Abdullah's favorite wife, Hissah, and another daughter, Sita.

Several of the drivers were there, admiring the subversive photos of faceless women, including one of a woman's ghostly outline on a couch.

They did not believe the royal presence signaled that the driving ban might soon end. "People never will be ready," said one. Agreed another: "I never thought the day would come when my daughter would not be able to drive. It seems such a simple, necessary part of life."

Now they are more angry at the U.S. than their own rulers. They feel the American media are playing up the repression of Saudi women post-9/11 as a way to demonize Saudi Arabia, just as George and Laura Bush played up the repression of Afghan women post-9/11 as a way to demonize the Taliban.

"Americans are always saying they're concerned with freedom and the democratic will of people," said one of the drivers, a professor. "But they didn't care about what was happening inside our country in 1990. And they still don't care. We are seen only as the ladies in black."

November 27, 2002

A Golden Couple Chasing
Away a Black Cloud

■

Prince Bandar is known as the Arab Gatsby.

Rising from a murky past in a racist society, born in a Bedouin tent as the son of an African palace servant impregnated by a Saudi prince, to a glamorous present as dean of the Washington diplomatic corps.

Tossing glittery parties with celebrity entertainment at his sumptuous mansions in Aspen and England's Wychwood, a royal hunting ground once used by Norman and Plantagenet kings.

Smoking cigars and bragging about his fighter-jock exploits—flying upside down fifty feet above the ground—at parties at his McLean, Virginia, estate overlooking the Potomac, "where there was more chilled vodka in little shot glasses than I've ever seen," as one guest recalled.

Flying off in his private Airbus to hunt birds in Spain with his friends George Bush, Sr., and Norman Schwarzkopf, entertaining the current President Bush's sister, Doro, at his Virginia farm, and palling around on the D.C. social circuit with Dick Cheney, Colin Powell, George Tenet, Brent Scowcroft and Bob Woodward.

Spinning a smoky web of intrigue with his cigars and CIA operations, helping finance the contras.

So if Bandar bin Sultan is Gatsby, his wife, Princess Haifa, must be like the careless Daisy, her voice full of money that could have ended up supporting two of the Saudi hijackers. And those fifteen Saudi hijackers would be "the foul dust that floated in the wake" of the Arab Gatsby's dreams.

His new dream is that Saudi Arabia will help America get rid of Saddam, and then the anger over Saudi involvement in 9/11 will fade and the cozy, oily alliance between the countries can get back on track.

All the millions the Saudis have spent since 9/11 on a charm offensive could not save them from *Newsweek*'s Michael Isikoff and Evan Thomas, who drew fresh tracks between charitable checks Princess Haifa wrote and two hijackers.

The princess says she feels as if a bomb had been dropped on her head—an unfortunate metaphor given the fact that Saudi terrorists funded by Saudi charities turned planes carrying innocent Americans into bombs.

She is rarely seen around Washington, abiding by Saudi customs sheltering women. But she entertains at her many homes, and powerful friends—including Barbara Bush and Alma Powell—called on Monday night to buck her up.

The case inflamed public suspicion that the Saudi government is more involved than it admits, and that the Bushies are less zealous about getting to the bottom of the Saudi role than they should be.

Some senators charge that the FBI has pulled its punches, and that the royal family, as Richard Shelby puts it, has "got a lot of answering to do."

General Tommy Franks has already spent a fortune setting up a new base in Qatar because the Saudis are still dithering about letting us use our old bases in their country.

Noncommittal on the future, and uncooperative on the past, the Saudis have been stingy about helping the FBI with 9/11. The administration has helped the Saudis be evasive, with Dick Cheney stonewalling congressional investigators.

It would probably be far easier for America to reduce its dependence on Saudi oil than for the House of Saud and the House of Bush to untangle their decades-long symbiosis.

Prince Bandar, the representative of an oil kingdom, is so close to the Bushes, an oil dynasty, that they nicknamed him "Bandar Bush." He contributed over $1 million to the Bush presidential library. The former president is affiliated with the Carlyle Group, which does extensive business with the Saudis.

It was terribly inconvenient for all the friends of the bin Sultans when the trail of checks led to the Saudi embassy. Many influential people in Washington were averting their eyes from the embarrassment. The prince and his panicky wife were defending themselves to the *Times*'s Pat Tyler while Bandar anxiously flipped among seven television screens in their pool house to catch the latest news.

The Bush crowd was praying it wasn't a last-days-of-disco scene similar to the one when the shah of Iran was overthrown by Islamic fundamentalists, and the jet-setting Iranian diplomats had to pour all the liquor down the drain at their embassy. Will the Arab Gatsby end like the original—"borne back ceaselessly into the past"?

July 23, 2003

Weapons of Mass Redaction

■

This correspondence from the Office of the Vice President to the ██████ ███████ ambassador to the U.S. was redacted by the Office of the Vice President for national and electoral security reasons:

Dear Prince ████████ bin █████████,

Thank you, my friend, for the falcon. It survived the trip on your Gulfstream. It is now eating small endangered woodland creatures at my Jackson Hole ranch.

We are pumped about the double rubout of the Hussein boys. We really needed that win. It could be a game-changer for us. The stock market killed on the killings. And the timing will help cover your royal ██████, too.

When the 9/11 committee report comes out tomorrow, I think you will be well satisfied with our efforts to keep you guys out of it.

We have almost as much experience as you at keeping private matters veiled. It's not good to overburden the American people with too much complicated information.

We didn't let a thing slip on our private energy meetings where we took care of our mutual friends in the ▮▮▮ industry; we kept the bidding closed on the Halliburton contracts to rebuild Iraq, and we set up our own CIA within the Pentagon to produce the intelligence we wanted to link Al Qaeda to Saddam rather than to your country.

We've classified the entire section of the 9/11 report that deals with the ▮▮▮▮ family's support of charitable groups that benefit terrorists, including mentions of your wife's checks inexplicably winding up in the bank accounts of two of the hijackers. (Lynne says to tell Princess ▮▮▮▮ we have four tickets for the ▮▮▮▮ ballet at the Kennedy Center.)

We're not even letting Bob Graham mention the name of your country. We threatened to throw him in the federal slammer if he calls ▮▮▮▮ ▮▮▮▮ anything but "a foreign government."

Not to worry that the report will shed any light on the ties between the hijackers and your government agent ▮▮▮▮ al-▮▮▮▮.

I know you're worried that the whiny widows of 9/11 will throw another hissy fit when they see all the blacked-out material, like they did when you whisked Osama's family out of the U.S. on a private jet right after the attacks. But we didn't go this far down the road of pushing aside incriminating evidence about you guys and blaming 9/11 on Saddam to turn back now because a few thousand families can't get their darn closure.

Buddy, we go back a long way. You've been a great host to the Bushes and you've been generous with rides on your Airbus and Gulfstream and with invites to your beautiful estates in ▮▮▮▮ and ▮▮▮▮ and ▮▮▮▮.

But now you have to throw us a bone. Al Qaeda cells are crawling all over your kingdom, planning attacks around the world. They've gotten even stronger since the May bombing of Western compounds in ███████. We need a little more than lip service about quelling anti-American fervor over there and cracking down on phony charities. You've got to at least give the FBI something to work with. Don't worry. They'll screw it up anyway.

Rest assured that the FBI's taking the heat for 9/11 in the report tomorrow, not you.

I hear you want to behead that ex-spook Robert Baer, who's been all over TV talking about the way you lavish money to influence U.S. politics, donating millions to presidential libraries, etc. But after all, every million spent on a congressman's favorite charity is one less million spent on a terrorist's fake charity.

Here in the ██████ House, we've mastered the art of moving beyond what people once thought was important to look for. First, we switched from looking for Osama to looking for Saddam. Then we switched from looking for "weapons" to looking for "weapons programs." Now Wolfie has informed the public that we need to worry less about finding weapons in Iraq than building democracy.

The trick is to keep moving. Just yesterday, we shifted the blame for the uranium debacle in the president's State of the ███████ speech from George Tenet at the CIA to Stephen Hadley at the NSC.

I'd like to return your many acts of generosity. Why not come to dinner at my Secret Undisclosed Location? Here's the address: ██████ ███████ in ███████.

All the best, Dick.

As the World Turns on Us

In Which Furious George Upends His Sire's Friendly Diplomacy

May 26, 2002

W.'s Grand Tour

■

T his used to be the Evil Empire.

But now we need the old Evil Empire to help us with the new Axis of Evil and the Evildoers. (Even though the ex–Evil Empire is helping the country that dubbed us the Great Satan gain nuclear capability.) So now Russia is the Good Empire.

We were watching the Kremlin signing ceremony for the arms treaty. Before a blindingly gold czarist throne draped in ermine, Mr. Bush hailed the new spirit of trust this way: "That's good. It's good for the people of Russia; it's good for the people of the United States. . . . For decades, Russia and NATO were adversaries. Those days are gone, and that's good. And that's good for the Russian people, it's good for the people of my country, it's good for the people of Europe, and it's good for the people of the world."

In other words, it's good.

Vladimir Putin, once regarded by the foreign-policy nanny Condi Rice as a suspect former KGB chief, is now W.'s beloved "Pootie-

Poot." In Bushworld, especially since 9/11, it's always either good or evil. The Bush doctrine is as basic as a Texas two-step: Either you're with us on terrorism, or agin' us.

W. is Manichaean Man. He used to be his father's White House loyalty enforcer, but had no interest in foreign affairs. Now he's the global loyalty enforcer. Before Mr. Bush left Washington, some Europeans sneered that "Bully Bush" had turned into something even more irritating: a missionary.

In Berlin, Mr. Bush's first stop on a trip full of fabulous cities he had never visited, he was asked by a snippy local peacenik reporter to "try to explain to the German people what your goals are when it comes to Iraq." The president huffed: "He's a dictator who gassed his own people."

It had to be the most powerful statement in postwar Germany, but the president seemed oblivious to its power. He had used the line before, but never in a country that had actually had a dictator who gassed his own people. Afterward, he told German lawmakers that the terrorists were like those who had "killed in the name of racial purity. . . . We are defending civilization itself."

Like Ronald Reagan, W.'s appeal is that he is an all-American who believes what he believes. And he trusted his gut to create a new dynamic with a Russian leader. But such a lack of nuance over the long term could be worrisome. As Murray Kempton said, there is "the evil of lesser evilism." The Bushes exhibit a moral myopia, thinking anything they do must be virtuous because they see themselves as virtuous.

W. has embraced Pakistan because it is helping in our fight against terrorism. But the general is not doing enough to fight his own militants, who are pushing India to the brink of nuclear war. Pakistan does not share our democratic values; this is a place where a young woman was recently sentenced to death by stoning. Her crime? She was raped by a relative.

The Mideast mess also shows the limits of a Manichaean presidency.

The president's trip has a Henry James tone to it, as the brash American president collides with the world-weary relativism of the Europeans. But Mr. Putin threw Mr. Bush's good-bad schemata back at him, slyly observing that when Mr. Bush complains to him about Iran: "I'd like to point out also that the U.S. has taken a commitment upon themselves to build similar nuclear power plants in North Korea. . . . We have some questions concerning development of missile programs in Taiwan."

A German reporter advised the president to "look beyond Iraq" and see that "Syria, too, in U.S. terminology, is a state sponsor of terrorism" and that "Saudi Arabia is anything but a democratic pluralistic society."

As a European ambassador to NATO said about Bush's fixation with Saddam, "You Americans want to kill the crocodile, and we think it's safer to drain the swamp."

This trip has shown why Bush likes a world so starkly colored. He does not seem curious about exploring cities he has never seen. He likes to avoid casual contact with the press and stay within his own self-affirming circle (including Deputy Secretary of State Karl Rove).

In Berlin, Mr. Bush called the presidency "life in the bubble." Since 9/11, he has tried to put America in a black-and-white bubble. His pals Gerhard and Vladimir have tried to show him some different shades, Berlin gray and Kremlin red.

W.'s Spaghetti Western

■

As Jacques Chirac droned on and on beneath the capering sylphides at Élysée Palace, orating about consequences and consultations, dialogues and divergences, President Bush's face transparently—and hilariously—reflected his thoughts. (And mine, as I sat in the audience watching.)

There may as well have been a bubble over W.'s head with the words "What a windbag." Or, since we were in Paris, "What a wind-baguette."

And when Mr. Bush got irritated and called an NBC reporter a pretentious "intercontinental" for asking the French president a question in French, and then noted that his pal Jacques was "always saying that the food here is fantastic, and I'm going to give him a chance to show me tonight," the bubble appeared over Mr. Chirac's head just as clearly.

"*Quel* hick," the French president's expression murmured.

Mr. Bush's trip was designed to soothe anxious allies by showing that the U.S. is not a warmongering, pollution-spewing, unfree-trading, terrorist-obsessing bully.

Or at least to show that the U.S. will consult with the Europeans while it continues to be a warmongering, pollution-spewing, unfree-trading, terrorist-obsessing bully.

But the sojourn has not been the sop the White House had hoped for; rather, it has reinforced stereotypes on both sides of the Atlantic.

Parisians were indifferent to the president's arrival, and a few gave his motorcade the intercontinental finger of disapproval, as had some Berliners.

The French actually seemed pleased when Mr. Bush played up his own political caricature, acting like a rodeo rider in King Louis's court, because it allowed them to indulge in their own favorite stereotypical behavior: looking down their Gallic noses at Americans.

"Bush is so . . . Texan," a French journalist told me with a grimace at the press conference.

The only one who did not typecast himself was the latest pledge to the NATO fraternity. President Vladimir Putin banged no shoes and threw no drunken fits. The clever, cold-eyed Russian leader even began to purloin some of Mr. Bush's trademark moves for himself. After watching him holding hands with Laura at the museum, Mr. Putin grabbed his surprised wife's hand.

He also began adopting Mr. Bush's jocular shtick. At the summit here yesterday, Mr. Putin dryly suggested that the NATO headquarters in Brussels be renamed: "We should call ourselves the 'House of the Soviets.'"

Naturellement, the Frenchies were both jealous and contemptuous of Mr. Bush's buddy act with Mr. Putin, sniffing that the American was getting played by the former KGB chief in a roundelay called "The snoop and the dupe."

After Bill Clinton beat George Bush, Sr., 41's press secretary, Marlin Fitzwater, told me that perhaps the patrician from Greenwich with the pork-rind façade should not have strained to straddle two worlds. "Maybe it would have been better to be all Eastern elite or all Texas populist," Mr. Fitzwater mused.

So now comes the son, who so desperately wants to be all-Texas-all-the-time that he overdoes the antielitist, anti-intellectual sneer.

After NBC's David Gregory asked Mr. Chirac, who speaks English, in French if he would like to comment on a question he'd asked Mr. Bush about Europe's view of America as imperious, Mr. Bush had a petit fit.

"Very good, the guy memorizes four words, and he plays like he's intercontinental," he said sarcastically as a bemused Mr. Chirac looked on. "I'm impressed. *Que bueno.* Now I'm literate in two languages." Mr. Bush did not care that foreign reporters usually ask him questions in English, or that he often sprinkles Spanish into his speeches with Hispanic groups.

He felt he was being mocked or tricked in some way, even though the question wasn't even directed at him. He was tired and he let his famously thin skin show too easily.

There is something bizarre about watching an Andover-, Yale- and Harvard-educated president, the grandson of an elegant Connecticut senator and the son of a gracious internationalist president, have a hissy fit because a reporter asks a legitimate question about European angst and talks to a Frenchman in French.

W.'s antielitism is sometimes refreshing, but does he have to carry it around all the time? He shouldn't be forced to be a chip off the old block, but he should lose the chip on his shoulder.

Lemon Fizzes on the Banks of the Euphrates

∎

The trap is sprung. The name of the game is containment.
Contain the wild man, the leader with the messianic and relentless glint who is scaring the world.

Surround him, throw Lilliputian nets on him, tie him up with a lot of UN inspection demands, humor him long enough to stop him from using his weapons and blowing up the Middle East.

But this time, the object of the containment strategy is not Saddam Hussein, but George W. Bush, the president with real bombs, not the predator with plans to make them.

America's European and Arab allies now act more nervous about the cowboy in the Oval Office who likes to brag on America as "the greatest nation on the face of the Earth" than the thug in the Baghdad bunker.

"We don't want another war in this region," says an adviser to the Saudi royal family. "When Afghanistan is bombed, they just hit rocks. When there's bombing in our neighborhood, they hit oil fields."

Gerhard Schroder's campaign prospects soared when he started running against Mr. Bush. "Many Germans," wrote the *Times*'s Steven Erlanger, "seem to fear American military action in Iraq more than they fear Mr. Hussein."

With assists from the rump cabinet of internationalists, including Colin Powell and Brent Scowcroft, America's allies have been engaged in a benevolent conspiracy to ensnare the president in the web of UN rules for war and diplomacy.

The Saudi foreign minister, Prince Saud al-Faisal, insists that the Iraqi threat must be taken care of without "the firing of a single shot or the loss of a single soldier." He added a big sweetener, promising that American bombers could use Saudi bases if Mr. Bush would work through the UN.

Privately, Saudi officials said they are alarmed by the Bush team's military strutting, and think it would have been much better to get rid of Saddam with a covert operation. They agree with the president that Saddam is a monster who not only eliminates his enemies, real and perceived, but also their wives, children and friends. But if he has nothing to lose, they worry, he might fire his chemical and biological weapons at the Saudis or the Israelis or give them to terrorists to use on the U.S.

By wrapping Mr. Bush in a warm embrace, the Persian Gulf allies hope to waltz him closer to where they want him to be. Meanwhile, the Egyptians and the Jordanians pinned Saddam to the mat and told him that if he had any chance of avoiding Armageddon, he should open up his country to inspectors.

Thus, in just a few days, the Iraq crisis went from Saddam having a noose around his neck to W. being bound by multilateral macramé.

"All the reasons for an attack have been eliminated," crowed Tariq Aziz, Iraq's deputy prime minister.

But the allies—and especially Mr. Aziz—should not underestimate the zeal of the Bush warriors.

Saddam can admit a legion of inspectors, but that may not stop Mr. Bush from wriggling out of the UN restraints and declaring the despot's compliance a sham.

The Arabs tut-tut that America should focus on rebuilding Afghanistan, getting a state for the Palestinians and pursuing the war on terror.

But the Bushies have gotten a taste of empire building in Afghanistan and they like it.

Karl Rove is building a Republican empire. Richard Perle, Paul Wolfowitz and Scooter Libby are building an ideological empire. Dick Cheney is building a unilateral empire. And Donald Rumsfeld is building a military empire.

As Henry Kissinger told *Newsweek*, Rummy wants "to beat back the attitudes of the Vietnam generation that was focused on American imperfection and limitations."

Besides, why should former CEOs Cheney and Rummy settle for mere Jack Welch–style perks when they can have the perks of empire?

They can restore civilization to the cradle of civilization. Lemon fizzes, cribbage and cricket by the Tower of Babel. A thirty-six-hole golf course on the banks of the Tigris and Euphrates. ArabDisney in the hanging gardens of Babylon. Oil on tap at the Baghdad Hilton. Huge contracts for buddies in the defense and oil industries. Halliburton's Brown & Root construction company building a six-lane highway from Baghdad to Tel Aviv.

How long can it be before the empire strikes back?

A Cynical Chapter

Feeding the Fear and Stoking the Homeland Insecurity

Dept. of Political Security

■

With the most daring reorganization of government in half a century, George W. Bush hopes to protect something he holds dear: himself.

After weeks of scalding revelations about a cascade of leads and warnings prefiguring the 9/11 attacks that were ignored by the U.S. government, the president created the Department of Political Security.

Or, as the White House calls it for public consumption, the "Department of Homeland Security."

Mr. Bush's surprise move was a complete 180, designed to knock FBI Cassandra Coleen Rowley off front pages. He had resisted the idea of a cabinet department focusing on domestic defense for nine months.

But clearly, Iago Rove saw his master's invincibility cracking and did a little whispering in W.'s ear. Why not use national security policy for scandal management?

So the minimalist Texan who had sneered about the larded federal bureaucracy all through his presidential campaign stepped before the cameras to slather on a little more lard—and nervous Republicans all over town found themselves suddenly praying that bigger government could save those in need (of reelection), after all.

By introducing yet another color-coded flow chart, the president tried to recapture his fading aura of wartime omnipotence. The White House even gave lawmakers "sample op-ed" pieces they could rewrite and submit to their local papers, beginning: "President Bush's most important job is to protect and defend the American people."

Even that champion of bloated government, Teddy Kennedy, seemed dubious: "The question is whether shifting the deck chairs on the *Titanic* is the way to go."

And others wondered whether it would be too unwieldy to have a department with twenty-two agencies devoted to eradicating both Al Qaeda and boll weevils. (The proposed Homeland behemoth does not include the FBI or CIA, but it would envelop the Animal and Plant Health Inspection Service.)

All day Thursday, before Mr. Bush addressed the nation, Special Agent Rowley, who was sporting a special badge allowing her to pack heat in the Capitol, and Bobby "Three Sticks" Mueller, who wasn't, had given the Senate Intelligence Committee a stunning and gruesome portrait of just how far gone the bureau is.

Their testimony made clear that there is no point in creating a huge new department of dysfunction to gather more intelligence on terrorists when counterterrorism agents don't even bother to read, analyze and disseminate the torrent of intelligence they already get.

"I think at the present time it's not done very well," Ms. Rowley said about the clogged-up information flow. Looking at the bureaucratic trellis of the FBI reorganization chart, she asked: "Why create more? It's not going to be an answer."

There are already too many pompous gatekeepers between the FBI chief and the field offices, she said. And the computers are ridiculous, unable to send e-mail or access the Internet or to search for two words together, like "aviation" and "school."

The blunt Midwesterner with the oversized glasses suggested that the disarray was less about modernity than the ancient flaws of ego and ambition—"careerists" with a don't-rock-the-boat attitude that hampered aggressive investigations. (Mr. Bush's plan would do nothing to disempower them.)

Mr. Mueller was confessing all kinds of dysfunction, as well. "When I first came in, I did a tour," he recalled. "There's a computer room downstairs . . . there were a number of different computer systems. There were Sun Microsystems, there were Apples, there were Compaqs, there were Dells. And I said, 'What's this?' And the response was, every division had a separate computer system until a year or two ago."

Asked how long it would take to get their computers up to snuff, Mr. Mueller replied: two to three years.

If we're really in a national emergency, couldn't the president call America's software geniuses and tell them to wire up the FBI this week?

Maybe if Mr. Bush brings Rudy Giuliani in as the new cabinet officer, he can work magic. But reorganization is an old dodge here.

The shape of the government is not as important as the policy of the government. If he makes the policy aggressive and preemptive, the president can conduct the war on terror from the National Gallery of Art.

Aloft on Bozoloft

■

T he makers of antidepressants are going to have to start testing their own products.

Drug companies peddling to our Zombie Nation are now frantically trying to climb out of a marketing valley of the dolls, a slump in the pace of sales of their little bliss pills.

A front-page article in the *The New York Times* chronicled how antidepressants have lost their aura as miracle drugs. As profits declined, efficacy plateaued and side effects increased ("Side effects may include dry mouth, flopsweat, deadened emotions, tremors, lassitude, insomnia, constipation, incontinence, deflated libido, inflated libido, overeating, no appetite and your spleen going SPLAT! all over a blind date at a swanky restaurant"), drug companies have been desperately trying to find new molecules to mine and new neurotransmitters to zap.

Addicted to their billion-dollar sales, the companies have been sneakily repackaging old pills for new uses, hawking their not-so-magic elixirs for everything from shyness to smoking to work stress to supermom jits to severe premenstrual blues to muscle tension to dating anxiety.

Some psychiatrists admitted in the *Times* article that "the impression often conveyed by commercials for the drugs is clear: Almost anyone could benefit from them."

Even though they seem to be straining, with new names that sound more like luxury cars than lifestyle pills, new drugs—Lexapro and Cymbalta—will soon pack the shelves next to Zoloft, Paxil, Prozac, Effexor, Celexa and Wellbutrin.

The more anxious the companies feel about profits, the more generalized the generalized anxiety disorders get.

As psychopharmacology becomes more and more highly targeted, we will be able to tweak molecules to soothe any specific unpleasantness in life. We can't be far away from such customized antidepressants as:

Gorzac: Works to counteract nausea that occurs when you turn on the TV and see Al promising to "let it rip" and lay his heart bare. Tell your doctors what medicines you are taking. Dangerous side effects if taken in combination with Liebertin, Edwardsox or Kerrytonin. Severe headaches could drive you to consider voting for the incumbent.

Elitex: Settles your stomach when you learn that the president, who says he is outraged by the insider trading and accounting shenanigans in corporate America, may have enjoyed his own sweetheart deal when he was a director of Harken Energy, a Texas oil firm.

Hallibutrin: Treats the everyday stresses of SEC scrutiny of accounting tricks at Halliburton, where Dick Cheney was once CEO and became a multimillionaire. Side effect: excessive secrecy and delusions of presidency. (This lasts 115 minutes.)

Marthax: Works to correct the fear, for those who are socially phobic and sitting alone in their hot little apartments, that everyone else is at fun cocktail parties in the Hamptons, trading insider stock tips that ensure that they get bigger mansions there and you stay trapped in your hot little apartment. Side effect: The only color you want to paint your walls is plain old white.

Moral Claritin: Relieves the confusion and whiplash you feel over President Bush's Middle East policy. Allays your dark suspicions that the president's abrupt decision to stop dealing with Yasir Arafat was dictated by his fidgetiness at having to sit through any more of Condi's wonkish briefings on Arafat. Side effect: May induce Napoleonic pretensions in Israeli prime minister.

Ashcroxx: Combats irritability and sleep disruptions brought on by unfathomable color-coded charts, politically timed terror warnings and dismantling of civil liberties. Side effects: compulsive love of Second Amendment, compulsive aversion to First Amendment, inexplicable affection for capital punishment.

Carmelexa: Relieves the combination of annoyance and despair you feel when told that new *Sopranos* episodes have been delayed another two years while they fine-tune first five minutes of third episode. Side effects: May cause temporary loss of interest in *Godfather* movies and irrational aversion to New Jersey.

Bozoloft: Alleviates anger and fear triggered when you hear administration officials claim that Al Qaeda has been disrupted and you know Osama is still out there plotting to pounce. Side effect: May induce uncontrollable urge to vote for Al Gore.

Desert Spring, Sprung

■

S uch a Fiestaware color for such an Armageddon moment. We're orange, but our officials tell us not to be blue.

Mayor Bloomberg says that New York City is a top target, including its hotels, apartment buildings, sports arenas and subways, but that we should "leave the worrying to the professionals." Tom Ridge, putting the terror throttle on high in the nation's capital, agreed that we should stick with our routines.

Right.

The country is in a constant state of stress. The space shuttle plunges down. The terror threat goes up. The 101st Airborne moves out to the Persian Gulf, along with the *Kitty Hawk*.

The Dow goes down. Deficits and job losses go up. American embassy staffs in the Mideast are moved out.

We plot to attack Iraq. Al Qaeda plots to attack us. We have "contingencies" for North Korea. And I'm sure it has "contingencies" for us.

Hollywood producers have instructed writers conjuring up villains to think French.

With or without those pesky Frenchies, we're on track for a mid-March invasion of Baghdad, known wryly around the Pentagon as "Desert Spring."

Some military reporters have been to Pentagon boot camp or expensive private self-protection courses; others are finalizing their lucrative deals to write war books and jockeying for plummy access to Rummy, who was jetting around the world on Friday, trying to insult Old Europe at closer range.

Network anchors are packing their bespoke flak jackets and zooming off to Turkey, Syria and Kuwait. The new chic thing here is an "embed"—a journalist slated to be "embedded" with the troops in the Gulf.

The Marine Corps Times and *The Navy Times* are full of advice for departing troops, like, "If you're single and have a pet, you need to arrange for someone to take care of it," as well as "sperm storage facts" for those worried about stories of infertility and sterility after the last gulf war. "Frozen assets"—a term Clare Boothe Luce used to describe virgins in *The Women*—is now military patois for "banking genetic material before deployment."

The orange alert made me wonder again why the Bush administration has spent the last year and a half hyping the Iraqi menace instead of single-mindedly hunting Al Qaeda.

Mr. Bush's presidency came into focus when he made his bullhorn vow to get "the people who knocked these buildings down." But we're not getting the creeps who knocked the buildings down. We're getting the creeps whose address we know.

Most Americans are willing to give Mr. Bush his war even though they are dubious that it will curb terror.

A CNN online poll shows that 82 percent think going to war with Iraq will provoke another attack on the U.S., as opposed to 13 percent who think it will prevent one.

The orange alert was expected. We're about to invade and occupy an Arab country, so Islamic radicals all around the world are angry at us. That's also why the FBI warned Jewish leaders on Friday that synagogues and Jewish-owned hotels might be especially vulnerable.

The hawks say things have to get worse before they get better. "By setting up our military in Iraq," one said, "we can get rid of the weapons and squelch the sources of terrorism. And we can set an example to other countries: 'If you cooperate with terrorists or menace us in any way or even look cross-eyed at us, this could happen to you.'"

The Bush team is infatuated with solving old problems—Israel, terrorism, oil—in a bold new way.

Americans and the allies have been watching St. Colin for months. No one knew if he was softening the bellicosity of the Bush inner circle or if the inner circle was using him as the human shield for its plan to change Arab history.

But in his appearances at the UN and on Capitol Hill last week, General Powell played General Patton.

The case was less persuasive than the presenter. And it was not clear why the presenter had jumped to the warlike side. But if the man who always resisted occupying Iraq had succumbed to the plan to occupy Iraq, more diplomacy is a charade.

Once they scratch their Saddam itch, maybe the Bush team can zero in on the terrorists who have put us on code orange, and the North Koreans who have put us on nuclear notice.

Meanwhile, Iraq had better ratchet up its own alert.

Ready or Not . . .

■

Nobody in America makes me feel more insecure than Tom Ridge.

The man who is supposed to restore my confidence in the prospect of my safety gives me the uneasy sense that the door's unlocked, the alarm's off and there's a ladder leaning up against the house.

He seems like a pleasant, well-meaning guy, and admits, "It's not always easy to know the right thing to say or the right thing to do."

But in George Bush's pulp Western, Mr. Ridge should be a square-jawed extra with no lines.

Last week, the head of Homeland Insecurity unveiled the big strategy he's been working on for nearly a year: a $1.2 million "ready campaign," a p.r. concoction complete with a "D'oh!" Web site. There are TV ads starring cute New York City firemen telling people to store water and get flashlights, and close-ups of Mr. Ridge spouting simpleminded axioms like "Have a good communications plan for your family."

The new campaign was developed with the help of focus groups convened by the Advertising Council.

George Bush has always mocked Washington's dependence on focus groups. Only last week, he derided mass European protests against the war, saying listening to the marchers would be like relying on focus groups to set foreign policy. (Millions of people marching in the streets of world capitals is not a sampling of opinion; it is opinion.)

Mr. Bush leads a West Wing that thinks politically all the time. Andy Card talks about rolling out the war with Iraq like a marketing campaign, and now Mr. Ridge runs his agency according to the principles of consumer marketing. (And maybe fund-raising, too. According to Al Kamen of *The Washington Post*, almost half the duct tape sold in the U.S. comes from a company whose founder gave more than $100,000 to Republicans in 2000.)

What can the Bush administration learn from a focus group of understandably confused Americans about making our borders and ports more secure? Do they have a preferred thickness of duct tape? Should they head straight to the bomb shelter or stop by Blockbuster first?

Peggy Conlon of the Ad Council told the *Times*'s Lynette Clemetson that they asked focus group panels if it would be effective for Mr. Ridge to use celebrities to instruct the public on safety.

The group participants thankfully recoiled from that idea, knowing that they share little common ground with stars who already have "safe rooms" in their mansions stocked with Pellegrino, Dom and Botox and their "human shield" minions running around buying Prada emergency packs.

The focus groupers also nixed a proposal to have Mr. Ridge's ad campaign advise Americans to "be a soldier in your own home."

They did not like to think about a terrorist attack in terms of war,

Ms. Conlon said, but more as a disaster like a tornado or earthquake that they could weather.

Anyhow, that's just another way of saying, you're on your own, buddy, you're an army of one, be all that you can be in the short time that remains.

In encouraging people to be prepared, the ready.gov Web site notes that you may be in a "moving vehicle at the time of an attack. Know what you can do." How about keep moving? The site's drawing illustrating a radiation threat shows a map of Texas, with the radioactive arrow pointed to the vicinity of Crawford.

The Republicans are afraid that Democrats are going to get traction with the argument that the White House has shortchanged national security in its Ahab pursuit of Saddam.

An upcoming article in *The New Republic*, contending that the president has not done enough, cites an American Association of Port Authorities estimate that it would cost $2 billion to make the ports secure. But since September 11, only $318 million has been spent. Although Mr. Bush himself endorsed a program to screen cargo at foreign ports, his budget provides no money for it.

What Mr. Ridge is supposed to be doing is getting the best scientific and technical expertise, as it relates to all threats, and developing concrete plans and suggestions for every possible contingency.

He's not supposed to be selling security, or spinning it; he's supposed to be providing it.

He doesn't need to make security more alluring to us. We already find it absolutely alluring. We'd just like to get some more of it.

November 23, 2003

Scaring Up Votes

■

First came the preemptive military policy. Now comes the preemptive campaign strategy.

Before the president even knows his opponent, his first political ad is blanketing Iowa today.

"It would take one vial, one canister, one crate slipped into this country to bring a day of horror like none we have ever known," Mr. Bush says, in a State of the Union clip.

Well, that's a comforting message from our commander in chief. Do we really need his cold, clammy hand on our spine at a time when we're already rattled by fresh terror threats at home and abroad? When we're chilled by the metastasizing Al Qaeda, the resurgent Taliban and Baathist thugs armed with deadly booby traps; the countless, nameless terror groups emerging in Turkey, Morocco, Indonesia and elsewhere; the vicious attacks on Americans, Brits, aid workers and their supporters in Iraq, Afghanistan and Turkey? The latest illustration of the low-tech ingenuity of Iraqi foes impervious to our latest cascade of high-tech missiles: a hapless, singed donkey that carted rockets to a Baghdad hotel.

Yet the Bush crowd is seizing the moment to scare us even more.

Flashing the words "terrorists" and "self-defense" in crimson, the Republican National Committee spot urges Americans "to support the president's policy of pre-emptive self-defense"—a policy Colin Powell claimed was overblown by the press.

"Since when have terrorists and tyrants announced their intentions, politely putting us on notice before they strike?" Mr. Bush says.

With this ad, Republicans have announced their intention: to scare us stupid, hoping we won't remember that this was the same State of the Union in which Mr. Bush made a misleading statement about the Iraq-Niger uranium connection, or remark that the imperial idyll in Iraq has created more terrorists.

Richard Clarke, the former U.S. counterterrorism chief, told Ted Koppel that Mr. Bush's habit of putting Xs through the pictures of arrested or killed Qaeda managers was very reminiscent of a scene in the movie *The Battle of Algiers*, in which the French authorities did the same to the Algerian terrorists: "Unfortunately, after all the known Algerian terrorists were arrested or killed, the French lost. And that could be the thing that's happening here, that even though we're getting all the known Al Qaeda leaders, we're breeding new ones. Ones we don't know about and will be harder to find."

This view of Al Qaeda was echoed by a European counterterrorism official in the *Times*: "There are fewer leaders but more followers."

The president is trying to make the campaign about guts: He has the guts to persevere in the war on terror.

But the real issue is trust: Should we trust leaders who cynically manipulated intelligence, diverted 9/11 anger and lost focus on Osama so they could pursue an old cause near to neocon hearts: sacking Saddam?

The Bush war left our chief villains operating, revved up the terrorist threat, ravaged our international alliances and sparked the resentment of a world that ached for us after 9/11.

Now Mr. Bush says that poor Turkey, a critical ally in the Muslim world, is the newest front in the war on terror. "Iraq is a front," he said. "Turkey is a front. Anywhere the terrorists think they can strike is a front." Here a front, there a front, everywhere a terror front.

In his Hobbesian gloom—"Fear and I were born twins," Hobbes said—Dick Cheney thought an Iraq whupping would make surly young anti-American Arab men scuttle away. Instead, it stoked their ire.

James Goodby and Kenneth Weisbrode wrote in *The Financial Times* last week that the Bush crew has snuffed the optimism of FDR, Ronald Reagan and Bush *père*: "Fear has been used as a basis for curtailing freedom of expression and for questioning legal rights long taken for granted. It has crept into political discourse and been used to discredit patriotic public servants. Ronald Reagan's favorite image, borrowed from an earlier visionary, of America as 'a shining city on a hill' has been unnecessarily dimmed by another image: a nation motivated by fear and ready to lash out at any country it defines as the source of a gathering threat."

Instead of a shining city, we have a dark bunker.

But the only thing we really have to fear is fearmongering itself.

■

On Piety and Pettifoggery

■

The God Squad

■

T alk about profiles in courage.

After Columbine, the politicians in Congress assembled, worked up their nerve and pounded together some legislation to help stop horrific high school shootings.

Their solution: Take two tablets; slap them above every blackboard in American classrooms.

They could have gone with the obvious approach—do something to make it harder for teenagers and crazy people to get guns. But noooooo. This is Washington, home of the opportunistic and the polled.

So they went the craven (i.e., the usual) route, passing a measure to allow the Ten Commandments in classrooms.

These tablets are a noble guide for living. But since Moses carried them down from Mount Sinai way back in B.C., they have never been known to prevent violence. Indeed, the first sight of the commandments at that pagan party with the golden calf actually incited a riot.

What happens after the next school shooting? Will Congress mandate that the rest of the Bible be stenciled across high school walls?

The politicians are giving virtue a bad name again.

Morality cannot be reduced to gestures. Simply exhibiting the Ten Commandments has nothing to do with teaching the meaning or the truth or the value of them.

Since Littleton, a rare consensus has developed that the American love affair with guns has to cool down. Just as in the impeachment debacle, the public understands that a few compromises can bring about a sensible solution. And just as in impeachment, the House is ignoring the public and going off on nutty tangents.

Tom (the Exterminator) DeLay orchestrated watering down the gun control provisions. His chief accomplice was Democratic boss John Dingell, who sold out his party in the dark of night. Here's a commandment for Democrats: Thou shalt not be hugged on the House floor by Tom DeLay.

The Torquemada from Texas let the whole bill collapse, forcing Republicans to take the heat for thwarting gun control in the wake of Columbine—an outcome no one outside NRA headquarters wanted.

This is the season of cheap virtue. Politicians are rushing to take God's name in vain (thereby violating commandment number three).

After linking Columbine to the culture of abortion and the teaching of evolution, Mr. DeLay went to a rally of ministers waving Bibles Wednesday and blamed separation of church and state for the tragedy. "All of this knee-jerk lawmaking is a waste of time," he said. Odd remark for the House whip.

Mr. DeLay has so debased the discourse that he included this charming anecdote as proof of the culture crisis: "I got an e-mail this morning that said it all. The student writes, Dear God: Why didn't you stop the shootings at Columbine? And God writes, Dear student: I would have, but I wasn't allowed in school."

The season of sanctimony isn't confined to the legislative branch. According to *Time*, George W. Bush decided to run for president at a private prayer service with his family last January: "Pastor Mark Craig started preaching about duty, about how Moses tried to resist God's call, and the sacrifice that leadership requires. And as they sat there, Barbara Bush leaned over to the son who has always been most like her and said, 'He's talking to you, George.'"

You'd think W. would be aware of the perils of religiosity after he had to spend all that time clarifying his 1993 comment that people who do not accept Jesus Christ as a personal savior cannot go to heaven.

In his announcement speech in Carthage, Al Gore joined the God Squad, intoning that "most Americans are hungry for a deeper connection between politics and moral values; many would say 'spiritual values.' Without values of conscience, our political life degenerates."

Faith is an intensely personal matter. It should not be treated as a credential or reduced to a sound bite. History teaches that when religion is injected into politics—the Crusades, Henry VIII, Salem, Father Coughlin, Hitler, Kosovo—disaster follows.

Before they hang the Ten Commandments in the schools, they should make sure they are hanging where they are broken daily: Congress and the White House.

They also might consider adding an eleventh: Thou shalt not pander.

Playing the Jesus Card

■

My father had two prized possessions: a scrapbook full of newspaper clippings about the Irish Catholic who didn't make it to the White House in 1928, and a huge framed photo of the Irish Catholic who did in 1960.

JFK once joked that after Al Smith lost to Herbert Hoover, whose slogan was "A vote for Smith is a vote for the pope," the New York governor had to cable the pope: "Unpack." President Kennedy added that after he refused to help the U.S. Catholic bishops get federal aid for parochial schools, the pope cabled him: "Pack."

Jack Kennedy's shimmering wit could lighten any tense moment. But as he went through his crusade in '60 to convince voters that a Catholic president would not build a pipeline to the Vatican, Catholics held their breaths in fear, murmuring Please, please, please, let him be president and he'll never, never, never mention religion.

Kennedy vowed to keep a wall between church and state: "I believe in a president whose views on religion are his own private affairs."

How odd that only forty years ago a presidential candidate could not win unless he left religion out; now candidates think they cannot win unless they bring religion in.

As H. L. Mencken pointed out, religion "is used as a club and a cloak by both politicians and moralists, all of them lusting for power and most of them palpable frauds."

George W. Bush finally scored some debate points on Monday night by supporting the holy trinity of ethanol, Jesus and soft money. (Didn't Jesus throw those soft-money changers out of the temple?) When the Republican candidates were asked to name their favorite political philosophers, Mr. Bush replied: "Christ, because he changed my heart."

Pressed to elaborate, the Texas governor again showed his inability to go deep. To borrow a Dorothy Parker quip, he ran the gamut from A to B. Just as in the last debate, when he was asked to expound on a biography of Dean Acheson, he gave the impression that he thought coughing up an impressive name was quite enough.

His mouth curled down into that famous smirky look. "Well, if they don't know, it's going to be hard to explain," he said. "When you turn your heart and your life over to Christ, when you accept Christ as the Savior, it changes your heart. It changes your life. And that's what happened to me."

Translation: You're either in the Christ club or out of it, on the J.C. team or off. This is the same exclusionary attitude, so offensive to those with different beliefs, that he showed in 1993 when he said that you must believe in Jesus Christ to enter heaven. (Mr. Bush has since conceded that only "God decides who goes to heaven, not George W. Bush.")

Dick Morris, the man who told President Clinton that Monica would not play well with the public, immediately proclaimed that

Jesus would play well with the public. The pollster enthused on Fox News that W. had "cut right into the evangelical vote."

This is the era of niche marketing, and Jesus is a niche. Why not use the son of God to help the son of Bush appeal to voters? W. is checking Jesus' numbers, and Jesus is polling well in Iowa. Christ, the new wedge issue.

When you take something deeply personal and parade it for political gain, you are guilty either of cynicism or exhibitionism. Exhibit A: Al Gore's skin-crawling speeches at the Democratic conventions about his son's accident and his sister's death.

Mr. Gore has sunk to the same level on religion. On *60 Minutes* last week, the vice president declared himself to be a born-again Christian. And in an earlier interview with *The Washington Post*'s Sally Quinn, he said he often asked himself "W.W.J.D.—for a saying that's popular now in my faith, 'What would Jesus do?'"

When the Kansas board of education removed evolution from the science curriculum testing to make way for creationism, neither Mr. Gore nor Mr. Bush could bring himself to utter a word in defense of scientific truth.

It raises the question of whether the vice president and the governor want Jesus as their personal savior or political savior.

Genuinely religious people are humbled by religion and are guided by it on the inside. They don't need to wear Jesus on the outside as a designer label.

A Blue Burka for Justice

■

I had to call Attorney General John Ashcroft recently to ask if he had instructed his advance team to remove naked lady statues and calico cats from his vicinity because they were wicked.

I know it sounds loopy. But with these guys, you never know.

Andrew Tobias, the financial writer and Democratic Party treasurer, had written in his Web column in November that an Ashcroft advance team "had shown up at the American Embassy in The Hague to check out the digs, saw cats in residence, and got nervous. They were worried there might be a calico cat. No, they were told, no calicos. Visible relief. Their boss, they explained, believes calico cats are signs of the devil. (The advance team also spotted a naked woman in the courtyard and discussed its being covered for the visit, though that request was not ultimately made.)"

Mindy Tucker, then Mr. Ashcroft's press secretary, told me he had laughed and said it was silly.

I laughed it off, too. Everybody knows that black cats, not calico, are the sign of the devil.

But then a few days later, a friend who had worked with Bobby Kennedy at Justice and had attended the ceremony naming the building for RFK, told me that the Art Deco statue of Justice, twelve and a half feet high, buxom and partly nude under a toga, which had been in the Great Hall since the department was built as a WPA project, had been hidden behind a "blue-nosed blue curtain."

Again I called Ms. Tucker. She said the curtains concealing the aluminum *Spirit of Justice* and her male counterpart, the *Majesty of Law*, were just up for that one event.

Now it turns out the prudish curtains are a permanent fixture of the Ashcroft era—at $8,650, $1,375 more than the two statues cost.

On ABC.com, Beverley Lumpkin, ABC's Justice Department reporter, revealed that Mr. Ashcroft had decided to throw the equivalent of a blue burka over the exultant "Minnie Lou," as the statue is fondly nicknamed, after seeing pictures of her breast hovering over his head as he announced plans to fight terrorism.

His new spokeswoman, Barbara Comstock, said the drapes, a shade she calls "TV blue," are more photogenic than the statues and the "yellow marbly color of the background." She said Lani Miller, an advance woman, had decided to expurgate art for aesthetic reasons, and that Mr. Ashcroft was not involved.

"He doesn't look at his press coverage a lot, himself," Ms. Comstock said. "He spends his time dealing with threat assessments and more important business."

But if he pays no mind to his press, why would he hide historic art behind "TV blue" curtains? Couldn't he just move his podium over a little?

Everyone here knows that cover-ups are what get you in trouble, but they just keep doing it.

Dick Cheney has pulled a TV blue curtain over Enron and the rest of the energy industry's blueprint for fashioning America's energy policy.

His highfalutin rationale is that the White House must "preserve the principle" of getting "unvarnished advice from any source." Translated, "unvarnished advice" means a corporate wish list and "any source" is the wealthy white guys who gave us big campaign contributions.

Who'd have guessed privacy would be the watchword of this administration? Justice Louis Brandeis, in a dissenting opinion for a 1928 wiretapping decision, defined privacy as "the right to be left alone," to be secure in your private life. Bush judges don't believe in that.

Mr. Cheney loftily argues that "privacy" means you can do things while hiding behind the cloak of anonymity. But no one has ever said there was a right to remain private in the course of trying to influence federal policy. That's one reason lobbyists have to register and why there are strict ex parte rules requiring disclosure of contacts with lobbyists at many federal agencies.

The vice president and president are really concerned about the privacy of power. They want to do what they want to do, and be accountable to no one. The stonewalling on the energy task force and the unilateralism on Camp X Ray are two sides of the same coin.

The theme of Bush I is now the theme of Bush II: Trust us, even if we won't let you verify. We know we're right. We answer to no one.

I, for one, want some answers. Let's start with those calico cats and Enron rats.

October 9, 2002

Tribulation Worketh Patience

■

WJD at the FDA?

We may soon find out, if W. David Hager becomes chairman of the powerful Food and Drug Administration panel on women's health policy. His résumé seems more impressive for theology than gynecology.

"Jesus stood up for women at a time when women were second-class citizens," Dr. Hager says. "I often say, if you are liberated, a woman's libber, you can thank Jesus for that."

A professor of obstetrics and gynecology at the University of Kentucky, he has a considerable body of work about Jesus' role in healing women, and last summer he helped the Christian Medical Association with a "citizens' petitions" calling on the FDA to reverse its approval of RU-486, the "abortion pill," claiming it puts women at risk. (RU-486 or RU-4Jesus?)

Karen Tumulty reports in *Time* that the FDA senior associate commissioner, Linda Arey Skladany, a former drug-industry lobbyist with Bush family ties, has rejected doctors proposed by FDA staffers and is pushing Dr. Hager.

The policy panel, which helped get RU-486 approved, will lead the study on the hot issue of hormone replacement therapy for menopausal women. As *Time* notes: "Some conservatives are trying to use doubts about such therapy to discredit the use of birth control pills, which contain similar compounds."

Dr. Hager wrote *As Jesus Cared for Women*, blending biblical accounts of Christ healing women with case studies from his own practice. "Jesus still longs to bring wholeness to women today," the jacket says.

He writes about a young patient named Sparkle who gets a job at a strip joint in Kentucky and becomes promiscuous and gets several sexually transmitted diseases. Sparkle reminds him of "a woman Jesus met who was generally known in her town as a sinner, but whom Jesus saw through eyes of love."

With his wife, Linda, he wrote *Stress and the Woman's Body*, which puts "an emphasis on the restorative power of Jesus Christ in one's life" and recommends Scripture readings to treat headaches (Matthew 13:44–46); eating disorders (II Corinthians 10:2–5) and premenstrual syndrome (Romans 5:1–11, "Tribulation worketh patience").

To exorcise affairs, the Hagers suggest a spiritual exercise: "Picture Jesus coming into the room. He walks over to you and folds you gently into his arms. He tousles your hair and kisses you gently on the cheek. . . . Let this love begin to heal you from the inside out."

Dr. Hager is also an editor of *The Reproduction Revolution: A Christian Appraisal of Sexuality, Reproductive Technologies, and the Family*. One of the pieces, "Using the Birth Control Pill Is Ethically Unacceptable," says scientific data show that the pill causes abortions.

Dr. Hager said he disagreed with that piece. He says he prefers not to prescribe contraceptives to single women, but will if they insist and reject his advice to abstain.

He says he does not do abortions, will not prescribe RU-486 and will not insert IUDs. "I am pro-life," he says. "I believe sex outside of marriage is a sin. But I am not against medication. The fact that I'm a person of faith does not deter me from also being a person of science."

But unlike C. Everett Koop, who did not let his evangelical beliefs influence his work as surgeon general, Dr. Hager has written that it is "dangerous" to compartmentalize life into "categories of Christian truth and secular truth."

Once again, the Bush administration seems to be sowing skepticism about science for the sake of politics. It has smothered the promise of stem cell research to extend and improve life with the right wing's reverence for "life."

A *Washington Post* article last month reported that the Bush crowd was restructuring scientific advisory committees on patients' rights and public health, "eliminating some committees that were coming to conclusions at odds with the president's views and in other cases replacing members with handpicked choices."

Dr. David Kessler, the former FDA commissioner who is now dean of the Yale University School of Medicine, warns: "If the criteria to be on an advisory committee are based on a political litmus test, that will set this country back."

Are we so worried about medieval villains abroad that we no longer worry about medievalism at home?

April 20, 2003

A Tale of Two Fridays

■

The Pentagon, aka the International Trust for Historic Preservation, has once more shown the world its deep cultural sensitivity.

Franklin Graham, the Christian evangelist who has branded Islam a "very wicked and evil" religion, was the honored speaker at the Pentagon's Good Friday service.

After Kenna West, a Christian singer, crooned, "There is one God and one faith," Mr. Graham told an auditorium of soldiers in camouflage, civilian staffers and his son, a West Point cadet: "There's no other way to God except through Christ. . . . Jesus Christ is alive because he is risen, and friends, he's coming back, and I believe he's coming back soon."

When Muslim groups complained that the Pentagon was "endorsing" his attacks on Islam, Mr. Graham asked for a photo op with Muslim Pentagon employees. They declined.

Muslims suspicious that America is on a crusade against Islam were inflamed to learn that Mr. Graham is taking his missionary act to Iraq. They are still scorched by his remarks to NBC News after 9/11: "It wasn't Methodists flying into those buildings, and it wasn't Lutherans. It was an attack on this country by people of the Islamic faith."

He wrote in his last book that Christianity and Islam were "as different as lightness and darkness," and recently told the *Sunday Times* of London, "The true God is the God of the Bible, not the Koran."

Workers from Mr. Graham's Christian relief organization, Samaritan's Purse, were in Jordan, waiting to inveigle Iraqi infidels with a blend of kitchen pantry and Elmer Gantry.

Treating Operation Iraqi Freedom as a lucky break for Jesus, Mr. Graham told the religious Web site Beliefnet: "We are there to reach out to love them and to save them, and as a Christian I do this in the name of Jesus Christ."

The fifty-year-old son of Billy Graham has close connections to the president, who was in charge of evangelical outreach during his father's '88 campaign and who pressed war in Iraq by calling liberty "God's gift to humanity."

Both scions "recommitted" to Jesus Christ after periods of rebellion. Franklin Graham gave the prayer at W.'s inaugural. The president said Billy Graham "planted a seed in my heart" to stop drinking and embrace Jesus.

In Baghdad, it was Bad Friday. On the Islamic holy day, thousands of Iraqis marched through downtown, shouting for America to "leave our country." Looters, continuing their rampage, stole vials of polio virus from a public health laboratory and set the Information Ministry on fire.

Mullahs were happy to talk—and balk—after suffocating under Saddam. "You are masters today," Sheik Ahmed al-Kubeisy lectured America in one Baghdad mosque. "But I warn you against thinking of staying. Get out before we force you out." (Isn't this how Osama got started?)

Back here, the neocons and war planners were too busy gloating to worry about the ambient sound of civilizations clashing.

Rummy, once a Bechtel Iraqi pipeline booster and now busy planning to load American military bases into Iraq, seemed almost perversely determined to act as though the vandalizing of relics of the birth of civilization was insignificant, something only sissies could cry over.

"It's the same picture of some person walking out of some building with a vase," he said, "and you see it 20 times and you think, my goodness, were there that many vases? Is it possible that there were that many vases in the whole country?"

The Pentagon could easily have saved the national museum and library if they had redeployed the American troops assigned to guard Ahmad Chalabi, the Richard Perle pal, Pentagon candidate and convicted embezzler who is back in Iraq trying to ingratiate himself with the country he left forty years ago.

Instead of hectoring those who expressed any doubt about the difficulty of occupying Iraq, the conservatives should worry about their own self-parody: pandering to the base by blessing evangelical Christians who want to proselytize Muslims; protecting their interests by backing a shady expat puppet; pleasing their contributors by preemptively awarding rebuilding contracts to Halliburton and Bechtel; and swaggering like Goths as Iraq's cultural heritage goes up in flames.

Talk about a baptism by fire.

Could Thomas Be Right?

■

What a cunning man Clarence Thomas is.

He knew that he could not make a powerful legal argument against racial preferences, given the fact that he got into Yale Law School and got picked for the Supreme Court thanks to his race.

So he made a powerful psychological argument against what the British call "positive discrimination," known here as affirmative action.

Justice Thomas's dissent in the 5 to 4 decision preserving affirmative action in university admissions has persuaded me that affirmative action is not the way to go.

The dissent is a clinical study of a man who has been driven barking mad by the beneficial treatment he has received.

It's poignant, really. It makes him crazy that people think he is where he is because of his race, but he is where he is because of his race.

Other justices rely on clerks and legal footnotes to help with their opinions; Justice Thomas relies on his id, turning an opinion on race into a therapeutic outburst.

In his dissent, he snidely dismisses the University of Michigan Law School's desire to see minority faces in the mix as "racial aesthetics," giving the effort to balance bigotry in society the moral weight of a Benetton ad. The phrase "racial aesthetics" would be more appropriately applied to W.'s nominating convention in Philadelphia, when the Republicans put on a minstrel show for the white fat cats in the audience.

Justice Thomas scorns affirmative action as "a faddish slogan of the cognoscenti." Quoting Frederick Douglass on the "Negro" 140 years ago, he urges: " 'All I ask is, give him a chance to stand on his own legs! Let him alone! . . . Your interference is doing him positive injury.' "

He is at the pinnacle, an African American who succeeded in getting past the Anita Hill sexual harassment scandal by playing the race card, calling the hearing "a high-tech lynching," and who got a $1.5 million advance to write his African American Horatio Alger story, *From Pin Point to Points After.*

So why, despite his racial blessings, does he come across as an angry, bitter, self-pitying victim?

It's impossible not to be disgusted at someone who could benefit so much from affirmative action and then pull up the ladder after himself. So maybe he is disgusted with his own great historic ingratitude.

When he switched from a Democrat to a conservative as a young man, he knew that he would be a hotter commodity in politics. But he also knew that it would bring him the scorn of blacks who deemed him a pawn of the white establishment—people like Justice Thurgood Marshall, who ridiculed Clarence Thomas and others as "goddamn black sellouts" for benefiting from affirmative action and then denigrating it.

As Jill Abramson and Jane Mayer write in *Strange Justice*, Mr. Thomas himself complained in a 1987 speech that, to win acceptance in conservative ranks, "a black was required to become a caricature of sorts, providing sideshows of anti-black quips and attacks." (Just as blond conservative pundettes flash long legs and sneer at feminism.)

When the forty-three-year-old was nominated by Bush 41 with the preposterous claim that he was "the best qualified" man for the job, GOP strategists diverted attention away from the judge's scant credentials and controversial record by pushing his inspiring life story, grandson of a sharecropper and son of a Georgia woman who picked the meat out of crab shells.

But it's as if Justice Thomas has been swallowed by his own personal drama, just as Bob Dole and Bob Kerrey were swallowed by their gripping personal dramas on the presidential campaign trail. Mr. Thomas is so blinded by his own autobiography he can no longer focus on bigger issues of morality and justice. Having used his personal story to get on the court, he is now left to worry that his success is not personal enough.

President Bush, the Yale legacy who also disdains affirmative action, is playing affirmative action politics in the preliminary vetting of a prospective Supreme Court nominee, Alberto Gonzales. No doubt Bush 43 will call Mr. Gonzales the best qualified man for the job, rather than the one best qualified to help harvest the 2004 Hispanic vote.

President Bush and Justice Thomas have brought me around. I don't want affirmative action. I want whatever they got.

Nino's Opera Bouffe

■

Antonin Scalia fancies himself the intellectual of the Supreme Court, an aesthete who likes opera and wines, a bon vivant who loves poker and plays songs like "It's a Grand Old Flag" on the piano; a real man who hunts and reads *Ducks Unlimited* magazine; a Catholic father of nine who once told a prayer breakfast: "We are fools for Christ's sake. We must pray for the courage to endure the scorn of the sophisticated world."

Like other conservatives, he enjoys acting besieged while belittling the other side. "Alas," he dryly told the journalist Hanna Rosin, "being tough and traditional is a heavy cross to bear. Duresse oblige."

He's so Old School, he's Old Testament, misty over the era when military institutes did not have to accept women, when elite schools did not have to make special efforts with blacks, when a gay couple in their own bedroom could be clapped in irons, when women were packed off to Our Lady of Perpetual Abstinence Home for Unwed Mothers.

He relishes eternal principles, like helping a son of the establishment dispense with the messiness of a presidential vote count. (His wife met him at the door after Bush vs. Gore with a chilled martini.)

He's an American archetype, or Archie type. Full of blustery rants against modernity and nostalgia for "the way Glenn Miller played, songs that made the hit parade . . . girls were girls and men were men." Antonin Scalia is Archie Bunker in a high-backed chair. Like Archie, Nino is the last one to realize that his intolerance is risibly out of date.

The court issued a bracing 6 to 3 decision declaring it illegitimate to punish people for who they are, and Justice Scalia fulminated in a last gasp of the old Pat Buchanan/Bill Bennett homophobic conservatism.

In his dissent to the decision striking down a Texas sodomy law and declaring that gays are "entitled to respect for their private lives," Justice Scalia raved that the court had "largely signed on to the so-called homosexual agenda" and predicted a "massive disruption of the current social order." (Has this man never seen a Rupert Everett movie?)

State laws could tumble, he huffed, barring masturbation. Next, Sister Scalia will tell us it makes you go blind. He also tut-tutted that laws against bestiality might fall away. (Maybe he should be warning fellow dissenter Clarence Thomas. Anita Hill told Congress he had been beastly to her by describing an X-rated film about bestiality.)

The stegosaurus Scalia roared that the court had "taken sides in the culture war." Conservatives shrieked the door was open to everything from lap dancing to gay marriage. (Note to the panicked right: *Newsweek* just reported married heterosexuals were strangers to sex. So, if you want gay couples to stop having sex, let them get married.)

Mr. Scalia has frothed about "Kulturkampf" since 1996, when he did an Archie screed on gays having "high disposable income" and "disproportionate political power." Sounds just like people at Bush fund-raisers. (One here Friday was headlined by the First Nephew, George P. Bush, to buck-rake for a group promoting conservative court nominees.)

Most Americans, even Republicans, have a more tolerant and happy vision of the country than Mr. Scalia and other nattering nabobs of negativism. Their jeremiads yearn for an airbrushed fifties America that never really existed. (The pedophile scandal in the Catholic Church, which condemns homosexuality, proves that.) And the America they feared—everyone having orgies, getting stoned and burning the flag—never came to pass.

Nino is too blinded by his own bloviation to notice that Americans are not as censorious as he is. They like the complicated national mosaic—that Dick Cheney has a gay daughter, that Jeb Bush has a Latina wife, that Clarence Thomas has a white wife. Newt Gingrich can leave two wives for younger women and Bill (Virtues) Bennett can blow $8 million on slot machines. Even many of those who did not like Bill Clinton cringed at Ken Starr's giddy voyeurism.

Justice Scalia may play patriotic songs on the piano, but Justice Anthony Kennedy gave patriotism true meaning in time for the Fourth of July. His ruling eloquently reminded the country, "Liberty presumes an autonomy of self that includes freedom of thought, belief, expression, and certain intimate conduct."

In the immortal words of John Riggins, loosen up, Nino, baby.

Butch, Butch Bush!

■

L et's get it straight. The president and the pope aren't riding the new gay wave.

"I believe a marriage is between a man and a woman," said President Bush last week. "And I think we ought to codify that one way or the other. And we've got lawyers looking at the best way to do that." Trying to add a tolerant note to an intolerant policy, he allowed that he was "mindful that we're all sinners."

Last time I checked, we had separation of church and state, so I don't know why the president is talking about sin, or why he is implying that gays who want to make a permanent commitment in a world full of divorce and loneliness are sinners.

If we follow Mr. Bush's logic, shouldn't we have a one-strike-and-you're-out constitutional amendment: no marriage for gays, but no second marriage for straights who prove they're not up to it?

The Vatican, always eager to erase lines between church and state, warned Catholic lawmakers it would be "gravely immoral" to vote for gay marriage or gay adoption. Such preaching seems tinny coming after revelations about the scope of homosexuality in the priesthood.

Until last week's denunciations, this had been a giddy Summer of Gays. First the Supreme Court blessing. Then Hollywood's raft of gay-themed projects, from J.Lo's lesbian turn in *Gigli* to the Bravo reality shows *Boy Meets Boy* and *Queer Eye for the Straight Guy*.

Queer Eye, the summer makeover hit, on the cover of *Entertainment Weekly*, features five gay guys who swoop in to give the Cinderfella treatment to unexfoliated straight guys, while scattering catty comments about their grooming and decor, such as, "This place screams women's correctional facility." (Colin Powell told his staff he found the show quite amusing.)

Maybe we should pity President Bush, stranded in his fifties world of hypermasculinity as his country goes gay and metrosexual (straight men with femme tastes like facials). Even the uptight Wal-Mart stores have expanded antidiscrimination policy to protect gay employees, and *Bride's* magazine is offering its first feature on same-sex weddings.

Maybe the president and his swaggering circle should think about a *Queer Eye* makeover. I asked a gay political reporter friend if he could offer some tips:

On the vice president: "I'd love to see Cheney with a pierced ear and a diamond stud. Or in a body-hugging black T-shirt, just for the pure sport of it.

"He needs new eyewear. With his big face and lantern jaw, he should lose those five-pound glasses. There are some fabulous frames out there.

"About his hair, all I can offer is my sincere regrets."

On the defense secretary: "In his own sort of antediluvian way,

Rummy is a metrosexual. He works. He may be a warmonger, he may be intemperate, but just about every third woman I know wants him."

When it came to the president's possibilities, he got really excited: "Cowboy boots are fine for a certain kind of saucy backyard barbecue. But wearing them as often as he does, with those big belt buckles in the shape of Texas, it seems like he's trying too hard to prove his masculinity.

"He's definitely on the right track with low-stress weight lifting, but if he really wants a physique for the ages, a little yoga would help uncoil that gunslinger hunch.

"His hair is too tightly clipped. It looks painted on. And he's a huge squinter. The corner of his eyes are starting to look lined. Botox alert!

"He needs to dip into the merciful world of cosmetic products and avail himself of some kind of lip balm or gloss that helps mask the fact that he misplaced his lips somewhere.

"In open-collar shirts, he has a tiny little island of lost chest hair. It is too low to be a shaving oversight and too high to be a peripheral outgrowth of Alec Baldwin chest mat. It's neither fish nor fowl, so he should wax it out of there.

"Everything else about him just shouts 'Butch, butch, butch!' But to throw Bush a metrosexual bone, whenever you see him walking off Air Force One with that little furball Barney under his arm, that canine puff of air that most drag queens wouldn't be caught dead with, it's like he's halfway to a Chanel rabbit fur handbag.

"Bush does such a good job of seeming blissfully laid-back and vacantly bubbly that he might as well go blond. It might help with California's electoral votes, too."

Stations of the Crass

■

F ather, forgive them, for they know not what they do.

Mel Gibson and George W. Bush are courting bigotry in the name of sanctity.

The moviemaker wants to promote *The Passion of the Christ* and the president wants to prevent the passion of the gays.

Opening on two screens: W.'s stigmatizing as political strategy and Mel's stigmata as marketing strategy.

Mr. Gibson, who told Diane Sawyer that he was inspired to make the movie after suffering through addictions, found the ultimate 12-step program: the Stations of the Cross.

I went to the first show of *The Passion* at the Loews on 84th Street and Broadway; it was about a quarter filled. This is not, as you may have read, a popcorn movie. In Latin and Aramaic with English subtitles, it's two gory hours of Jesus getting flayed by brutish Romans at the behest of heartless Jews.

Perhaps fittingly for a production that licensed a jeweler to sell

$12.99 nail necklaces (what's next? crown-of-thorns prom tiaras?), *The Passion* has the cartoonish violence of a Sergio Leone Western. You might even call it a spaghetti crucifixion, *A Fistful of Nails.*

Writing in *The New Republic*, Leon Wieseltier, the literary editor, scorns it as "a repulsive, masochistic fantasy, a sacred snuff film" that uses "classically anti-Semitic images."

I went with a Jewish pal, who tried to stay sanguine. "The Jews may have killed Jesus," he said. "But they also gave us *Easter Parade.*"

The movie's message, as Jesus says, is that you must love not only those who love you, but more importantly those who hate you.

So presumably you should come out of the theater suffused with charity toward your fellow man.

But this is a Mel Gibson film, so you come out wanting to kick somebody's teeth in.

In *Braveheart* and *The Patriot*, his other emotionally manipulative historical epics, you came out wanting to swing an ax into the skull of the nearest Englishman. Here, you want to kick in some Jewish and Roman teeth. And since the Romans have melted into history . . .

Like Mr. Gibson, Mr. Bush is whipping up intolerance but calling it a sacred cause.

At first, the preacher in chief resisted conservative calls for a constitutional ban on gay marriage. He felt, as Jesus put it in the Gibson script (otherwise known as the Gospels), "If it is possible, let this chalice pass from me."

But under pressure from the Christian right, he grabbed the chalice with both hands and swigged—seeking to set a precedent in codifying discrimination in the Constitution, a document that in the past has been amended to correct discrimination by giving fuller citizenship rights to blacks, women and young people.

If the president is truly concerned about preserving the sanctity of marriage, as one of my readers suggested, why not make divorce illegal and stone adulterers?

Our soldiers are being killed in Iraq; Osama's still on the loose; jobs are being exported all over the world; the deficit has reached biblical proportions.

And our president is worrying about Mars and marriage?

When reporters tried to pin down White House spokesman Scott McClellan yesterday on why gay marriage is threatening, he spouted a bunch of gobbledygook about "the fabric of society" and civilization.

The pols keep arguing that institutions can't be changed when, in fact, they change all the time. Haven't they ever heard of the institution of slavery?

The government should not be trying to legislate what's sacred.

When Bushes get in trouble, they look around for a politically advantageous bogeyman. Lee Atwater tried to make Americans shudder over the prospect of Willie Horton arriving on their doorstep; and now Karl Rove wants Americans to shudder at the prospect of a lesbian—Dick Cheney's daughter Mary, say—setting up housekeeping next door with her "wife."

When it comes to the Bushes' willingness to stir up base instincts of the base, it is as it was.

As the Max von Sydow character said in Woody Allen's *Hannah and Her Sisters*, while watching a TV evangelist appealing for money: "If Jesus came back and saw what's going on in his name, he'd never stop throwing up."

Quid Pro Quack

∎

T hat incandescent intellect, the Stephen Hawking of jurisprudence, has been kind enough to take time from his busy schedule to explain to us how the Republic really works.

Antonin Scalia has devoted twenty-one pages to illuminating the impertinence of those who suggest that it is wrong for a Supreme Court justice to take favors from a friend with a case before the court.

Res ipsa loquitur, baby. Why should the justice who put Dick Cheney in the White House stop helping him now? It's the logrolling, stupid!

"Many justices have reached this court precisely because they were friends of the incumbent president or other senior officials," the justice sniffs.

That elite old boy network can really help in those dicey moments when you need to stop the wrong sort, like Al Gore, from getting ahead.

You don't stop ingratiating yourself with your powerful friends and accepting "social courtesies" from them just because you get on the court. Ingratitude is a terrible vice.

Anyway, what's the point of being in the ultimate insiders' club if you have to fly coach, eat at IHOP and follow silly rules on conflict of interest?

Justice Scalia proffers that while he accepted the vice president's offer of a ride on Air Force Two to Louisiana for a duck-hunting trip, taking along his son and son-in-law, there was no quid pro quack. "I never hunted in the same blind as the vice president," he says. No need for justice to be blind when the blinds are just.

Not since Tony Soprano discovered ducks in his swimming pool have ducks revealed so much about the man.

The justice elucidates that if he and his family had not accepted a free ride on Air Force Two, there would have been "considerable inconvenience" to his other friends, who would have had to meet a commercial plane in New Orleans and arrange car and boat trips to the hunting camp.

What is integrity compared to inconvenience?

"I daresay that, at a hypothetical charity auction, much more would be bid for dinner for two at the White House than for a one-way flight to Louisiana on the vice president's jet," he writes wittily. "Justices accept the former with regularity." Now there's an argument that requires a first-rate mind: Everybody does it.

Only a few casuistical steps away from parsing the meaning of "is," Justice Scalia writes that it is fine for him to be friends with Mr. Cheney and hear his case as long as it doesn't concern "the personal fortune or the personal freedom of the friend."

Holy Halliburton, whatever were we thinking?

The Sierra Club suit is against Mr. Cheney in his official capacity, not in his camouflage capacity.

"Political consequences are not my concern," says the justice. Unless, of course, it's about picking the president of the United States.

He reassures us that "Washington officials know the rules, and know that discussing with judges pending cases—their own or anyone else's—is forbidden." We must simply trust them, for they were bred to lead. Watching Mr. Cheney and Justice Scalia in action is all the proof one needs that Washington officials would never break the rules or engage in cronyism.

"If it is reasonable to think that a Supreme Court justice can be bought so cheap, the nation is in deeper trouble than I had imagined," the justice scoffs.

That's for sure.

Justice Scalia says, "The people must have confidence in the integrity of the justices, and that cannot exist in a system that assumes them to be corruptible by the slightest friendship or favor, in an atmosphere where the press will be eager to find foot faults." He observes that it would be nonsensical for him to recuse himself simply because the press has the effrontery to point out when someone has done something wrong.

We, the press, are supposed to be the handmaidens and the manservants of our rulers. If we fulfilled our duties properly, our reports would go something like this:

In an admirable spirit of uncommon objectivity, in the pursuit of truth, justice and the American way, Associate Justice Scalia made time to poke around in the marshes of Louisiana with the equally scrupulous Dick Cheney, and then, refreshed by a well-deserved plane trip at our expense, he continued to transmit his enlightenment to a grateful nation.

In Which Cheney, Rummy, Wolfie, Condi, Chalabi and the Neocon Gang Hijack the War on Terror

June 23, 2002

Hans, Franz and W.

■

A s I sit in my office, munching Pirate's Booty, sipping my cara-
mel macchiato and watching a sweaty President Bush on TV
extolling the glories of exercise and nutrition, I have four questions:

Why is the most fitness-crazed president in the nation's history
sometimes so short on stamina?

Why does someone who bench-presses 185 pounds still have an
aura that's more scrawny than brawny? ("The chair," one Republican moaned, "has a way of swallowing him up.")

Why does the leader of the free world, a man with limitless opportunities for stimulation, seem to get really jazzed only when he
can run his 6:45 miles?

Does it ever occur to Mr. Bush and his aides to vacate the gym and
nail down a Middle East policy?

The president was scheduled to deliver a speech on the Middle
East to tell us how he would help stop the cycle of violence there.
But then, after another bombing in Israel, he postponed it. If he's

supposed to have a plan to stop the killing, why let the killing stop the plan?

Nothing ever forces W. to postpone his daily workout, even when a gunman shot up the White House lawn one morning at 11:30 A.M. while he was on the treadmill, or when the Supreme Court met on the deadlocked presidential election.

He even sometimes takes along a treadmill on Air Force One, sticking it in the plane's conference room, and takes one to hotel suites. (If you do the treadmill in an airplane and press the INCLINE button really hard, are you a space traveler?)

W. doesn't even like to watch TV news while he works out. Aides say he likes to focus on "the fitness."

Maybe, given all the things he can't get a handle on—terrorists regrouping in every corner of the globe, Arafat pretending he's in control, and the FBI and CIA pretending to get along, not to mention the problem of trying to explain the reshuffling of the bureaucracy after he told us there was no need to reshuffle the bureaucracy—the president wants to spend time on a few things he can control: pecs, glutes, abs, quads and delts.

This is not exactly what the Pentagon has in mind when it calls on the president to show American muscle.

On Thursday at the White House Fitness Expo, Mr. Bush said that exercise helped him with stress and mental agility, so he hoped it could do the same for his staff. Yet the most striking thing about watching the president on his recent trip abroad was that he had so little stamina—especially compared with the hyperactive traveling style of his father.

After staying up with Vladimir Putin two nights until midnight, W. was exhausted and cranky in Paris. What is the point of going to bed nearly every night at 9:30 and working out maniacally if you get the wind knocked out of you so easily?

At every company, underlings ape the boss's passions to curry favor. So naturally, four hundred administration employees rushed to sign up to trot along with the president in a three-mile run this weekend. The big question among the fittest staff members, as the *Times*'s Elisabeth Bumiller noted, was whether they should allow the president to win.

Dana Milbank reported in *The Washington Post* that the White House Athletic Center "has become a pungent-smelling beehive of 24-hour athleticism. Bush aides say they are cutting back on caffeine and alcohol in favor of soy milk and three liters of water a day." Mary Matalin and Karen Hughes have been hanging out there, pumping Arnies, as in Schwarzenegger, a combination of the biceps curl and triceps press.

Some West Wingers admit that they are jealous of Richard Armitage, the State Department honcho who is built like Bluto, because Mr. Bush likes to chat with him about lifting weights (as opposed to throw weights). And they are envious of Condi Rice, who has bonded with W. by working out with him in Crawford while they talk sports and world leaders. A geovascular experience.

Mr. Bush once told a friend that he was a gym rat because he was afraid that his inner fat boy might come out. Why doesn't he ever worry about the emergence of his inner brain boy?

What this president desperately needs is a few more geeky, scholarly analysts with thick glasses and shameful physiques, poring over memos and intelligence feeds at the CIA, FBI and NSA.

Toned bodies are well and good. But how about some toned minds?

Junior Gets a Spanking

■

O edipus, Shmoedipus.

Why cite a Greek hero when we can cite the president's favorite British hero?

In *Goldmember*, Austin Powers has "Earn Daddy's Respect" on his To Do list. So the teary but still groovy spy confronts his prodigal father, played by Michael Caine.

"Got an issue?" Daddy breezily responds. "Here's a tissue."

Tissue issues between the two Bush presidents spilled into public view on Thursday when that most faithful family retainer, Brent Scowcroft, wrote a jaw-dropping op-ed piece in *The Wall Street Journal* headlined: "Don't Attack Saddam."

Mr. Scowcroft gave the back of his hand to conservatives' strenuous attempts to link Saddam to 9/11.

Bellicose Bushies have yet to offer a sustained and persuasive rationale for jumping Saddam, beyond yammering about how "evil" he is, as if he had a monopoly on that.

In the *Journal*, Mr. Scowcroft, one of the team that drew that fateful line in the sand a decade ago, ticked off all the reasons why invading Iraq makes no sense: it would jeopardize, and maybe destroy, our global campaign against terrorism; it would unite the Arab world against us; it would require us to stay there forever; it would force Saddam to use the weapons against us or Israel.

"Scowcroft is now more critical of Bush's foreign policy than Sandy Berger, which is mind-boggling," says Bill Kristol, a Bush I veteran who edits *The Weekly Standard*.

No one who knows how close Mr. Scowcroft is to former president Bush—they wrote a foreign-policy memoir so symbiotic they alternated writing paragraphs—believes he didn't check with Poppy first. Did 41 allow his old foreign-policy valet to send a message to 43 that he could not bear to impart himself?

The father is hypersensitive about meddling and reluctant to give advice. He doesn't want his pride to get in the way of his son's making up his own mind on what's right.

"It's a very strange relationship," a former aide to the father says. "He's so careful about his son's prerogatives that I don't think he would tell him his own views."

But Bush the elder must be fed up with being his son's political punching bag. On everything from taxes to Iraq, the son has tried to use his father's failures in the eyes of conservatives as a reverse playbook.

It must be galling for Bush *père* to hear conservatives braying that the son has to finish the job in Iraq that the father wimped out on.

His proudest legacy, after all, was painstakingly stitching together a global coalition to stand up for the principle that one country cannot simply invade another without provocation. Now the son may blow off the coalition so he can invade a country without provocation.

Junior could also have made the case that Dad's tax increase, which got him into so much trouble, led to ten years of prosperity. Instead he has philosophically joined the right-wingers who erroneously think that the tax increase caused a recession.

But W. has spent his life running from his father's long shadow, trying to usurp Dad's preppy moderate Republicanism with good ol' boy conservative Republicanism.

Poppy bequeathed his son, a foreign affairs neophyte, his own trusted Desert Storm team, with Dick Cheney as surrogate father.

But Mr. Cheney brought in Don Rumsfeld, an old rival of Poppy's, and he was joined at the Pentagon by Paul Wolfowitz and Richard Perle. This group is far more conservative, unilateral, ideological and belligerent than the worldly realists: 41, Scowcroft, Colin Powell and James Baker.

"The father and Scowcroft were about tying the coalition and the New World Order with a neat little bow," a Bush I official said. "Wolfowitz and Perle are: 'We're the new sheriff in town. We'll go it alone.'"

The Bush I moderates worry that the Bush II ideologues will use terrorism as an alibi for imperialism. Bush II thinks Bush I is trapped in self-justification.

Mr. Kristol writes in the upcoming *Weekly Standard* that Mr. Scowcroft and Mr. Powell are "appeasers" who "hate the idea of a morally grounded foreign policy that seeks aggressively and unapologetically to advance American principles around the world."

What does that make the old man? The Chamberlain of Kennebunkport?

Who needs a war plan? We need family therapy.

Who's Your Daddy?

◼

In the Bush family, the gravest insult is to be called a wimp.

When *Newsweek* published its "Fighting the 'Wimp Factor'" cover about Bush Senior when he was running for president in 1987, he was so angry he refused to talk to the magazine again until he had a meeting with the editors and the publisher, Katharine Graham. Mr. Bush even knew the precise number of times the word "wimp" appeared in the article.

In his memoir, Bush Junior wrote: "My blood pressure still goes up when I remember the cover."

The Bushes arranged their whole lives to put a veneer of Texas lock-'n'-load over Greenwich lockjaw.

After he buried Iraq as commander in chief, Bush Senior assumed he'd buried the W-word. And yet here it is again, the nightmare from which it is impossible for a Bush to awake, hurled at him by his own son's supporters.

As crazy Al Haig said Sunday on Fox, Bush 43 "has to be careful of the old gang. These are the people that created the problems in the first place by not handling Saddam Hussein correctly. . . . I'm talking about the previous administration and their spokesmen, Jim Baker, Scowcroft, and a very wise daddy who's not talking at all and he shouldn't."

The pathologically blunt General Haig simply spit out what other conservatives imply: Daddy wimped out in Iraq and Junior has to fix it.

You might think the United States would have an elevated debate before deciding to launch a major war against another country. But we've simply had a childish game of chicken, with different factions sneering at one another: "You're a wimp!" "No, you're a wimp!"

The clique of conservative intellectuals pushing the war has labeled Colin Powell and the Bush I crowd wimpy "appeasers."

Richard Perle, Paul Wolfowitz and Bill Kristol echo the message of Eliot Cohen, author of *Supreme Command*: "As Lord Salisbury said, 'If you ask the soldiers, nothing is safe.' To which the politicians must respond, 'Neither is inaction.'"

They paint the military brass as wimpy. "Powell did not want to do Bosnia," said a whack-Iraq'er. "The Pentagon was reluctant on Kosovo. On Iraq, Powell and Schwarzkopf dragged their feet on the first war. And the civilians are right this time, too. Iraq has had 11 years to comply with cease-fire arrangements on weapons of mass destruction."

The military types snipe back that the loudly squawking hawks—Cheney, Wolfowitz, Perle—are war wimps. "All the generals see it the same way," said the retired Marine Corps general Anthony Zinni, a Powell adviser, "and all the others who have never fired a shot and are hot to go to war see it another way."

And Senator Chuck Hagel, a hero in Vietnam, chimed in: "Maybe

Mr. Perle would like to be in the first wave of those who go into Baghdad." (Maybe he would.)

Giving a new definition of chutzpah, the conservatives pushing for war began taunting W., saying he had gone too far on Iraq to turn back now without being a wimp.

"The failure to take on Saddam after what the president said," Mr. Perle said, "would produce such a collapse of confidence in the president that it would set back the war on terrorism." Or: Nice little administration you have here; pity if something should happen to it.

The Bushies figured if they went after Saddam, whom they could find, as opposed to the vanished Osama, they would not seem wimpy.

But the more the president let Dick Cheney make the case for him, the more he risked being seen as wimpy. He was saved only by the Democrats, silent all summer, too wimpy to take on the White House and carve out their own case on Iraq.

It seems that Mr. Cheney now regards the end of the gulf war as a great historic gaffe and wants to earn his immortality correcting it.

But the more Junior goes along with his vice president and surrogate daddy and stakes his entire presidency on trying to finish the job, the more he underscores the contention that his real daddy went wobbly.

Last night conservatives were muttering that the inscrutable president was losing control of the debate. He could not simply persuade the congressional leaders gathering at the White House today, they argued. He had to do something really forceful, like asking for a resolution authorizing the use of force against Saddam.

Otherwise, they warned, W. might inherit the W-word.

Culture War with B-2s

■

Don't feel bad if you have the uneasy feeling that you're being steamrolled. You are not alone.

As my girlfriend Dana said: "Bush is like the guy who reserves a hotel room and then asks you to the prom."

As the Pentagon moves troops, carriers, covert agents and B-2 bombers into the Persian Gulf, the president, Dick Cheney and Donald Rumsfeld continue their pantomime of consultation.

When Senator Mark Dayton of Minnesota asked the defense chief on Thursday, "What is compelling us to now make a precipitous decision and take precipitous actions?" an exasperated Mr. Rumsfeld sputtered: "What's different? What's different is 3,000 people were killed."

The casus belli is casuistry belli: We can't cuff Saddam to 9/11, but we'll clip Saddam because of 9/11.

Mr. Rumsfeld offered sophistry instead of a smoking gun: "I suggest that any who insist on perfect evidence are back in the 20th century and still thinking in pre-9/11 terms."

Ah, Rummy. Evidence, civil liberties, debating before we go to war . . . it's all sooo twentieth century.

Anyway, how can we have evidence when we learned last week that our evidence-gathering snoozy spooks are even more aggressively awful than we thought?

The administration isn't targeting Iraq because of 9/11. It's exploiting 9/11 to target Iraq. This new fight isn't logical—it's cultural. It is the latest chapter in the culture wars, the conservative dream of restoring America's sense of Manifest Destiny.

The Bush hawks don't simply want to go back in a time machine and make Desert Storm end with a turkey shoot. They want to travel back even farther to the Vietnam war and write a more muscular coda to that as well.

Extirpating Saddam is about proving how tough we are to a world that thinks we got soft when that last helicopter left the roof of the American embassy in Saigon in 1975.

We can't prove it with Al Qaeda. That's like grabbing smoke.

So former Nixon officials Cheney and Rummy are playing out their own "Four Feathers," rescuing the lost honor of the American empire in the sands of Arabia. They want to stomp on Saddam to exorcise the specters of Vietnam and Watergate—the ethical relativism, the lack of patriotism, the postmodern angst, the loss of moral authority, the feeling that America is in decline or in the wrong, the do-whatever-feels-good Clintonesque ethos.

Dick Cheney fought multinationalism and Lynne Cheney fought multiculturalism, defending the dead white males who made the republic great. She has written a children's book, *America: A Patriotic*

Primer, and urged that 9/11 be a day to remember the nation's glories rather than its "faults and failings."

The Cheneys, who have been known to invite dinner guests at the vice-presidential mansion to sing along to "Home on the Range," think they can restore a sunnier, more can-do mood to our society. Even if it takes incinerating Baghdad to do it.

Rummy is equally impatient with the post-Vietnam focus on imperfections and limitations. He wants to yank the boomers by their collars and make them, if not the Greatest Generation, at least a bit Greater.

This is fine with W., who stayed fifties through the sixties and stopped liking the Beatles when they got into their "weird psychedelic period." He arrived at Yale and Harvard Business School just as the white male WASP ascendancy was slipping. He was in that small coterie of bewildered guys in wide-wale corduroy trousers, Izod polo shirts and Sperry Top-Siders, surrounded by wild and crazy hippies protesting the war and smoking roaches.

The Bushies want to bring back the imperial, imperious presidency. The preemption proclamation had the tone of Cheney Caesar and Condi Ben-Her. And the resolution sent to Congress seeking authority to go after Iraq was the broadest request for executive military authority since LBJ got the Gulf of Tonkin resolution rubber-stamped in 1964. At least LBJ had to phony up the Tonkin Gulf provocation. Mr. Bush can't be bothered. "I cannot believe the gall and the arrogance of the White House," Senator Robert Byrd bellowed.

Things are getting dangerouser and dangerouser. Karl Rove's gunning for the Democrats. Ariel Sharon's gunning for Arafat. W.'s gunning for Saddam. And Al Qaeda's still gunning for us.

No More Bratwurst!

■

They rule their world ruthlessly and insolently, deciding who will get a cold shoulder, who will get locked out of the power clique and who will get withering glares until they grovel and obey the arbitrary dictates of the leaders.

We could be talking about the middle school alpha girls, smug cheerleaders with names like Darcy, Brittany and Whitney.

But, no, we're talking about the ostensibly mature and seasoned leaders of the Western world, a slender former cheerleader named W. and his high-hatting clique—Condi, Rummy and Cheney.

I used to think the Bush hawks suffered from testosterone poisoning, always throwing sharp elbows and cartoonishly blustering my-way-or-the-highway talk around the world, when a less belligerent tone would be classier and more effective.

But now we have the spectacle of the seventy-year-old Rummy acting like a sixteen-year-old Heather, vixen-slapping those lower in the global hierarchy, trying to dominate and silence the beta countries with less money and fewer designer weapons.

At a meeting of NATO defense ministers this week in Warsaw, the Pentagon chief snubbed his German counterpart, Peter Struck, refusing to meet with him, only deigning to shake his hand at a cocktail party.

Echoing Condi's peevishness, Rummy announced that the campaign of Gerhard Schröder, who eked out a victory by running against the Bush push to invade Iraq, "had the effect of poisoning a relationship."

In their eagerness to apply adolescent torture methods, Bush hawks seem to have forgotten history: Do we really want to punish the Germans for being pacifists? Once those guys get rolling in the other direction, they don't really know how to put the brakes on.

Mr. Schröder behaved like a good beta, trying to align himself with the American alphas, by dumping his embarrassing friends, the justice minister who linked Mr. Bush's tactics to Hitler's, and the parliamentary floor leader who compared W. to Augustus, the Roman emperor who subdued the Germanic tribes.

Mr. Struck and the German foreign minister, Joschka Fischer, were eager wannabes. Mr. Struck offered more German troops for Afghanistan and Mr. Fischer apologized to Colin Powell, the administration's gamma girl, the careful listener who'd always rather build relationships than run roughshod over them.

Gerhard will have to go through way more of a shame spiral. He can forget about getting Germany a permanent seat on the UN Security Council. And no more bratwurst on White House menus.

The State Department wanted the petulant president to make nice with the Germans. But W. was, like, enjoying his hissy fit, refusing to make the customary call to congratulate Mr. Schröder.

As with alpha girls, the president makes leadership all about him. He thinks there are only two places to be: with him on Iraq or with the terrorists.

After all, Germany is not Saudi Arabia—they have elections over there. And surely the Bushes have heard of candidates saying whatever it takes, and placating various special interests, to win an election—and then mending fences afterward. Three words: Bob Jones University. All pols know today's adversary is tomorrow's ally.

Maybe the Bush policy on Empire & Preemption allows us to decide not only who can run a country but what are the proper issues for other nations' election debates.

Bush Senior was a master of personal diplomacy, taking heads of state out on his cigarette boat, to Orioles games and to the Air and Space Museum to see the movie *To Fly*.

He was a foreign policy realist who used socializing, gossiping, notes and phone calls to lubricate relations with other leaders.

But W., who was always the hot-blooded hatchet man in the family, has turned his father's good manners upside down—consulting sparingly, leaving poor Tony Blair to make the case against his foes for him, and treating policy disagreements as personal slights.

Only the Saudis get away with disobliging the administration on Iraq without being frozen out. They're like the spoiled, foreign princesses in high school, dripping in Dolce & Gabbana and Asprey, who drive their Mercedes convertibles into the magic alpha circle.

But then, Germans merely make Mercedeses. Saudis control the oil.

Why? Because We Can

■

The Boy Emperor's head hurt.

All the oppressive obligations of statecraft were swimming through his brain like hungry koi.

He summoned the imperial war tutor to the oval throne.

"I'm confused, Wise Rummy," he confessed. "Is the war preemptive, preventive or preventable? Is Saddam fissile or fissible? What in creation is counterproliferation? Everything's moving so fast. It's a puzzlement. Why are we mad at Saddam?"

"Because he wants to attack our country," the mandarin replied.

"Why?" the Boy pressed.

"Because we want to attack his country," the tutor said.

"Why?" The Boy was insatiable.

"Because Saddam tried to destroy your dad."

"Why?"

"Because your dad tried to destroy Saddam."

"Why?"

"Because he's evil."

"Why?"

"Because he's pretending to go along with inspections so he can get bombs."

"Why?"

"Because we're pretending to go along with inspections so we can bomb."

"What is our smoking gun against Saddam?"

"Reply hazy. Ask again later."

"Why do you sound like a Magic 8 Ball, Teacher?"

"We don't have the intelligence on Iraq or we don't want to talk about it. You decide."

"But can we really tie Al Qaeda to Saddam?"

"Goodness gracious! Al Qaeda is dangerous. Iraq is dangerous. We have to connect the dots of the future and not dwell on the dots of the past. It's unhelpful to get into a lot of detail because it just changes our capabilities."

"I don't understand."

"It is not possible to find hard evidence that something is going to happen down the road because you will have known it happened only after it happens. It's very difficult to get perfect evidence before an event occurs or even after it occurs. Preemption requires only preevidence."

"You've flipped your cap, Rummy," the Boy Emperor wailed. "Get me Condi!"

"The problem with it," Rummy continued, ignoring the Boy's outburst, "is that when intelligence is gathered, it's gathered at a moment, and then that moment passes and then there's the next moment and the moment after that. It is not possible to know whether the information that was accurate is still accurate. Do you follow me?"

"But aren't we just killing our own Frankenstein monsters, Teacher? Didn't we help build up Saddam when he was fighting Iran, and Osama when he was fighting the Soviets? How do we know which people we like now might someday do something that we would hate if we knew what they might do?"

"Holy mackerel, my young Padawan! The risks of doing nothing are greater than the risks of knowing nothing and doing something."

"Why do we give intelligence to the terrorists in their jail cells, instead of getting intelligence on the terrorists that puts them in jail cells?"

"Our intelligence agencies are dumb."

"Why can't we make them smart?"

"Because we're too busy planning war with Iraq."

"Why are we attacking Iraq, which may someday team up with terrorists, instead of Iran, which has already teamed up with terrorists?"

"Midterms."

"Multiple choice, right? I hate those essay tests. But haven't Pakistan and Saudi Arabia also supported terrorists?"

"Those creeps are our creeps."

"Can you explain the Bush Doctrine again, Rummy Sensei?"

"We start with self-defense, which is legitimate, and journey up to anticipatory self-defense, which has to do with history and real estate. Then we follow the rising path of wisdom to prevention, which sounds somewhat more acceptable than preemption, and which is about oil at $17 a barrel."

"Is Tom Daschle right that our war is political?"

"Is the White House white?"

"Why is President Gore running against me again?"

"He's unpatriotic. We should give that guy a one-way ticket to Guantanamo."

"What's the difference between Guantanamo and Guantanamera?"

"Golly."

The Soufflé Doctrine

■

T he Boy Emperor picked up the morning paper and, stunned, dropped his Juicy Juice box with the little straw attached.

"Oh, man," he wailed. "North Korea's got nukes. Sheriff Musharraf was helping them. Al Qaeda's blowing stuff up again. The Pentagon's speculating that the Beltway sniper might really be Qaeda decoy teams trying to distract the law while they plan a bio-blitzkrieg or a dirty bomb attack on the capital. Tenet's broken out in hives about the next 9/11. Powell spends all his time kissing up to the Frenchies. Saddam's ranting about a river of American blood. Jebbie's in a world of hurt. The economy's cratering. At least Karl says our war strategy will open up a can of Election Day whoop on congressional Democrats.

"This is not the way my new doctrine was supposed to work. We are supposed to decide who we preempt and when we preempt them. The speechwriters called it an 'Axis of Evil,' but it was really just a 'Spoke of Evil.' Condi and Rummy said once we finished off

Saddam, nobody would mess with America again. But everything's gotten fuzzier than fuzzy math. Some people are actually talking about my doctrine leading to World War III!!! Karl says that would be bad."

The Boy Emperor was starting to feel bamboozled by his war tutors. He needed a fresh perspective. There was a guy on TV with a round face and deep voice running around Provence, London and Berlin, where he suggested Schröder resign. He was preeminent on preemption. The Boy summoned him to explain the Bush doctrine.

"Do I know you?" he asked his visitor.

"I am the chairman of your Defense Policy Board," an amused Richard Perle replied. "I am an adviser to Rumsfeld, a friend of Wolfowitz's and a thorn in Powell's medals. *Je suis un gourmand, Monsieur le President.* I have always dreamed of opening a chain of fast-food soufflé shops based on a machine that would automatically separate eggs, beat the yolks and combine them with hot milk and sugar, add the desired flavorings, whip the whites until stiff, fold them into the mixture and bake in individual pots without human intervention. Then conveyor belts would bring the glass-enclosed ovens to the table and patrons would get to see their meals rise. I've never found investors smart enough to realize the dazzling ingenuity of the Perle Soufflé Doctrine. Meanwhile, I'm killing time trying to get your foreign policy to rise. I'm known as the Prince of Darkness."

"Why?"

"I persuaded Reagan to ignore the weak-kneed, striped-pants set at the State Department and buy every weapon in sight until the Evil Empire was scared stiffer than a perfectly executed meringue."

"But why are we going after a lunatic in Iraq for planning to make a bomb and not a lunatic in North Korea who already has bombs?" the Boy asked.

"At the end of the day," Perle replied, his voice dripping with patience for his student, "Iraq is an easy kill."

"But if North Korea can deter us by brandishing a nuclear weapon," the Boy pressed, "why can't we deter Saddam by brandishing a nuclear weapon?"

"You must puncture the soufflé before it rises," Perle instructed.

"Why are we mad at North Korea for flouting its international agreements when we flout our international agreements?" the Boy wondered.

"You cannot make sublime crêpes suzette without a fire," Perle lectured.

"Didn't you insist that Saddam and Al Qaeda were linked?" the Boy persisted.

"We made that up," Perle shrugged. "You have to be imaginative, as Audrey Hepburn was in *Sabrina* when she offered to make Bogie a soufflé out of saltines and eggs. As the Baron told Sabrina: 'A woman happily in love, she burns the soufflé. A woman unhappily in love, she forgets to turn on the oven!'"

"Huh?" the Boy said. "Tony and Colin told me to stop talking about 'regime change' and instead say 'War is a last resort,' and stop talking about a 'preemptive strike' and instead say 'War is not imminent.'"

"They're sissies," Perle said, his lip curling with an epicene disdain. "You cannot deliver the sashimi unless you use the blade."

The Boy Emperor was more befuddled than ever.

"Get me Condi!" he yelled. "And a peanut butter and jelly sandwich."

The Empire Strikes First

■

T here was no smoking gun last night. There was merely a smoky allusion.

President Bush tried to sell skittish Americans on a war with Iraq by alluding to the possibility of a link between Saddam and Al Qaeda.

Outlaw regimes seeking bad weapons, Mr. Bush said, "could also give or sell those weapons to terrorist allies, who would use them without the least hesitation."

The Axis of Evil has shrunk to Saddam, evil incarnate. Iran and North Korea were put aside with the dismissive comment: "Different threats require different strategies."

The state of the union is skeptical.

At a moment when Americans were hungry for reassurance that the monomaniacal focus on Iraq makes sense when the economy is sputtering, Mr. Bush offered a rousing closing argument for war, but no convincing bill of particulars.

Republican senators tried to back up the president. While admitting that there was no evidence that Iraq had weapons of mass destruction yet, John Warner told reporters that an attack was justified "if you put together all the bits and pieces that are out there right now."

Americans will never understand the Bush rationale for war if they simply look at the bits and pieces of physical evidence.

They will understand the Bush rationale for war only if they look at the metaphysical evidence, the perfect storm of imperial schemes and ideological stratagems driving the desire to topple Saddam.

The Bush team thinks the way to galvanize the public is with fear, by coupling Saddam to 9/11 and building him up into a Hitler who could threaten the world, as the White House chief of staff, Andy Card, told Tim Russert last Sunday, "with a holocaust."

But their reasons for war predate 9/11. The conservatives have wanted Saddam's head for a dozen years.

Dick Cheney; his chief of staff, Scooter Libby; and the Pentagon official Paul Wolfowitz also think Saddam is the perfect lab rat on which to test their new preemptive "empire strikes first" national security strategy, which Mr. Wolfowitz and Mr. Libby first drafted back in 1992, during the Bush 41 administration, when Mr. Cheney was defense secretary.

The first President Bush found the ideas too far out. But now his son has put them into play. Bush 43, former prep school football yell leader, is reputed to be the author of the phrase in the new national security strategy that sums up the policy: "We recognize that our best defense is a good offense." (Didn't Sunday's Super Bowl prove that the best defense is a good defense?)

After removing the super-rat, Mr. Wolfowitz, Mr. Libby and their fellow hawk Richard Perle can turn his country into a laboratory for democracy in the Arab world—creating a domino effect to give Israel more security. Once they have planted Athenian democracy on Mesopotamian soil, they envision orchestrating more freedom throughout the Middle East—as long as the region plays ball with the new sheriff. They'll put pressure on Syria and Iran to abandon their support for terrorism. And then, with an American spigot, the oil will flow free—except to the French, who will pay dearly.

Mr. Rumsfeld sees a war with Iraq as a chance to exorcise American ambivalence about the use of force left over from Vietnam, and the "pinprick bombings" of the Clinton years. And Mr. Cheney sees it as an opportunity to exorcise all the ghosts of the sixties and the feel-good Clinton era—the loss of moral authority and the feeling that America is in decline or in the wrong.

The vice president jumped up last night to cheer brawny unilateralism when Mr. Bush said: "The course of this nation does not depend on the decisions of others."

Despite its fixation on Saddam, the administration hasn't completely forgotten about Osama. *The Economist* ran an ad this week that said: "For over 100 years Arab-Americans have served the nation. Today we need you more than ever. . . . For additional information and to apply online, please visit our website."

The CIA is seeking Arabic-speaking agents.

Now they get around to that?

In Which the Reader Roots for the Gallant Colin Powell to Prevail Against the Pentagon Visigoths

February 5, 2003

Powell Without Picasso

■

W hen Colin Powell goes to the United Nations today to make his case for war with Saddam, the UN plans to throw a blue cover over Picasso's antiwar masterpiece, *Guernica*.

Too much of a mixed message, diplomats say. As final preparations for the secretary's presentation were being made last night, a UN spokesman explained, "Tomorrow it will be covered and we will put the Security Council flags in front of it."

Mr. Powell can't very well seduce the world into bombing Iraq surrounded on camera by shrieking and mutilated women, men, children, bulls and horses.

Reporters and cameras will stake out the secretary of state at the entrance of the U.N. Security Council, where the tapestry reproduction of *Guernica*, contributed by Nelson Rockefeller, hangs.

The UN began covering the tapestry last week after getting nervous that Hans Blix's head would end up on TV next to a screaming horse head.

(Maybe the UN was inspired by John Ashcroft's throwing a blue cover over the *Spirit of Justice* statue last year, after her naked marble breast hovered over his head during a televised terrorism briefing.)

Nelson Rockefeller himself started the tradition of covering up art donated by Nelson Rockefeller when he sandblasted Diego Rivera's mural in the RCA Building in 1933 because it included a portrait of Lenin. (Rivera later took his revenge, reproducing the mural for display in Mexico City, but adding to it a portrait of John D. Rockefeller, Jr., drinking a martini with a group of "painted ladies.")

There has been too much sandblasting in Washington lately.

After leading the charge for months that there were ties between Iraq and Al Qaeda, Defense Secretary Donald Rumsfeld chastised the media yesterday for expecting dramatic, explicit evidence from Mr. Powell. "The fixation on a smoking gun is fascinating to me," he said impatiently, adding: "You all . . . have been watching *L.A. Law* or something too much."

The administration's argument for war has shifted in a dizzying Cubist cascade over the last months. Last summer, Bush officials warned that Saddam was close to building nuclear bombs. Now, with intelligence on aluminum tubes, once deemed proof of an Iraqi nuclear program, in dispute, the administration's emphasis has tacked back to germ and chemical weapons. With no proof that Saddam has given weapons to terrorists, another once-crucial part of the case for going to war, Mr. Rumsfeld and others now frame their casus belli prospectively: that we must get rid of Saddam because he will soon become the Gulf's leading weapons supplier to terrorists.

Secretary Powell was huddling on the evidence in New York yesterday with the CIA director, George Tenet. Mr. Tenet was there to make sure nothing too sensitive was revealed at the UN, but mainly to lend credibility to Mr. Powell's brief, since there have been many reports that the intelligence agency has been skeptical about some of the Pentagon and White House claims on Iraq. It was Mr. Tenet who warned Congress in a letter last fall that there was only one circumstance in which the U.S. need worry about Iraq sharing weapons with terrorists: if Washington attacked Saddam.

When Mr. Bush wanted to sway opinion on Iraq before his State of the Union speech last week, he invited columnists to the White House. But he invited only conservative columnists, who went from gushing about the president to gushing more about the president.

The columnists did not use Mr. Bush's name, writing about him as "a senior administration official," even though the White House had announced the meeting in advance.

They quoted "the official" about the president's determination on war. That's just silly.

Calling in only like-minded journalists is like campaigning for a war only in the red states that Mr. Bush won in 2000, and not the blue states won by Al Gore.

When France and Germany acted skeptical, Mr. Rumsfeld simply booted them out of modern Europe, creating a pro-Bush red part of the European map (led by Poland, Italy and Britain) and the left-behind blue of "Old Europe."

When the evidence is not black and white, the president must persuade everyone. There is no red and blue. There is just red, white and blue.

Bush's Warsaw War Pact

■

The diplomatic motorcade pulled up to the White House yesterday with great fanfare. The two Marine guards at the door of the colonnaded West Wing saluted smartly. TV cameras pressed close to get pictures of the vital American ally alighting from the black sedan for his one-on-one with President Bush.

It was a summit of the two great strategic partners, America and Bulgaria.

Bulgaria?

As the world's only remaining superpower was conferring honor upon one of its only remaining friends, America smashed through the global looking glass.

To get Saddam, the Bush administration has dizzily turned the world upside down and inside out.

Our new best friends are the very people we used to protect our old best friends from. During the cold war, we safeguarded Old Europe from the Evil Empire. Now we have embraced the former So-

viet bloc satellites to protect us from the Security Council machina-
tions of our former paramours France and Germany. NATO was
created to protect Western Europe from the Communist hordes—
namely the Bulgarians, who tried to outdo the bizarro Albanians as
the most Stalinist regime in Eastern Europe and were renowned for
the "thick necks" who did wet work for the KGB.

The U.S. is now in the process of wooing the "minnows"—as
some in the Pentagon disparagingly call the small countries that
could deliver the votes for a Security Council resolution on going to
war with Iraq.

It's the battle of the pipsqueak powers: We dragoon Bulgaria to
offset France dragooning Cameroon.

The Bulgarians used to be the lowest of the low here. In 1998, just
before the visit of the Bulgarian president, Prime Minister Benjamin Netanyahu of Israel met with President Clinton. The visit
was so icy that a Clinton aide joked to reporters about Mr. Netanyahu: "We're treating him like the president of Bulgaria. Actually, I
think Clinton will go jogging with the president of Bulgaria, so
that's not fair."

Now Secretary Don Evans flies off to Bulgaria to discuss trade,
and Rummy hints we may move U.S. troops from Germany to Bulgaria.

In diplomatic circles, our new allies from Eastern Europe are
dryly referred to as "Bush's Warsaw Pact." As one Soviet expert put
it, "Bulgaria used to be Russia's lapdog. Now it's America's lapdog."

The Bulgarians were such sycophants to Russia that in the sixties
they proposed becoming the sixteenth republic of the Soviet Union.

Mr. Bush will not be the only one having trouble with the Bulgarian prime minister's name. We all will. In some press reports
it's spelled Simeon Saxcoburggotski, and in others Simeon Saxe-

Coburg-Gotha. The tall, balding, bearded prime minister was formerly King Simeon II, a deposed child czar. He is a distant relative of Prince Albert, Queen Victoria's consort, but not Count Dracula. That's our other new best friend, Romania.

Is this a good trade, the French for the Bulgarians?

Sketchy facts about Bulgaria rattle around: It has a town called Plovdiv; it wants to become big in the skiing industry; its secret service stabbed an exiled dissident writer in London with a poison-tipped umbrella—a ricin-tipped umbrella, in fact; its weight-lifting team was expelled from the Olympics in a drug scandal in 2000; it sent agents to kill the pope.

During the cold war Bulgaria was valued by Moscow for the canned tomatoes it sent in winter, and by France for sending attar of roses, distilled rose oil that was the binding agent for French perfume.

Three famous Bulgarians: Carl Djerassi, who invented birth control pills; Christo, the original wrap artist; Boris Christof, the opera singer. In *Casablanca* there was the Bulgarian girl who offered herself to Claude Rains to get plane tickets.

Avis Bohlen, a former second-in-command at the American embassy in France and an ambassador to Sofia in the late nineties, calls Bulgaria "a very gutsy little country" that has worked hard to improve.

Ms. Bohlen is dubious about the Bush administration's volatile snits at old allies. "You can't build a foreign policy on pique," she says.

She says Bulgaria will be a good ally: "They're really brilliant at math and science, and they have famous wine."

So, we don't need French wine after all.

Bush Ex Machina

■

George W. Bush has often talked wickedly about his days as the black sheep of a blue-blooded family. But the younger rebellion pales before the adult revolt, now sparking epochal changes.

The president is about to upend the internationalist order nurtured by his father and grandfather, replacing the Bush code of noblesse oblige with one of force majeure.

Bush 41, a doting dad, would never disagree with his son in public, but in a speech at Tufts last week, he defended his decision to leave Saddam Hussein in power after Desert Storm.

"If we had tried to go in there and created more instability in Iraq, I think it would have been very bad for the neighborhood," he told the crowd of 4,800. (Was he referring to Baghdad or Kennebunkport?)

He conceded that getting a coalition together is harder now, because the evidence about Saddam's weapons of mass destruction is "a little fuzzier" than was his evident invasion of Kuwait. But 41 still thinks coalitions work: "The more pressure there is, the more chance this matter will be resolved in a peaceful manner." (Maybe he should enter the Democratic primary.)

At the very same moment the father was pushing peace, the son was treating the war as a fait accompli. At the American Enterprise Institute, he finally coughed up the real reason for war: trickle-down democracy.

Unable to handcuff Osama and Saddam, he soft-pedaled his previous cry for a war of retribution for 9/11. Now he was being more forthright, calling for a war of reengineering.

"A new regime in Iraq would serve as a dramatic and inspiring example of freedom for other nations in the region," he said, adding: "Success in Iraq could also begin a new stage for Middle Eastern peace, and set in motion progress towards a truly democratic Palestinian state."

Conservatives began drawing up steroid-fueled plans to reorder the world a decade ago, imperial blueprints fantastical enough to make "Star Wars" look achievable.

In 1992, Dick Cheney, the defense secretary for Bush 41, and his aides, Paul Wolfowitz and Scooter Libby, drafted a document asserting that America should prepare to cast off formal alliances and throw its military weight around to prevent the rise of any "potential future global competitor" and to preclude the spread of nuclear weapons.

The solipsistic grandiosity of the plan was offputting to 41, who loved nothing better than chatting up the other members of the global club. To Poppy and Colin Powell, this looked like voodoo foreign policy, and they splashed cold water on it.

In 1996, Richard Perle, now a Pentagon adviser, and Douglas

Feith, now a Rumsfeld aide, helped write a report about how Israel could transcend the problems with the Palestinians by changing the "balance of power" in the Middle East, and by replacing Saddam.

The hawks saw their big chance after 9/11, but they feared that it would be hard to sell an eschatological scheme to stomp out Islamic terrorism by re-creating the Arab world. So they found Saddam guilty of a crime he could commit later: helping Osama unleash hell on us.

Mr. Bush is his father's son in his "trust us, we know best" attitude.

After obscuring the real reasons for war, the Bushies are now obscuring the Pentagon's assessments of the cost of war ($60 billion to $200 billion?), the size of the occupation force (100,000 to 400,000?) and the length of time American troops will stay in Iraq (two to ten years?).

A Delphic Mr. Wolfowitz tried to blow off House Democrats who pressed him on these issues: "We will stay as long as necessary and leave as soon as possible."

Rahm Emanuel, a congressman from Chicago, chided Mr. Wolfowitz, saying, "In the very week that we negotiated with Turkey, the administration also told the governors there wasn't any more money for education and health care."

The president's humongously expensive tax cuts leave less for all programs except the military.

Asked if we should give up the tax cut to underwrite the war, the president demurred, replying, "Americans are paying the bill."

Nobody knows if the Bush team's hubristic vision for redrawing the Middle East map will end up tamping down terrorism or inflaming it.

Either way, deus ex machina doesn't come cheap.

What Would Genghis Do?

◼

It's easy to picture Rummy in a big metal breastplate, a skirt and lace-up gladiator sandals.

Rummius Maximus Pompeius.

During the innocent summer before 9/11, the defense secretary's office sponsored a study of ancient empires—Macedonia, Rome, the Mongols—to figure out how they maintained dominance.

What tips could Rummy glean from Alexander the Great, Julius Caesar and Genghis Khan?

Mr. Rumsfeld would be impressed, after all, if he knew that Genghis Khan had invented the first crude MIRV (a missile that spews out multiple warheads to their predetermined targets). As David Morgan writes in *The Mongols*, when the bloodthirsty chieftain began his subjugation of the Chinese empire in 1211, he had to figure out a way to take China's walled cities:

"Genghis Khan offered to raise the siege if he were given 1,000 cats and 10,000 swallows. These were duly handed over. Material was tied to their tails, and this was set on fire. The animals were released and fled home, setting the city ablaze, and in the ensuing confusion the city was stormed."

In her new book *The Mission*, about America's growing dependence on the military to manage world affairs, Dana Priest says that the Pentagon commissioned the study at a time when Rummy did not yet have designs on the world.

To the dismay of his four-star generals, the new secretary was talking about pulling American soldiers out of Saudi Arabia, the Sinai Desert, Kosovo and Bosnia. He thought using our military to fight the South American drug trade was "nonsense."

He hated to travel and scorned "international hand-holding," Ms. Priest writes, adding that the defense chief was thinking that "maybe the United States didn't need all these entanglements to remain on top." He canceled multinational exercises, and even banned the word "engagement." His only interest in colonization was in putting weapons in space.

Then 9/11 changed everything. At the Pentagon, Paul Wolfowitz talked about "ending states who sponsor terrorism." He and Richard Perle said our best bet for stomping out Islamic terrorism was to take over Iraq, rewrite those anti-American textbooks and spur a democratic domino effect.

Now, with the rest of the world outraged at the administration's barbed and swaggering style, the Bushies have grown tetchy about the word "empire." They insist they are not interested in hegemony, even as the Pentagon proconsuls prepare to rule in Iraq, the ancient Mesopotamian empire.

Bernard Lewis of Princeton, Newt Gingrich and others worked on the August 2001 report on empires, which noted: "Without strong political and economic institutions, the Mongols and the Macedonians could not maintain extensive empires. What made the Roman Empire great was not just its military power but its 'franchise of empire.' What made the Chinese Empire great was not just its military power but the immense power and might of its culture.

"If we can take any lesson from history it is this: For the United States to sustain predominance it must remain militarily dominant, but it must also maintain its pre-eminence across the other pillars of power."

Some demur. A classical scholar, Bernard Knox, said, "Empires are pretty well dead; their day is gone."

Niall Ferguson, a professor at Oxford and New York University who wrote the coming book *Empire*, said that while "it was rather sweet" that the Pentagon was studying ancient empires, he thought the lessons were no longer relevant.

"The technological and economic differences between modernity and premodernity are colossal," he said.

Besides, he says Americans aren't temperamentally suited to empire building. "The British didn't mind living for years in Iraq or India for 100-plus years," he said. "Americans aren't attracted to the idea of taking up residence in hot, poor places."

He's right. America doesn't like to occupy. We like to buy our territory, like the bargain Louisiana Purchase and the overpriced amount we were going to pay Turkey (the old Ottoman Empire) to use its bases, before its Parliament balked. At the outside, we prefer to time-share.

As the brazen Bush imperialists try to install a new democracy in Iraq, they are finding the old democracy of our reluctant allies inconvenient.

The Xanax Cowboy

■

You might sum up the president's call to war Thursday night as "Message: I scare."

As he rolls up to America's first preemptive invasion, bouncing from motive to motive, Mr. Bush is trying to sound rational, not rash. Determined not to be petulant, he seemed tranquilized.

But the Xanax cowboy made it clear that Saddam is going to pay for 9/11. Even if the fiendish Iraqi dictator was not involved with Al Qaeda, he has supported "Al Qaeda–type organizations," as the president fudged, or "Al Qaeda types" or "a terrorist network like Al Qaeda."

We are scared of the world now, and the world is scared of us. (It's really scary to think we are even scaring Russia and China.)

Bush officials believe that making the world more scared of us is the best way to make us safer and less scared. So they want a spectacular show of American invincibility to make the wicked and the wayward think twice before crossing us.

Of course, our plan to sack Saddam has not cowed the North Koreans and Iranians, who are scrambling to get nukes to cow us.

It still confuses many Americans that, in a world full of vicious slimeballs, we're about to bomb one that didn't attack us on 9/11 (like Osama); that isn't intercepting our planes (like North Korea); that isn't financing Al Qaeda (like Saudi Arabia); that isn't home to Osama and his lieutenants (like Pakistan); that isn't a host body for terrorists (like Iran, Lebanon and Syria).

I think the president is genuinely obsessed with protecting Americans and believes that smoking Saddam will reduce the chances of Islamic terrorists' snatching catastrophic weapons. That is why no cost—shattering the UN, NATO, the European alliance, Tony Blair's career and the U.S. budget—is too high.

Even straining for serenity, Mr. Bush sounded rattled at moments: "My job is to protect America, and that is exactly what I'm going to do. . . . I swore to protect and defend the Constitution; that's what I swore to do. I put my hand on the Bible and took that oath, and that's exactly what I am going to do."

But citing 9/11 eight times in his news conference was exploitative, given that the administration concedes there is no evidence tying Iraq to the 9/11 plot. By stressing that totem, Mr. Bush tried to alchemize American anger at Al Qaeda into support for smashing Saddam.

William Greider writes in *The Nation*, "As a bogus rallying cry, 'Remember 9/11' ranks with 'Remember the *Maine*' of 1898 for war with Spain or the Gulf of Tonkin resolution of 1964. . . ." A culture more besotted with inane "reality" TV than scary reality is easily misled. Mr. Greider pointed out that in a *Times*/CBS News survey, 42 percent believe Saddam was personally responsible for the attack on the World Trade Center and Pentagon, and in an ABC News poll, 55 percent believe he gives direct support to Al Qaeda.

The case for war has been incoherent due to overlapping reasons conservatives want to get Saddam.

The president wants to avenge his father, and please his base by changing the historical ellipsis on the Persian Gulf war to a period. Donald Rumsfeld wants to exorcise the post-Vietnam focus on American imperfections and limitations. Dick Cheney wants to establish America's primacy as the sole superpower. Richard Perle wants to liberate Iraq and remove a mortal threat to Israel. After Desert Storm, Paul Wolfowitz posited that containment is a relic, and that America must aggressively preempt nuclear threats.

And in 1997, Bill Kristol of *The Weekly Standard* and Fox News, and other conservatives, published a "statement of principles," signed by Jeb Bush and future Bush officials—Mr. Rumsfeld, Mr. Cheney, Mr. Wolfowitz, Scooter Libby and Elliott Abrams. Rejecting 41's realpolitik and shaping what would become 43's preemption strategy, they exhorted a "Reaganite policy of military strength and moral clarity," with America extending its domain by challenging "regimes hostile to our interests and values."

Saddam would be the squealing guinea pig proving America could impose its will on the world.

With W., conservatives got a Bush who wanted to be Reagan. With 9/11, they found a new tragedy to breathe life into their old dreams.

I Vant to Be Alone

■

It will go down as a great mystery of history how Mr. Popularity at Yale metamorphosed into President Persona Non Grata of the world.

The genial cheerleader and stickball commissioner with the gregarious parents, the frat president who had little nicknames and jokes for everyone, fell in with a rough crowd.

Just when you thought it couldn't get more Strangelovian, it does. The Bush bullies, having driven off all the other kids in the international schoolyard, are now resorting to imaginary friends.

Paul Wolfowitz, the deputy secretary of defense, spoke to the Veterans of Foreign Wars here yesterday and reassured the group that America would have "a formidable coalition" to attack Iraq. "The number of countries involved will be in the substantial double digits," he boasted. Unfortunately, he could not actually name one of the supposed allies. "Some of them would prefer not to be named now," he said coyly, "but they will be known with pride in due time."

Perhaps the hawks' fixation on being the messiahs of the Middle East has unhinged them. I could just picture Wolfie sauntering down the road to Baghdad with our new ally Harvey, his very own pooka, a six-foot-tall invisible rabbit that the U.S. wants to put on the U.N. Security Council.

Ari Fleischer upped the ante, conjuring up an entire international forum filled with imaginary allies.

He suggested that if the UN remained recalcitrant, we would replace it with "another international body" to disarm Saddam Hussein. It wasn't clear what he was talking about. What other international body? Salma Hayek? The World Bank? The Hollywood Foreign Press Association?

The not-so-splendid isolation of the White House got worse this afternoon when Donald Rumsfeld suggested the unthinkable at his Pentagon briefing: We might have to go to war without Britain.

Even though Tony Blair said he was working "night and day" to get us international support (and beating back a revolt in his own party), Mr. Rumsfeld dismissively remarked that it was "unclear" just what the British role would be in a war.

Asked whether the U.S. would go to war without "our closest ally," he replied, "That is an issue that the president will be addressing in the days ahead, one would assume."

The Brits covered up their fury with typical understatement, calling Rummy's comment "curious." But behind the scene, Downing Street went nuts and began ringing Pennsylvania Avenue, demanding an explanation. How could Rummy be so callous about "the special relationship" after Mr. Blair had stuck his neck out for President Bush and courageously put his career on the line, and after he had sent one quarter of the British military to the Persian Gulf?

Even though Mr. Rumsfeld scrambled later to mollify the British, one BBC commentator dryly said that perhaps he was trying to be sensitive, but "as we all know, Donald Rumsfeld doesn't do sensitive very well."

Now we've managed to alienate our last best friend. We are making the rest of the world recoil. But that may be part of the Bush hawks' master plan. Maybe they have really always wanted to go it alone.

Maybe it has been their strategy all along to sideline the UN, deflate Colin Powell and cut the restraining cords of traditional coalitions. Their decision last summer to get rid of Saddam was driven by their desire to display raw, naked American power. This time, they don't want Colin Powell or pesky allies counseling restraint in Baghdad.

Rummy was unfazed by Turkey's decision not to let our troops in, and he seemed just as unruffled about the prospect of the Brits' falling out of the war effort. And in a well-timed display of American military might, the Air Force tested a huge new bomb called "MOAB" in Florida. Tremors traveled through the ground, and the scary dust cloud could be seen for miles.

"These guys at the Pentagon—Wolfowitz, Perle, Doug Feith—when they lie in bed at night, they imagine a new book written by one of them or about them called *Present at the Recreation*," an American diplomat said. "They want to banish the wimpy Europeanist traditional balance of power, and use the Iraq seedbed of democracy to impose America's will on the world."

The more America goes it alone, the more "robust," as the Pentagon likes to say, the win will be.

Mashing Our Monster

■

E veryone thinks the Bush diplomacy on Iraq is a wreck.

It isn't. It's a success because it was never meant to succeed.

For the hawks, it's a succès d'estime. (If I may be so gauche as to use a French phrase in a city where federal employees are slapping stickers over the word "French" on packets of French dressing and on machines dispensing French vanilla yogurt at the Capitol. Seeing this made me long for the cold war, when you could eat your Russian dressing in peace and when Jackie Kennedy brought France to heel with élan, brains and charm, rather than scattershot embargos and inane suggestions in the capital L'Enfant planned that we disinter our war dead in France.)

Sure, the Bushies might be feeling a bit rattled right now, with the old international system and the North Atlantic alliance crashing down around their ears.

But you can't transfigure the world without ticking off the world.

It's not a simple task, carving new divisions in Europe, just as Europe is moving past the divisions that led to the greatest tragedies of the twentieth century.

The Bush hawks never intended to give peace a chance. They intended to give preemption a chance.

They never wanted to merely disarm the slimy Saddam. They wanted to dislodge and dispose of him.

The president's slapped-together Azores summit is not meant to "go the last mile" on diplomacy, as Ari Fleischer put it.

If Mr. Bush really wanted to do that, he'd try to persuade some leaders who disagree with him; he'd confront the antiwar throngs in London, Paris or Berlin and not leave poor, exhausted Tony Blair to always make the case.

The hidden huddle in the Azores is trompe l'oeil diplomacy, giving Mr. Blair a little cover, making Poppy Bush a little happy. Just three pals feigning sitting around the campfire singing "Kumbaya," as the final U.S. troops and matériel move into place in the Persian Gulf and the president's "Interim Iraqi Authority" postwar occupation plan is collated.

The hawks despise the UN and if they'd gotten its support, they never would have been able to establish the principle that the U.S. can act wherever and whenever it wants to—a Lone Ranger, no Tontos.

Cheney, Rummy, Wolfie, etc., never wanted Colin Powell to find a diplomatic solution. They hate diplomatic solutions. That's why they gleefully junked so many international treaties, multilateral exercises and transatlantic engagements.

They blame the popular Mr. Powell for persuading Bush 41 to end Desert Storm with Saddam still in power, so that the Army would not look as if it was slaughtering the retreating Iraqi Republican Guard.

Once the war stopped, American troops could not intervene to help Shiite Muslims rising up in the south, a rebellion encouraged by Bush 41. Saddam massacred the rebels.

Mr. Powell embodies what the hard-liners want to root out of the American psyche: an "enfeebling" caution, bred by Vietnam, about sending American troops to impose American values.

We'll soon know if the hawks' ambitious foreign policy experiment has a miraculous result, or an anarchic one.

The Los Angeles Times reported on Friday that a classified State Department report debunks the hawks' domino theory and expresses doubt that installing a new regime in Iraq will foster democracy.

And Don Van Natta, Jr., of *The New York Times* reveals that Al Qaeda is using rising anger among young Muslims about the plan to overthrow Saddam to recruit and groom a new generation of terrorists.

It's not easy to superimpose morality with certainty.

As Roger Morris, the author of a Nixon biography, wrote in the *Times* last week: "Forty years ago, the C.I.A., under President John F. Kennedy, conducted its own regime change in Baghdad, carried out in collaboration with Saddam Hussein."

And America is not known for its long attention span or talent for empire building. As Bob Woodward reports in his book *Bush at War*, a month into the bombing of Afghanistan, when the Taliban stronghold of Mazar-i-Sharif fell, Mr. Bush turned to Condoleezza Rice, in a moment straight out of *The Candidate*, and asked: "Well, what next?"

March 19, 2003

The Perpendicular Pronoun

■

S ometimes I feel as if I've spent half my adult life covering a President Bush squaring off against Saddam Hussein, an evil dictator who invades his neighbors and gasses his own people.

But while on the surface this seems like Groundhog War, the father-and-son duels in the sun with Saddam are breathtakingly different. The philosophical gulf between 41's gulf war and 43's gulf war is profound and cataclysmic—it has sent the whole world into a frenzy—yet it can be summed up in a single pronoun.

"The big I," as Bush Senior calls it.

The first President Bush was often teased about his loopy syntax. But it was a way of speaking that signified the modesty and self-effacement his mother had insisted upon. He was so afraid to sound arrogant if he used the first-person singular that he often just dropped the subject of a sentence and went straight to the verb.

"Mother always lectured us—in a kinder, gentler way—against

using the big I," said Poppy, who is so shy of "I" he has never written a personal memoir.

Even though he came to politics with a sparse résumé, compared with his dad's stuffed one, the cocky W. was always more comfortable with the first-person perpendicular.

When I asked him during the 2000 campaign about why he hadn't inherited his father's phobia about the dread singular pronoun, he laughed and self-deprecatingly replied, "That's the difference between a Phi Beta Kappa and a gentleman's C."

During his war overture on Monday night, W. was not afraid of the first-person spotlight: "This danger will be removed. . . . That duty falls to me as commander in chief by the oath I have sworn, by the oath I will keep."

The whole approach of the father, who had once served as ambassador to the UN and loved nothing more than to drag world leaders out on his cigarette boat and give them mal de mer, was a clubby "we." He and James Baker had a coalition of thirty-six countries for Desert Storm to affirm the principle that one country can't arbitrarily invade another. They constantly schmoozed world leaders and tried to maintain international order.

The hawks of Bush II are not afraid of disorder in the pursuit of American dominance. They have no interest in any permanent coalition—except their own. They see the international "we" as an impediment to joy—and to destiny. The Bush doctrine is animated by "the big I." That self-regarding doctrine, concocted by Bill Kristol, Paul Wolfowitz and Richard Perle back when W. was still merely a presidential gleam in Karl Rove's eye, preaches preventive preemptive preternatural preeminence.

The only holdover from the first Bush administration's land of "us" is Colin Powell. When the secretary of state was asked yesterday whether the decision to go to war reflected the preemptive Bush doctrine, he recoiled, crying, "No, no, no."

While the president seemed to endorse Mr. Powell's attempt at diplomacy, it's now clear that he simultaneously adopted Dick Cheney's plan for a military buildup that was bound to upend the diplomatic effort.

The Wall Street Journal reported on Monday that even though Mr. Cheney receded into the background for months, he was choreographing events like Pluto, lord of the underworld. In his undisclosed locations, he had dinner parties with anti-Saddam intellectuals, reached out to Iraqi dissidents and plotted the war with his old pal Rummy, letting Colin Powell vainly spend his prestige at the mealymouthed UN.

We'll never know from the ultrasecretive vice president whether he also touched base with oil industry types, since Halliburton and other big construction companies that give to Republicans now stand to make millions in contracts for reconstructing Iraq and reviving its oil industry.

And so we arrive at this remarkable moment, when a Bush who squeaked into office with an ordinary guy's appeal, not knowing very much at all about the globe but promising a humble foreign policy, has turned decades of American foreign policy on its head.

Asked on *Meet the Press* about the ire the president's go-it-alone approach has provoked around the world, Mr. Cheney was dismissive, proclaiming Mr. Bush to be "Reaganesque." But President Reagan always said to aides, "You have to be both revered and feared."

This crowd has the fear part down cold. They have a long way to go on the other.

Perle's Plunder Blunder

■

I t's Richard Perle's world. We're just fighting in it.

The Prince of Darkness, a man who whips up revelatory souf-flés and revolutionary preemption doctrines with equal ease, took a victory lap at the American Enterprise Institute on Friday morning.

The critical battle for Baghdad was yet to come and "Shock and Awe" was still a few hours away. (The hawks, who are trying to send a message to the world not to mess with America, might have pre-ferred an even more intimidating bombing campaign title, like "Operation Who's Your Daddy?")

Yet Mr. Perle, an adviser to Donald Rumsfeld, could not resist a little preemptive crowing about preemption, predicting "a general recognition that high moral purpose has been achieved here. Mil-lions of people have been liberated."

His conservative audience at the Reagan shrine's "black coffee briefing" (they're too macho for milk and sugar) was buzzed that their cherished dream of saving Iraq by bombing it was under way.

The bossy "you repent, we decide" Bush doctrine was cooked up pre-Bush, fashioned over the last twelve years by conservatives like Mr. Perle, Mr. Rumsfeld, Dick Cheney, Paul Wolfowitz, Scooter Libby, Douglas Feith and Bill Kristol.

The preemption doctrine prefers ad hoc coalitions, allowing an unfettered America to strike at threats and potential threats. At AEI, Mr. Perle boasted that far from going it alone, the Bush administration had a coalition of "more than 40 countries and . . . growing." (Including Micronesia, Mongolia and the Marshall Islands—all of them.)

And he was already looking forward to giving makeovers to other rogue regimes. "I'm rather optimistic that we will see regime change in Iran without any use of military power by the United States," he said.

Michael Ledeen, an AEI scholar on the same panel, called Iraq "just one battle in a broader war. Iran is . . . the mother of modern terrorism."

As Bush 41 learned, waging holy wars can be dicey. After pressing the morality of Desert Storm, he faced questions about his postwar conduct. Critics excoriated Mr. Bush, who had labeled Saddam another Hitler, for turning his back as Saddam laid waste to Kurdish refugees and to Kurds and Shiite Muslims rising up against him after the war.

Now Mr. Perle, who urged America to war with moral certitude, finds himself subject to questions about his own standards of right and wrong.

Stephen Labaton wrote in *The New York Times* on Friday that Mr. Perle was advising the Pentagon on war even as he was retained by Global Crossing, the bankrupt telecommunications company, to help overcome Pentagon resistance to its proposed sale to a joint venture involving a Hong Kong billionaire.

The confidant of Rummy and Wolfie serves as the chairman of the Defense Policy Board, an influential Pentagon advisory panel. That's why Global Crossing agreed to pay Mr. Perle a fat fee: $725,000. The fee structure is especially smelly because $600,000 of the windfall is contingent on government approval of the sale. (In his original agreement, Mr. Perle also asked the company to shell out for "working meals," which could add up, given his status as a gourmand from the Potomac to Provence, where he keeps a vacation home among the feckless French.)

Although his position on the Defense Policy Board is not paid, Mr. Perle is still bound by government ethics rules that forbid officials from reaping financial benefit from their government positions. He and his lawyer told Mr. Labaton that his work for Global Crossing did not violate the rules because he did not lobby for the company and was serving in an advisory capacity to its lawyers.

But that distinction is silly because Global Crossing has so many other big names on its roster of influence peddlers that it doesn't need Mr. Perle's Guccis for actual lobbying footwork or advice on the process. His name alone could be worth the $725,000 if it helps win the Pentagon's seal of approval.

His convictions of right and wrong extend to the right and wrong investments. On Wednesday he participated in a Goldman Sachs conference call to advise clients on investment opportunities arising from the war, titled "Implications of an Imminent War: Iraq Now. North Korea Next?"

Maybe Mr. Perle should remove the laurel wreath from his head and replace it with a paper bag.

No More Saddam TV

■

R ummy was grumpy.

TV generals and Pentagon reporters were poking at his war plan, wondering if he had enough troops and armor on the ground to take Baghdad and protect the rear of his advancing infantry.

"It's a good plan," the war czar insisted with a grimace, adding that battle is "a tough business."

The cocky theorists of the administration, and their neocon gurus, are now faced with reality and history: the treacherous challenge, and the cost in lives and money, of bringing order out of chaos in Iraq.

With sandstorms blackening their TV screens, with POWs and casualties tearing at their hearts, Americans are coming to grips with the triptych of bold transformation experiments that are now in play.

There is the president's dream of remaking the Middle East to make America safer from terrorists.

There is Dick Cheney's desire to transform America into a place that flexes its power in the face of any evil.

There is Donald Rumsfeld's transformation of the American military, changing from the old heavy ground forces to smaller, more flexible units with high-tech weapons.

When Tommy Franks and other generals fought Rummy last summer, telling him he could not invade Iraq without overwhelming force, the defense chief treated them like Old Europe, acting as if they just didn't get it.

He was going to send a smaller force on a lightning-quick race to Baghdad, relying on air strikes and psychological operations—leaflets to civilians and e-mail and calls to Iraqi generals—to encourage Iraqis to revolt against Saddam.

(The Pentagon has downgraded Saddam, the way it did Osama when it just missed getting him. Now the war in Iraq is "not about one man," as General Franks put it.)

The administration was afraid that with too many Iraqis dead, we would lose the support of the world. But some generals worry that by avoiding tactics that could kill Iraqi civilians and "baby-talking" the Iraqi military, we have emboldened the enemy and endangered American troops.

As Ralph Peters, a retired military officer, wrote in a *Washington Post* op-ed article: "Some things do not change. The best way to shock and awe an enemy is still to kill him."

Despite the vast sums we spend on our intelligence and diplomatic services, American officials often seem clueless about the culture of our adversaries. After Vietnam, Robert McNamara admitted that he and other war planners had never understood Vietnamese history and culture. Our intelligence services didn't see the Iranian revolution coming, or the Soviet Union's breakup.

It's hard to know why the administration seems so surprised at Iraqi ruses. As Sun-tzu, the ancient Chinese military tactician who inspired the "shock and awe" campaign, noted, "All war is deception." Besides, the Iraqis used similar fake surrender tricks in the last gulf war.

It's also hard to know why the Pentagon is surprised at Iraqi brutality, or at the failure of Iraqi ethnic groups, deserted by America after the last gulf war, to celebrate their "liberation" by the U.S., or by the hardened resistance of Saddam loyalists like the fedayeen, who have no escape hatch this time around.

American war planners were privately experiencing some shock and awe at Iraqi obliviousness to shock and awe, which we can see on TV, as Iraqis crowd into restaurants and onto roofs to watch the bombing.

Miscalculating, the Pentagon delayed trying to take down Iraqi TV until last night because it hoped to use the network after the war. But that target should have been one of the first so the Iraqis could not have peddled their propaganda, paraded our POWs and shown brazen speeches by Saddam, or Stepford-Saddam, and the mockery of Iraqi officials over the predictions of a quick victory.

The Pentagon started last year with an "inside out" strategy that would rely on a quick capture of Baghdad, with U.S. forces then taking over the rest of the country. That was scrapped in favor of the "outside in" strategy that we're now witnessing.

But Saddam responded to our "outside in" strategy with his own "inside out" strategy.

Tragically for everybody, the Iraqi fiend is still inside, dug in and diabolically determined to kill as many people as he can on the way out.

March 30, 2003

Back Off, Syria and Iran!

■

W e're shocked that the enemy forces don't observe the rules of war. We're shocked that it's hard to tell civilians from combatants, and friends from foes. Adversaries use guerrilla tactics; they are irregulars; they take advantage of the hostile local weather and terrain; they refuse to stay in uniform. Golly, as our secretary of war likes to say, it's unfair.

Some of their soldiers are mere children. We know we have overwhelming, superior power, yet we can't use it all. We're stunned to discover that the local population treats our well-armed, high-tech troops like invaders.

Why is all this a surprise again? I know our hawks avoided serving in Vietnam, but didn't they, like, read about it?

"The U.S. was planning on walking in here like it was easy and all," a young marine named Jimmy Paiz told ABC News this weekend with a rueful smile. "It's not that easy to conquer a country, is it?"

We will conquer the country, and it will be gratifying to see the satanic Saddam running like a rat through the rubble of his palaces. But it was hard not to have a few acid flashbacks to Vietnam at warp speed.

The hawks want Iraq to be the un-Vietnam, to persuade us that war is a necessary disciplinary tool of the only superpower, that America has a moral duty to spread democracy. This time, we crush the opposition swiftly. This time, the domino theory works in reverse, as repressive regimes in the Middle East fall in a chain reaction set off by a democratic Baghdad. Yet in just a week we've seen peace marches, world opinion painting us as belligerent, and draining battlefield TV images.

We saw American commanders expressing doubts about a war plan that the Pentagon insisted was going splendidly while being vague about the body count. "The enemy we're fighting is a bit different than the one we war-gamed against," Lieutenant General William Wallace, the Army's senior ground commander, told reporters. (No doubt, that truthful heads-up will earn General Wallace a slap down.)

Retired generals were even more critical of the Rumsfeld doctrine of underwhelming force. The defense chief is so enamored of technology and air power that he overrode the risk of pitting 130,000-strong American ground forces—the vast majority of the frontline troops have never fired at a live enemy before—against 350,000 Iraqi fighters, who have kept their aim sharp on their own people.

The incoherence of the battle plan—which some retired generals say is three infantry divisions short—has made the guts and stamina and ingenuity of American forces even more remarkable.

Rummy was beginning to erase his fingerprints. "The war plan," he said, "is Tom Franks's war plan." Tommy, we hardly knew ye.

Paul Wolfowitz conceded that the war planners may have under-estimated the hardiness of the heartless Iraqi fighters.

This admission is galling. You can't pound the drums for war by saying Saddam is Hitler and then act surprised when he proves ruth-less on the battlefield.

In their wild dreamscape, the hawks envision Iraq as the rolling start of a broader campaign to bring other rogue states, like Iran and North Korea, to heel.

But in pursuit of what they call a "moral" foreign policy, they stretched and obscured the truth. First, they hyped CIA intelligence to fit their contention that Saddam and Al Qaeda were linked. Then they sent Colin Powell out with hyped evidence about Iraq's weapons of mass destruction. Then, when they were drawing up the battle plan, they soft-pedaled CIA and Pentagon intelligence warn-ings that U.S. troops would face significant resistance from Saddam's guerrilla fighters.

In cranking up their war plan with expurgated intelligence, the hawks left the ground troops exposed and insufficiently briefed on the fedayeen. Ideology should not shape facts when lives are at stake.

Asked about General Wallace's remarks, Donald Rumsfeld shrugged them off, noting that anyone who read Amnesty Interna-tional reports should have known the Iraqis were barbarians.

Rummy was too busy shaking his fist at Syria and Iran to worry about the shortage of troops in Iraq.

As one administration official marveled: "Hasn't the guy bitten off enough this week?"

Dances with Wolfowitz

■

There is an unforgettable scene in *Lawrence of Arabia* when an agonized Lawrence resists as a British commander in Cairo presses him to return to the desert to lead the Arabs revolting against the Ottoman Turks.

LAWRENCE: "I killed two people. One was yesterday. He was just a boy, and I led him into quicksand. The other was . . . well . . . before Aqaba. I had to execute him with my pistol, and there was something about it that I didn't like."

GENERAL ALLENBY: "That's to be expected."

LAWRENCE: "No, something else."

GENERAL ALLENBY: "Well, then let it be a lesson."

LAWRENCE: "No . . . something else."

GENERAL ALLENBY: "What then?"

LAWRENCE: "I enjoyed it."

We were always going to win the war with Iraq. We were always going to get to some triumphant moment, like the great one on Fox at 1:30 A.M. eastern time on Monday morning, when two GIs from Georgia held up a University of Georgia bulldog flag in front of Saddam's presidential palace in Baghdad, and others mischievously headed upstairs to try out Saddam's gold fixtures in the master bathroom.

The big question about the war was, How much blood could Americans bear?

Donald Rumsfeld and Dick Cheney were determined to lead America out of its post-Vietnam, post-Mogadishu queasiness with force and casualties, to change the culture to accept war as a more natural part of a superpower's role in the world.

Their strategy might be described as Black Hawk Up.

Mr. Cheney's war guru, Victor Davis Hanson, writes in his book *An Autumn of War* that war can be good, and that sometimes nations are better off using devastation than suasion. Mr. Hanson cites Sherman's march through Georgia, the nineteenth century's great instance of shock and awe, as a positive role model.

Polls and interviews show that in their goal of making Americans less rattled by battle, Mr. Rumsfeld and Mr. Cheney have succeeded: Most Americans are showing a stoic attitude about the dead and the wounded so far.

(Perhaps the American tolerance for pain is owed to the fact that much of the pain is not shown on television, embeddedness not-withstanding.)

Wolfowitz of Arabia and the other administration hawks are thrilled with U.S. hawkishness. When Mr. Wolfowitz was on *Meet the Press* on Sunday his aides sat in the green room watching the monitor and high-fiving their boss's performance.

As American forces made their first armored thrusts into Baghdad, visions of a JDAM strike on Damascus danced in the hawks' heads.

The former CIA director James Woolsey, a Wolfie pal and a prospective administrator in occupied Iraq, bluntly told UCLA students last week that to reshape the Middle East, the U.S. would have to spend years and maybe decades waging World War IV. (He counted the cold war as World War III.)

He identified America's enemies as the Islamist Shia who run Iran, the Iranian-supported Hezbollah, the fascist Baathists in Iraq and Syria, and the Islamist Sunnis who run Al Qaeda and affiliated terrorist groups.

Mr. Wolfowitz, however, played the diplomat on Sunday, gliding past Tim Russert's probing on whether the neocons' dreams of other campaigns in Syria, Iran and North Korea would come true. Pressed, he said, "There's got to be change in Syria as well."

And the *Times*'s David Sanger reported that when a Bush aide stepped into the Oval Office recently to tell the president that the hard-boiled Rummy had also been shaking a fist at Syria, Mr. Bush smiled and said one word: "Good."

The administration already sounds as triumphalist as Lawrence at his giddiest. Today's satirical *Onion* headline reads: "Bush Sub-consciously Sizes Up Spain for Invasion."

The success of this war should not leave us infatuated with war. Americans' tolerance for these casualties should not be mistaken for a willingness to absorb endless American sacrifice on endless battle-fields.

Victory in Iraq will be a truly historic event, but it will be exceedingly weird and dangerous if this administration turns America into Sparta.

There remains the unfinished business of Osama bin Laden. But the end of Operation Iraqi Freedom should not mark the beginning of Operation Eternal War.

April 27, 2003

He's Out with the In Crowd

■

The swank cocktail party celebrating the fall of Baghdad was the hot ticket on Embassy Row.

The host was the Bush administration's vicar of foreign policy. The guests on Saturday, April 12, included Tony Brenton, acting head of the British embassy, and dozens of ambassadors from the smaller countries that fashioned the fig leaf known as the coalition of the willing.

The ambassador of Eritrea was welcomed to the house on Kalorama Road, even as the French ambassador, who lives directly across the street in a grand château, was snubbed. The German ambassador is kaput, but the ambassador of the Netherlands mingled with Dick Cheney, Paul Wolfowitz, Doug Feith, and General Richard Myers and General Peter Pace of the Joint Chiefs. The winners were gaily lording it over the losers, sneering at the French.

Conspicuously absent was the nation's top diplomat. Asked if

Colin Powell was invited, a State Department official replied, "No. People here didn't know about the party."

The host was Rummy, top gun of a muscle-bound foreign policy summed up by the comic Jon Stewart as "You want a piece of this?"

Washington has a history of nasty rivalries, with competing camps. There were Aaron Burr people and Alexander Hamilton people; Lincoln people and McClellan people; Bobby people and Lyndon people.

Now, since Newt Gingrich aimed the MOAB of screeds at an already circumscribed Mr. Powell, the capital has been convulsed by the face-off between Defense and State.

There are Rummy people: Mr. Cheney, Mr. Wolfowitz, Mr. Feith, Bill Kristol, William Safire, Ariel Sharon, Fox News, *The National Review, The Weekly Standard, The Wall Street Journal* editorial board, the fedayeen of the Defense Policy Board—Richard Perle, James Woolsey, Mr. Gingrich, Ken Adelman—and the fifth column at State, John Bolton and Liz Cheney.

And there are Powell people: Brent Scowcroft, James Baker, Bush 41, Ken Duberstein, Richard Armitage, Richard Haass, the Foreign Service, Joe Biden, Bob Woodward, the wet media elite, the planet.

The dueling secretaries made a show of having lunch Wednesday at the Pentagon. Meanwhile, Mr. Armitage said Newt was "off his meds and out of therapy"; Mr. Baker called Mr. Gingrich "someone with no foreign policy or national security experience . . . who was in effect forced to resign" as House speaker; a Powell aide said it was "inconceivable that Newt could have made this extraordinary attack on his own" without running it past Rummy; and a Powell friend said the hard-liners had tormented the frustrated diplomat and made his life "hellish."

Newt, amateur historian, is part of Rummy's brain trust. The defense chief regularly forwards blathering Gingrich e-mail about military strategy to irritated Pentagon officials.

This clash is epochal because it's beyond ego. It's about whether America will lead by fear, aggression and force of arms or by diplomacy, moderation and example.

Rummy may merely be a front man for Dick Cheney, who tangled with Mr. Powell for being too cautious in the first Persian Gulf war, and scorned Mr. Powell's strategy of going to the UN before the second.

Karl Rove scolded Mr. Gingrich for overreaching; W. still dislikes Newt for leading the revolt against Poppy for breaking his tax pledge.

But the president has not spoken up for Mr. Powell, allowing his credibility to be undermined as he heads off to the Middle East to build the peace. And Mr. Bush has never reined in Rummy's rabid fedayeen.

W.'s gut leans toward the macho Cheney-Rummy idea that America is not bound by history, that the U.S. can help Israel and reshape the Arab world and the rest of the world and not care who is run over, or worry about what will happen if we don't get cooperation on terrorism, proliferation, AIDS, trading, or if people everywhere get up in the morning thinking about how to get back at us.

Nerviness, absolutism and smiting enemies are seductive. Nuance and ambivalence aren't.

The day before Rummy's party, senators were shown an organizational chart for remaking Iraq. Just below Jay Garner, who reports to Tommy Franks, was a line to Larry DiRita, who is a special assistant to the defense chief. Even the time on the chart was "1700," for 5 P.M.

Diplomacy in Washington now runs on military time.

Hypocrisy and Apple Pie

◼

R ichard Perle is at ease with neo-imperial swagger.

At the White House Correspondents Association dinner on Saturday night, the Pentagon's Prince of Darkness lectured Hans Blix as if he were a colonial subject, instructing him on why an invasion of Iraq had been justified even though no weapons of mass destruction had yet been found.

Asked afterward how Mr. Blix had reacted, Mr. Perle replied merrily: "He's a Swedish disarmament lawyer. He's used to a lot of abuse."

When one partygoer told Mr. Perle that she would miss the buzzy, standing-room-only "black coffee briefings" on Iraq held by hard-liners at the American Enterprise Institute, he suggested the neocons might hold another round.

"We'll have green tea briefings on North Korea," he said slyly.

On Fox News, Bill Kristol spoke up for a more brazen imperial attitude. "We need to err on the side of being strong," he said. "And if people want to say we're an imperial power, fine. If three years from now, we have beaten back these threats and have a decent regime there, it'll be worth it."

But imperial flair is rare. America is a furtive empire, afraid to raise its flag or linger too long or even call things by their real names. The U.S. is having a hard time figuring out how to wield its colonial power, how to balance collegiality with coercion, how to savor the fruits of imperialism without acknowledging its imperialist hubris.

When Kofi Annan called the Americans in Iraq an "occupying power" last week, Bush officials freaked. Maybe they would have preferred "Honored Guests."

The Pentagon once more outgunned the State Department this week, changing the name of a new governing body of Iraqis from "interim authority" to "transitional government" to signal that the U.S. would leave quickly and give its Armani-clad puppet, Ahmad Chalabi, an advantage. But it doesn't matter what euphemistic name is used; if there are too many militant Shiite clerics involved, Rummy, the real authority, will tell them to take their camels and vamoose.

"America is the empire that dare not speak its name," Niall Ferguson, the Oxford professor who wrote *Empire*, told a crowd at the Council on Foreign Relations here on Monday. He believes that America is so invested in its "creation myth," breaking away from a wicked empire, that Americans will always be self-deceiving—and even self-defeating—imperialists.

"The great thing about the American empire is that so many Americans disbelieve in its existence," he said. "Ever since the annexation of Texas and invasion of the Philippines, the U.S. has systematically pursued an imperial policy.

"It's simply a suspension of disbelief by Americans. They think they're so different that when they have bases in foreign territories, it's not an empire. When they invade sovereign territory, it's not an empire."

Asked in an interview about Viceroy Jay Garner's promise that U.S. military overlords would "leave fairly rapidly," Mr. Ferguson replied: "I'm hoping he's lying. Successful empires must be based on hypocrisy. The Americans can say they're doing things in the name of freedom, liberty and apple pie. But they must build a civil society and revive the economy before they have elections.

"From 1882 until 1922, the British promised the international community 66 times that they would leave Egypt, but they never did. If they leave Iraq to its own devices, the whole thing will blow up."

Afghanistan offers cautionary lessons. It was the abandonment by the U.S. after Afghanistan's war in 1989 with the Soviet Union that stoked the fury of Al Qaeda. The regime of the American puppet Hamid Karzai is still perilously fragile.

As Carlotta Gall wrote in the *Times* last weekend, after two U.S. soldiers were killed by Afghan rebels: "In a very real sense the war here has not ended.... Nearly every day, there are killings, explosions, shootings and targeted attacks on foreign aid workers, Afghan officials and American forces, as well as continuing feuding between warlords."

Exiled Taliban leaders have called for a holy war against the "occupying forces." The religious police are once more harassing and beating women over dress and behavior, and schools that take little girls are being attacked and threatened.

Until we can get democracy stabilized in our new colonies, Mr. Ferguson offers two words of advice: "Better puppets."

The Iceman Cometh

■

T he tail hook caught the last cable, jerking the fighter jet from 150 m.p.h. to zero in two seconds.

Out bounded the cocky, rule-breaking, daredevil flyboy, a man navigating the Highway to the Danger Zone, out along the edges where he was born to be, the further on the edge, the hotter the intensity.

He flashed that famous all-American grin as he swaggered around the deck of the aircraft carrier in his olive flight suit, ejection harness between his legs, helmet tucked under his arm, awestruck crew crowding around. Maverick was back, cooler and hotter than ever, throttling to the max with joystick politics.

Compared to Karl Rove's "revvin' up your engine" mythmaking cinematic style, Jerry Bruckheimer's movies look like *Lizzie McGuire*.

This time Maverick didn't just nail a few bogeys and do a 4G inverted dive with a MIG-28 at a range of two meters. This time the

Top Gun wasted a couple of nasty regimes, and promised this was just the beginning. Mav swaggered across the deck to high-five his old gang: his wise flight instructor, Viper; his amiable sidekick, Goose; his chiseled rival, Iceman.

MAVERICK: I feel the need . . .

GOOSE: The need for speed!

ICEMAN: You're really a cowboy.

MAVERICK: What's your problem?

ICEMAN: Your ego's writing checks your body can't cash. You didn't need to take all that water survival training in the White House swimming pool. The Abraham Lincoln was practically docked, only thirty miles off shore, after ten months at sea. They had to steer it away from land for you. If you'd waited a few hours, you could've just walked aboard. You and Rove are making a gorgeous campaign video on the Pacific to cast you as the warrior president for 2004, but back on shore, things are ugly. The California economy's bleeding, even worse than other states'. When you took office, the unemployment rate in San Jose was 1.7 percent; by February of this year, it had risen to 8.5 percent. Your motorcade didn't bother to stop in the depressed high-tech corridor in Silicon Valley. Every time you cut taxes and raise deficits while you're roaring ahead with a preemptive military policy, you're unsafe. National unemployment goes up to 6 percent and you just hammer Congress to pass your tax cut. The only guys sure about their jobs these days are defense contractors connected to Republicans and the Carlyle Group, which owns half of the defense plant you visited here. You're dangerous.

MAVERICK: That's right, Iceman. I am dangerous.

ICEMAN: You can fly, Maverick. But you, Cheney and Rummy are strutting around on a victory tour when you haven't found Osama or Saddam or WMD; you haven't figured out how you're going to stop tribal warfare and religious fanaticism and dangerous skirmishes with our soldiers; you don't yet know how to put Afghanistan and Iraq back together so that a lot of people over there don't hate us. And why can't you stop saying that getting rid of Saddam removed "an ally" of Al Qaeda and was payback for 9/11? You know we just needed to jump somebody in that part of the world.

MAVERICK: That part of the world is what I call a target-rich environment, sorta like a Democratic debate. Hey, Miss Iceman, why don't you head to the ladies' room? John Kerry and John Edwards are already there, fixin' their hair all pretty-like. Howard Dean's with 'em, trying on a dress, and Kucinich is hemming it for him.

VIPER: You're arrogant, son. I like that in a pilot. You're a hell of an instinctive flier. You're a lot like your old man. He was a natural, heroic son of a gun. I flew with him in his torpedo bomber in '44. Is that why you fly the way you do? Trying to prove something by doing the opposite? He tried to get deficits down. He did it right. And he knew you had to have wingmen among the allies. You can't buzz the tower of the world every time you go up. You can't just jettison the Top Gun global rules of engagement.

MAVERICK: Sure I can. Like greed, aggression is good. Aggression has marked the upward surge of mankind. Aggression breeds patriotism, and patriotism curbs dissent. Aggression has made Democrats cower, the press purr and the world quake. Aggression—you mark my words—will not only save humanity, but it will soon color all the states Republican red. Mission accomplished.

Who's Losing Iraq?

■

K arl Rove has got to be nervous.
The man who last year advised Republican candidates to "focus on war" is finding out that the Bush doctrine of preemption cannot preempt anarchy.

Now, General Rove will have to watch Democratic candidates focus on war.

We're getting into very volatile territory in the Middle East.

As Paul Bremer admitted last week, the cost of the Iraq adventure is going to be spectacular: $2 billion for electrical demands and $16 billion to deliver clean water.

We're losing one or two American soldiers every day. Saddam and Osama are still lurking and scheming—the "darkness which may be felt."

After a car bomb exploded outside a Najaf mosque on Friday, killing scores of people, including the most prominent pro-American Shiite cleric, we may have to interject our troops into an internecine

Shiite dispute—which Saddam's Baathist guerrillas are no doubt stoking.

With Iraqis in Najaf screaming, "There is no order! There is no government! We'd rather have Saddam than this!," we had one more ominous illustration that the Bush team is out of its depth and divided against itself.

You can't conduct a great historical experiment in a petty and bickering frame of mind. The agencies of the Bush administration are behaving like high school cliques. The policy in Iraq is paralyzed almost to the point of nonexistence, stalled by spats between the internationalists and unilateralists, with the national security director, Condoleezza Rice, abnegating her job as policy referee.

The State Department will have to stop sulking and being in denial about the Pentagon running the show in Iraq. And the Pentagon will have to stop being dogmatic, clinging to the quixotic notion that it only wants to succeed with its streamlined force and its faux coalition. Rummy has to accept the magnitude of the task and give up running the Department of Defense the way a misanthropic accountant would.

Big deeds need big spirits. You can't have a Marshall Plan and a tax cut at the same time.

It has also now become radiantly clear that we have to drag Dick Cheney out of the dark and smog. Less Hobbes, more Locke.

So far, American foreign policy has been guided by the vice president's gloomy theories that fear and force are the best motivators in the world, that war is man's natural state and that the last great superpower has sovereign authority to do as it pleases without much consultation with subjects or other nations.

We can now see the disturbing results of all the decisions Mr. Cheney made in secret meetings.

The General Accounting Office issued a report last week noting that the vice president shaped our energy policy with clandestine advice from "petroleum, coal, nuclear, natural gas, electricity industry representatives and lobbyists."

Favoritism to energy pals led to last week's insane decision to gut part of the Clean Air Act and allow power plants, refineries and other industrial sites to belch pollutants.

Another Bush-Cheney energy crony is Anthony Alexander of Ohio's FirstEnergy Corporation, which helped trigger the blackout after failing to upgrade its transmission system properly since deregulation. He was a Bush Pioneer, having raised at least $100,000 for the campaign.

This logrolling attitude has led to the U.S. Army Corps of Engineers allowing Halliburton—which made Mr. Cheney a rich man with $20 million worth of cashed-in stock—to get no-bid contracts in Iraq totaling $1.7 billion, and that's just a start.

All this, and high gas prices, too?

When he wasn't meeting secretly with energy lobbyists, Mr. Cheney was meeting secretly with Iraqi exiles. The Iraqi National Congress leader Ahmad Chalabi and other defectors conned Mr. Cheney, Rummy and the naive Wolfowitz of Arabia by playing up the danger of Saddam's WMDs and playing down the prospect of Iraqi resistance to a U.S. invasion.

According to *The Los Angeles Times*, U.S. and allied intelligence agencies are investigating to see if they were duped by Iraqi defectors giving bogus information to mislead the West before the war.

Some intelligence officials "now fear that key portions of the prewar information may have been flawed," the story said. "The issue raises fresh doubts as to whether illicit weapons will be found in Iraq."

Karl Rove has got to be nervous.

■

Hey Dude, Where's My Covert Action?

In Which Top Gun

Is Toppled by

Sputtering Spooks

■

May 25, 2003

Yo, Ayatollahs!

■

T he CIA is snooping around itself and other spy agencies to see if prewar reports of Iraqi weapons of mass destruction and ties to Al Qaeda were exaggerated.

The suspense is killing me.

The delicious part is that the review was suggested by Donald Rumsfeld, a main culprit in twisting the intelligence to justify a strike on Baghdad. It's like O.J. vowing to find the real killer.

When the CIA reports weren't incriminating enough about Saddam last fall, Rummy started his own little CIA within the Pentagon to ferret out information to back up the hawks' imperial schemes. It will be interesting to see how a man who never admits he's wrong wriggles out of admitting he's wrong, after his investigation fingers him for hyping.

When Colin Powell went to the UN in February to make the case for attacking Iraq, he raised the specter of 25,000 liters of anthrax, tons of chemical weapons and a dictator on the brink of a nuclear bomb.

Flash forward to May. Stymied U.S. arms inspectors are getting ready to leave Iraq, having uncovered moldy vacuum cleaners, pesticides and playground equipment, but nary a WMD. Those jungle gyms can be treacherous. One of the weapons hunters compared his work to a Scooby-Doo mystery—stuff seems pretty scary at first, but then turns out to be explainable.

Even before the war, some CIA analysts and British spymasters were complaining of puffed-up intelligence. Now Congress wants to know if it was flawed as well.

As Representative Jane Harman, the ranking Democrat on the House Intelligence Committee, put it: "This could conceivably be the greatest intelligence hoax of all time."

Her innocence is touching.

The Iraq WMD and ties to Al Qaeda were merely MacGuffins, as Alfred Hitchcock called devices that drove the plot but were otherwise inconsequential.

The plot was always to remake the Middle East, while remaking a Bush into a Reagan. And the Bushies were not above playing on American fears and desire for 9/11 payback.

Far from being chagrined about the little problem of having no casus belli, and no plan for smoothly delivering Pax Americana to Iraq and Afghanistan, the hawks are hawking the next regime change. If Iraq was not harboring Al Qaeda and going nuclear, then certainly Iran is.

"Of course, they have senior Al Qaeda in Iran, that's a fact," Rummy said at the Pentagon briefing on Wednesday. "Iran is one of the countries that is, in our view, assessed as developing a nuclear capability, and that's unfortunate."

Bushies were also hinting that Iran may have been involved in the attack on a Western compound in Saudi Arabia—before our intelligence sources are sure. And the U.S. cannot let Iran foment desire in Iraq for a Shiite fundamentalist government.

Citing newspaper reports that said one of the organizers of the Saudi attacks was hiding in Iran, Bill Kristol beat the drum on Fox News: "Indeed, bin Laden's son is probably in Iran. And that looks like the place where they are reconstituting Al Qaeda. Plus, Iran has been a larger sponsor of terror, including perhaps the terror, indirectly at least, that hit Jerusalem today. Are you willing to get serious about Iran?" (Mr. Kristol is obviously ready to watch another war from his living room.)

The administration is panicky about Iran's nuclear program, which the mullahs threw into overdrive after America attacked Iraq.

Some neocons would like Israel to take out Iran's nuclear reactor, as it did Iraq's in '81; but Israel wants America to do it. Some are pushing shah nostalgia, suggesting that Reza Pahlavi, the son of the last shah of Iran, could be the next Chalabi.

The Taliban and Al Qaeda are resurgent; Afghanistan and Iraq are a mess; the vice police are back arresting women in Afghanistan and looters are tearing up archaeological sites in Iraq; Saddam and Osama are still wanted, dead or alive. Yet the MacGuffin has moved on.

It is paradoxical that the hawks were passionate about breeding idealism by bringing democracy to the Middle East, but are unconcerned about breeding cynicism by refusing to admit mistakes or overreaching.

By the time the CIA delivers its report, it will be time to investigate how our intelligence was hyped in the prelude to the strike on Iran.

June 4, 2003

Bomb and Switch

■

Before 9/11, the administration had too little intelligence on Al Qaeda, badly coordinated by clashing officials.

Before the Iraq invasion, the administration had too much intelligence on Saddam, torqued up by conspiring officials.

As Secretary of State Colin Powell prepared to make his case for invading Iraq to the UN on February 5, a friend of his told me, he had to throw out a couple of hours' worth of sketchy intelligence other Bush officials were trying to stuff into his speech.

U.S. News & World Report reveals this week that when Mr. Powell was rehearsing the case with two dozen officials, he became so frustrated by the dubious intelligence about Saddam that he tossed several pages in the air and declared: "I'm not reading this. This is &*#."

First America has no intelligence. Then it has &*# intelligence.

So this is progress?

For the first time in history, Americans are searching for the reason we went to war after the war is over.

As the *Times*'s James Risen reports, a bedrock of the administration's weapons case—the National Intelligence Estimate that concluded that Iraq had chemical and biological weapons and was seeking nukes—is itself being reassessed. The document is at the center of a broad prewar-intelligence review, being conducted by the CIA to see whether the weapons evidence was cooked.

Conservatives are busily offering a bouquet of new justifications for a preemptive attack on Iraq that was sold as self-defense against Saddam's poised and thrumming weapons of mass destruction.

Pressed by reporters about whether Tony Blair and President Bush were guilty of hyperbole—Mr. Blair's foreign secretary claimed Saddam could deploy chemical and biological weapons in forty-five minutes—Senator John McCain replied, "The American people support what the president did, whether we find those weapons or not, and they did so the day they saw 9- and 10-year-old boys coming out of a prison in Baghdad."

Senator Pete Domenici noted that experts thought that Saddam's overthrow might pave the way for the Middle East road map to work. "For those kind of experts to say that has changed the dynamics in the Middle East, sufficient that we might get peace, seems to me to outweigh all the questions about did we have every bit of evidence that we say we had or not," he said.

In a *Vanity Fair* interview, Paul Wolfowitz said another "almost unnoticed but huge" reason for war was to promote Middle East peace by allowing the U.S. to take its troops out of Saudi Arabia— Osama's bête noire. But it was after the U.S. announced it would pull its troops from Saudi Arabia that a resurgent Qaeda struck Western compounds, killing eight Americans.

And it was after the U.S. tried to intimidate other foes by stomping on Saddam that Iran and North Korea ratcheted up their nukes.

Iran and North Korea actually do have scary nuclear programs, but if we express our alarm to the world now, will we be accused of crying Wolfowitz?

A new Pew survey of twenty-one nations shows a deepening skepticism toward the U.S. "The war had widened the rift between Americans and Western Europeans, further inflamed the Muslim world, softened support for the war on terrorism, and significantly weakened global public support for the pillars of the post–World War II era—the U.N. and the North Atlantic alliance," said Pew's director, Andrew Kohut.

Brits may be more upset with Mr. Blair than Americans are with Mr. Bush because they have the quaint idea that even if you think war was a good idea, you should level with the public about your objectives.

The Bush crowd practiced bait and switch, leaving many Americans with the impression that Saddam was involved in 9/11.

When James Woolsey, the former CIA director and current Pentagon adviser, appeared on *Nightline* five days after 9/11 and suggested that America had to strike Iraq for sponsoring terrorism, Ted Koppel rebutted: "Nobody right now is suggesting that Iraq had anything to do with this. In fact, quite the contrary."

Mr. Woolsey replied: "I don't think it matters. I don't think it matters." The Republicans will have to follow the maxim of Robert Moses, the autocratic New York builder who never let public opinion get in the way of his bulldozing: "If the ends don't justify the means, what does?"

June 22, 2003

Desert Double Feature

■

L ooking back, you have to wonder if Rummy and Saddam were in two completely different movies, Rummy starring in a heroic war adventure like *Sands of Iwo Jima* while Saddam was scheming in a slick heist caper like *Ocean's Eleven.* (With a soundtrack by Frank Sinatra using the Iraqi dictator's favorite song, "Strangers in the Night.")

Could we have been at war with someone who wasn't fighting back?

In Iraq, Rummy wanted to prove that the sleek, high-tech American military could be used to fight in unconventional ways. But maybe Saddam, who gives creepy new meaning to the phrase ultimate survivor, was playing an even more unconventional game.

What if he never meant to mount a last stand in Baghdad but merely spread word that there was a dread "red line" of chemical and germ warheads ringing the capital to give himself time to melt away into subterranean safety?

Two nights before the war began, Qusay or his minions were busy plundering a billion dollars from Iraq's central bank.

As U.S. tanks sped through Iraq, meeting surprisingly little opposition except for fedayeen harassment, Saddam may have been burning records of his weaponizing and terrorizing. He had probably already hidden or destroyed any bad stuff during the year the Bushies spent trash-talking about whupping him.

Maybe he decided that rather than hit America with biological warfare, he would use psychological warfare, discrediting the U.S. with allies by stripping the anthrax cupboards.

Was the tyrant sending out doubles in public while he plotted his getaway? Or making loyalists pretend to be double agents, dishing fake tips to the CIA about where the Ace of Spades was dining so the U.S. would bomb the wrong places?

Saddam knew how hard it would be for America to rely on trust and understanding in a part of the world that we don't understand and where no one trusts us.

He had twelve years between wars and Bushes, after all, to plot ruses.

His captured top lieutenant has told American interrogators that he fled to Syria with Saddam's sons after the war (until Syria expelled them) and that Saddam was hiding in Iraq.

Maybe Saddam has been chortling from the sidelines as his guerrillas and Islamic militants kill enough U.S. soldiers to make Americans queasy. Maybe he could inflame an Iraqi rebellion over chaotic conditions, to expel the occupiers who came with no occupation plan.

Or, if Saddam brought a plastic surgeon underground with him, perhaps he could resurface as a fresh face, a populist candidate in Viceroy Bremer's first democratic elections.

After all, Baath, the name of his party, translates as "Resurrection."

It's funny that the Bushies didn't recognize a heist when they saw one, given that they pulled off such a clever heist of their own: They cracked the safe of American foreign policy and made off with generations of resistance to preemptive and unilateral attacks.

On Friday, senators on the intelligence committee cut a deal that lets "a thorough review"—i.e., a Republican whitewash—go forward into whether the spy community ginned up prewar intelligence. The Democrats, already Fausted by their prewar fear of being pantywaists, naturally caved on open hearings.

Open, closed, who cares? Congress is looking in the wrong place. They're scrutinizing those who gathered the intelligence rather than those who pushed to distort it.

George Tenet might have buttered up his bosses by not objecting loud enough when the Bushies latched onto bogus or exaggerated claims, but if obsequiousness is a subject of congressional investigation, we're in for a busy summer.

The hawks started with Saddam's demise and worked backward.

The New Republic reports in its "Deception and Democracy" cover story: "In the summer of 2002, Vice President Cheney made several visits to the C.I.A.'s Langley headquarters, which were understood within the agency as an attempt to pressure the low-level specialists interpreting the raw intelligence. 'That would freak people out,' said one former C.I.A. official. 'It is supposed to be an ivory tower. And that kind of pressure would be enormous on these young guys.'"

It's scary, all right. Dick Cheney's hot breath on your raw files.

July 13, 2003

National House of Waffles

■

ore and more, with Bush administration pronouncements about
the Iraq war, it depends on what the meaning of the word
"is" is.

W. built his political identity on the idea that he was not Bill Clinton. He didn't parse words or prevaricate. He was the Texas straight shooter.

So why is he now presiding over a completely Clintonian environment, turning the White House into a Waffle House, where truth is camouflaged by word games and responsibility is obscured by shell games?

The president and Condi Rice can shuffle the shells and blame George Tenet, but it smells of mendacity.

Mr. Clinton indulged in casuistry to hide personal weakness. The Bush team indulges in casuistry to perpetuate its image of political steel.

Dissembling over peccadillos is pathetic. Dissembling over preemptive strikes is pathological, given over two hundred Americans dead and a thousand wounded in Iraq, and untold numbers of dead Iraqis. Our troops are in "a shooting gallery," as Teddy Kennedy put it, and our spy agencies warn that we are on the cusp of a new round of attacks by Saddam snipers.

Why does it always come to this in Washington? The people who ascend to power on the promise of doing things differently end up making the same unforced errors their predecessors did. Out of office, the Bush crowd mocked the Clinton propensity for stone-walling; in office, they have stonewalled the 9/11 families on the events that preceded the attacks, and the American public on how—and why—they maneuvered the nation into the Iraqi war.

Their defensive crouch and obsession with secrecy are positively Nixonian. (But instead of John Dean and an aggressive media, they have Howard Dean and a cowed media.)

In a hole, the president should have done some plain speaking: "The information I gave you in the State of the Union about Iraq seeking nuclear material from Africa has been revealed to be false. I'm deeply angry and I'm going to get to the bottom of this."

But of course he couldn't say that. He would be like Sheriff Bart in *Blazing Saddles*, holding the gun to his own head and saying, "Nobody move or POTUS gets it." The Bush administration has known all along that the evidence of the imminent threat of Saddam's weapons and the Al Qaeda connections were pumped up. They were manning the air hose.

Mr. Tenet, in his continuing effort to ingratiate himself to his bosses, agreed to take the fall, trying to minimize a year's worth of war-causing warping of intelligence as a slip of the keyboard. "These 16 words should never have been included in the text written for the president," he said, in fifteen words that were clearly written for him on behalf of the president. But it won't fly.

It was Ms. Rice's responsibility to vet the intelligence facts in the president's speech and take note of the red alert the tentative Tenet was raising. Colin Powell did when he set up camp at the CIA for a week before his UN speech, double-checking what he considered unsubstantiated charges that the Cheney chief of staff, Scooter Libby, and other hawks wanted to sluice into his talk.

When the president attributed the information about Iraq trying to get Niger yellowcake to British intelligence, it was a Clintonian bit of flimflam. Americans did not know what top Bush officials knew: that this "evidence" could not be attributed to American intelligence because the CIA had already debunked it.

Ms. Rice did not throw out the line, even though the CIA had warned her office that it was sketchy. Clearly, a higher power wanted it in.

And that had to be Dick Cheney's office. Joseph Wilson, former U.S. ambassador to Gabon, said he was asked to go to Niger to answer some questions from the vice president's office about that episode and reported back that it was highly doubtful.

But doubt is not the currency of the Bush hawks. Asked if he regretted using the Niger claim, Mr. Bush replied: "There is no doubt in my mind that Saddam Hussein was a threat to world peace. And there's no doubt in my mind that the United States, along with allies and friends, did the right thing in removing him from power. And there's no doubt in my mind, when it's all said and done, the facts will show the world the truth."

I'm happy that Mr. Bush's mental landscape is so cloudless. But it is our doubts he needs to assuage.

Let's Blame Canada

■

hey were wrong, of course. Soldiers should not go public in the
middle of a conflict and trash-talk their superiors or ask for the
resignation of the secretary of defense.

But it was inevitable that their gripes would bubble to the surface.
Many American troops in Iraq are exhausted, and perplexed about
the scary new guerrilla war they're caught up in. And they have
every right to be scared, because the coolly efficient Bush commanders have now been exposed as short-term tacticians who had no
strategy for dealing with a war of liberation that morphed into a
war of attrition.

The 3rd Infantry Division, which spearheaded the drive to Baghdad and has been away from home the longest, has had its departure
date yanked away twice. Last week, some soldiers from the 3rd in
Falluja—a treacherous place where many Americans have been
killed by guerrillas, including one on Friday—griped to the ABC

News correspondent Jeffrey Kofman. One soldier said, "If Donald Rumsfeld was here, I'd ask him for his resignation."

The complaints infuriated some in the Bush administration, and the new Tommy Franks, General John Abizaid, suggested that field commanders might mete out "a verbal reprimand or something more stringent."

Somebody at the White House decided not to wait. Matt Drudge, the conservative cybercolumnist, told Lloyd Grove, the *Washington Post* gossip columnist, that "someone from the White House communications shop" told him about the ABC story and also about a profile of the Canadian-born Mr. Kofman in *The Advocate*, a gay publication. Mr. Drudge quickly linked the two stories on his popular Web site, first headlining the *Advocate* piece, "ABC NEWS REPORTER WHO FILED TROOP COMPLAINTS STORY—OPENLY GAY CANADIAN." Eight minutes later, he amended the headline to read, "ABC NEWS REPORTER WHO FILED TROOP COMPLAINTS STORY IS CANADIAN," leaving readers to discover in the body of the story what the Bush provocateur apparently felt was Mr. Kofman's other vice.

Now that the right wing's bête noire, Peter Jennings, has gotten his American citizenship, conservatives may have needed another ABC Canadian to kick around. And the Christian Right is still smarting over the Supreme Court's telling police they could no longer storm gay bedrooms in search of sodomy.

Scott McClellan, the new Bush press secretary, said that if Mr. Drudge's contention about his source was true, it would be "totally inappropriate." He added, "If anyone on my staff did it, they would no longer be working for me." He said he had no way to trace an anonymous source.

But Bush loyalists regularly plant information they want known in the *Drudge Report*. Whoever dredged up the *Advocate* story was appealing to the baser nature of President Bush's base, seeking to discredit the ABC report by smearing the reporter for what he or she considers sins of private life (not straight) and passport (not American). Let's hope the fans of Ann (Have you no sense of decency?) Coulter aren't taking her revisionist view of McCarthyism too seriously and making character assassination fashionable again on the Potomac.

What we are witnessing is how ugly it can get when control freaks start losing control. Beset by problems, the Bush team responds by attacking those who point out the problems. These linear, Manichaean managers are flailing in an ever-more-chaotic environment. They are spending $3.9 billion a month trying to keep the lid on a festering mess in Iraq, even as Afghanistan simmers.

The more Bush officials try to explain how the president made the bogus uranium claim in his State of the Union address, despite the CIA red flags and the State Department warning that it was "highly dubious," the more inexplicable it seems. The list of evils the administration has not unearthed keeps getting longer—Osama, Saddam, WMD, the anthrax terrorist—as the deficit gets bigger ($455 billion, going to $475 billion).

After 9/11, this administration had everything going for it. Republicans ruled Congress. The president had enormously high approval ratings. Yet it overreached while trying to justify the reasons for going to war.

Even when conservatives have all the marbles, they still act as if they're under siege. Now that they are under siege, it is no time for them to act as if they're losing their marbles.

Blanket of Dread

■

There is no more delightful way to pass a summer's day in Washington than going up to Capitol Hill to watch senators jump ugly on Wolfie.

Many Democrats and Republicans on the Senate Foreign Relations Committee felt they had been snookered by Paul Wolfowitz, and they did not want to be played again.

They waited gimlet-eyed yesterday while Wolfowitz of Arabia shimmied away once more from giving the cost, in lives or troops or dollars, of remaking a roiling Iraq.

Instead, he offered a highly dramatic travelogue of his recent Iraq trip, sleeping in Saddam's palace and flying with members of the Tennessee National Guard, who made him "very unhappy" when they told him about their nearly two years of active duty. (Gee, whose fault is that?) He described Saddam's "torture tree," "unspeakable torture," "torture chamber" and "a smothering blanket of apprehension and dread woven by 35 years of repression."

"The military and rehabilitation efforts now under way in Iraq are an essential part of the war on terror," Mr. Wolfowitz proclaimed, capitalizing the *W* and the *T* in his written testimony, and underlining the sentence for those too dim to understand its essential importance.

Brazening out the failure to find the Saddam-Qaeda links and WMD the administration aggrandized before the war, Mr. Wolfowitz has simply done an Orwellian fan dance, covering up the lack of concrete ties to the 9/11 terrorists with feathery assertions that securing "the peace in Iraq is now the central battle in the war on terror."

It is a new line of defense that was also used by Dick Cheney in a speech last week ("In Iraq, we took another essential step in the war on terror") and by the president in a speech on Monday ("And our current mission in Iraq is essential to the broader war on terror; it's essential to the security of the American people").

Even now that it's clear the Bushies played up the terror angle because they thought it was the best way to whip up support for getting rid of Saddam, the administration refuses to level with the public.

It dishes out the same old sauerkraut—conjuring up images of Al Qaeda by calling Iraqi guerrillas and foreign fighters "terrorists." Meanwhile, the real Qaeda may be planning more suicide hijackings of passenger planes on the East Coast this summer, Homeland Security says.

Noting that the administration is tamping down Iraq while Al Qaeda is bubbling up elsewhere, Senator Russ Feingold pressed: "I would ask you, Secretary Wolfowitz, are you sure we have our eye on the ball?"

Senator Lincoln Chafee, Republican of Rhode Island, responded to Mr. Wolfowitz's oration about Saddam's tyranny by noting sharply that Liberia's Charles Taylor is also a vicious tyrant famous for dismembering and burning victims, and spreading war. "But we're doing nothing in Liberia," he said. He objected to Mr. Wolfowitz's using 9/11 to push regime change in Iraq, even though the hawk had advocated getting rid of Saddam all through the late nineties.

Senator Joseph Biden excoriated Mr. Wolfowitz for his lack of candor and said his own review of the Iraqi police force—"almost looked like the Katzenjammer Kids"—had convinced him democracy was way off.

"I no more agree, just for the record, with your assessment that Iraq is the hotbed of terror now than I did with your assertions about Al Qaeda connections at the front end," Mr. Biden said, adding that if officials did not tell the truth to the public about the costs in Iraq, they would lose credibility.

Spill all the facts? This crowd? Fat chance. Only yesterday, the administration showed ingenious new talent for insidious secrecy. President Bush refused to declassify the twenty-eight-page redaction about the Saudi government's role in financing the hijackings, even though the Saudi foreign minister flew to the U.S. to ask the president to do that. (You know you're in trouble when the Saudis are begging you to be more open.)

And Mr. Secrecy, John Poindexter, had another boneheaded scheme canceled at the Pentagon, when stunned senators learned that his department had started an online trading market, a dead pool, where investors could wager on terror attacks.

Even Mr. Wolfowitz, who has shown an audacious imagination in refashioning the Middle East, thought the death wagers were over the top: "It sounds like maybe they got too imaginative in this area."

Neocon Coup at the Department d'État

■

Let others fight over whether the war in Iraq was a neocon vigilante action disrupting diplomacy. The neocons have moved on to a vigilante action to occupy diplomacy.

The audacious ones have saddled up their preemptive steeds and headed off to force a regime change at Foggy Bottom.

President Bush staged a Texan tableau vivant last night, playing host at his ranch to the secretary of state, his wife, Alma, and his deputy, Richard Armitage. Mr. Bush wanted to show solidarity after a *Washington Post* story on Monday that said that Colin Powell, under pressure from his wife, said he would not be part of a second Bush term, nor would Mr. Armitage.

Mr. Bush might be trying to signal his respect for Mr. Powell, but the president is not always privy to the start of a grandiose neocon scheme.

The scene was reminiscent of last August in Crawford, when Mr. Bush dismissed press "churning" that the administration was on the verge of striking Iraq, saying, "When I say I'm a patient man, I mean I'm a patient man and that we will look at all options and we will consider all technologies available to us, and diplomacy and intelligence."

We all know how that turned out.

When the neocons want something done, they'll get it done, no matter what Mr. Bush thinks. And they think Mr. Powell has downgraded the top cabinet post into a human resources job, making nicey-nice with the UN and assorted bad guys instead of pursuing the neocon blueprint for world domination through what James Woolsey calls World War IV (World War III being the cold war).

Countering the *Post* story, Mr. Powell's posse claimed that neither the secretary of state nor his deputy had ever said they intended to step down, and charged that the neocons were leaking a canard to turn the two men they consider lame doves into lame ducks.

"This is the revenge of the neocons for two months of bad news, looking like they're falling all over themselves in Iraq," said a Powell confidant, noting that Alma Powell was furious she had been dragged in.

In the *Post*, nearly all of the names of those who could move up if Mr. Powell moves out are Iraq hawks: Condi Rice, Paul Wolfowitz and Newt Gingrich were mentioned as candidates for secretary of state; Wolfie, Cheney chief of staff Scooter Libby and Condi deputy Steve Hadley, who may be radioactive after the uranium mistake, were mentioned for national security chief.

Mr. Wolfowitz has been tacitly campaigning for the jobs. He told Charlie Rose about his vice-regal trip to Iraq, where he said at last grateful Iraqis were thronging. "As we would drive by, little kids would run up to the road and give us a thumbs-up sign," he said. (At least he thought it was the thumb.)

The move against the popular Powell had all the earmarks of the neocons' preemptive strike on Iraq.

1. Demonize. Reiterating his speech trashing Foggy Bottom last April for propping up dictators and coddling the corrupt, Mr. Gingrich—a Rummy ally who serves on the Defense Policy Board—called for "top-to-bottom reform and culture shock" at State in an article in the July *Foreign Policy* magazine.

2. Sex-up the intelligence. The leakers spread word that Mr. Armitage told Condi that he and Mr. Powell would leave on January 21, 2005, the day after the next presidential inauguration. "Nonsense," said Mr. Powell. "Nonsense," said Mr. Armitage.

3. Create a false rationale. Everyone knew the pair might not stay for a second term. But the neocons were impatient to give them a push, blaming poor Alma Powell for henpecking her husband when they were.

4. Bring about regime change.

5. Fail to prepare for the aftermath. "Newt as secretary of state?" sneered one Powell pal. "Hel-lo?"

6. Make sure it's good for Ariel Sharon. Just as the neocons made their move on Mr. Powell, pro-Israel hawks scorned the secretary for not being on their team in the peace process. Israel's supporters scoffed at the new threat to cut loan guarantees as a State Department policy, not a White House policy.

7. Ignore the real threat. While the neocons are preoccupying the country with Iraq and a coup at the department d'état, Al Qaeda may have blown up a Marriott in Indonesia and are plotting attacks here.

8. Change the subject. Next stop, North Korea.

The Jihad All-Stars

■

Yep, we've got 'em right where we want 'em.

We've brought the fight to their turf, they're swarming into Iraq and blowing up our troops and other Westerners every day, and that's just where we want to be.

Our exhausted and frustrated soldiers are in a hideously difficult environment they're not familiar with, dealing with a culture America only dimly understands, where our desperation for any intelligence has reduced us to recruiting Saddam's old spies, whom we didn't trust in the first place, and where we're so strapped that soldiers may have to face back-to-back yearlong overseas tours.

We don't know exactly which of our ghostly Arab enemies are which, how many there are, who's plotting with whom, what weapons they have, how they're getting into Iraq, where they're hiding, or who's financing and organizing them.

And we certainly don't understand the violent internecine religious battles we've set in motion. At first the Shiites were with us, and the Sunnis were giving us all the trouble. Now a new generation of radical Shiites is rising up and assassinating other Shiites aligned with us; they view us as the enemy and our quest as a chance to establish an Islamist state, which Rummy says won't be tolerated.

In yesterday's milestones, the number of U.S. soldiers who have died since the war now exceeds the number who died during the war, and next year's deficit was estimated at a whopping $480 billion, even without all the sky-high costs of Iraq.

But Republicans suggest that Iraq's turning into a terrorist magnet could be convenient—one-stop shopping against terrorism. As Rush Limbaugh observed: "We don't have to go anywhere to find them! They've fielded a Jihad All-Star Team."

The strutting, omniscient Bush administration would never address the possibility that our seizure of Iraq has left us more vulnerable to terrorists. So it is doing what it did during the war, when Centcom briefings routinely began with the iteration: "Coalition forces are on plan"; "We remain on plan"; "Our plan is working."

Even though the Middle East has become a phantasmagoria of evil spirits, and even though some Bush officials must be muttering to themselves that they should have listened to the weenies at State and nags at the CIA, Team Bush is sticking to its mantra that everything is going according to plan.

As Condoleezza Rice put it on Monday, the war to defend the homeland "must be fought on the offense."

Taking a breather from fund-raisers yesterday, Mr. Bush discreetly ignored his administration's chaotic occupation plan and declaimed, "No nation can be neutral in the struggle between civilization and chaos."

Echoing remarks by other officials implying that it's better to have one big moment of truth and fight our enemies on their turf

rather than ours, Mr. Bush said, "Our military is confronting terrorists in Iraq and Afghanistan and in other places so our people will
not have to confront terrorist violence in New York or St. Louis or
Los Angeles."

So that's the latest rationale for going into Iraq? We wanted an
Armageddon with our enemies, so we decided to conquer an Arab
country and drive the Muslim fanatics so crazy with their jihad
mentality that they'd flip out and storm in, and then we'd kill
them all?

Terrorism is not, as the president seems to suggest, a finite thing.

Asked at a recent Pentagon town hall meeting how he envisioned
the end state for the war on terror, Donald Rumsfeld replied, "I
guess the end state in the shortest response would be to not be
terrorized."

By doing their high-risk, audacious sociological and political
makeover in Iraq, Bush officials and neocons hoped to drain the terrorist swamp in the long run. But in the short run, they have created
new terrorist-breeding swamps full of angry young Arabs who see
America the same way Muslims saw Westerners in the Crusades: as
Christian expansionist imperialists motivated by piety and greed.

Just because the unholy alliance of Saddam loyalists, foreign fighters and Islamic terrorists has turned Iraq into a scary shooting
gallery for our troops doesn't mean Americans at home are any safer.
Since when did terrorists see terror as an either/or proposition?

"Bring 'em on" sounded like a tinny, reckless boast the first time
the president said it. It doesn't sound any better when Mr. Bush says
it louder with a chorus.

September 3, 2003

Empire of Novices

■

The Bush foreign-policy team always had contempt for Bill Clinton's herky-jerky, improvised interventions around the world. When it took control, it promised a global stewardship purring with gravity, finesse and farsightedness.

But now the Bush "dream team" is making the impetuous Clinton look like Rommel.

When your aim is remaking the Middle East, you don't want to get stuck making it up as you go along.

Even officials with a combined century of international experience can behave with jejeunosity—if they start believing their own spin.

The group that started out presuming it could shape the world is now getting shoved by the world.

Our unseen tormentors are the ones who seem canny and organized, not us. As they move from killing individual U.S. soldiers and Iraqis to sabotaging power plants, burning oil pipelines, blowing up mosques, demolishing the UN headquarters and now hitting the Baghdad police headquarters, our enemies seem better prepared and more committed to creating chaos in Iraq—and Afghanistan—than we are to creating order.

They've also proved more adept at putting together an effective coalition than the Bush team: a terrifying blend of terrorists from other countries, Al Qaeda and Ansar al-Islam fighters, radical Shiites and Saddam remnants, all pouring into Iraq and united by their hatred of America.

If we review the Bush war council's motives for conquering Iraq, the scorecard looks grim:

- We wanted to get rid of Osama and Saddam and the Taliban and Al Qaeda. We didn't. They're replicating and coming at us like cockroaches. According to *Newsweek*, Osama is in the mountains of Afghanistan, plotting to use biological weapons against America. If all those yuppies can climb Mount Everest, at 29,000 feet, can't we pay some locals to nab Osama at 14,000 feet?

- Bushies thought freeing Iraq from Saddam would be the first step toward the Middle East road map for peace, as well as a guarantee of greater security for Israel. But the road map blew up, and Israel seems farther away from making peace with the Arabs than ever. The U.S. has now pathetically called on Yasir Arafat to use his power to help after pretending for more than a year that he didn't exist.

- Rummy wanted to exorcise the stigma of Vietnam and prove you could use a lighter, faster force. But our adventures in Iraq and Afghanistan may not banish our fears of being mired in a place halfway around the world, where we don't understand the language or culture, and where our stretched-thin soldiers are picked off, guerrilla-style.

- The neocons wanted to marginalize the wimpy UN by barreling past them into Iraq. Now the Bush administration is crawling back to the UN, but other nations are suspicious of U.S. security and politics in Iraq.

- Dick Cheney and Rummy wanted to blow off multilateralism and snub what Bushies call "the chocolate-making countries" of France, Germany, Belgium and Luxembourg. But faced with untold billions in costs and mounting casualties in Iraq and Afghanistan, Americans are beginning to see the advantages of sidekicks who know the perils of empire.

- The Pentagon wanted to sideline the CIA and State and run the war and reconstruction itself. Now, overwhelmed, the Pentagon's special operations chiefs were reduced to screening a 1965 movie, *The Battle of Algiers*, last week, as David Ignatius reported in *The Washington Post*, to try to learn why the French suffered a colonial disaster in a guerrilla war against Muslims in Algiers.

- The neocons hoped democracy in Iraq would spread like a fever in the Mideast, even among our double-dealing friends like Saudi Arabia and Pakistan. But after the majestic handoff of democracy to the twenty-five-member Iraqi Governing Council, it seems the puppets (now nervous about bodyguards) don't even want to work late, much less govern. As one aide told the *Times*, "On the Council, someone makes a suggestion, then it goes around the room, with everyone talking about it, and then by that time, it's late afternoon and time to go home."

- The vice president wanted to banish that old sixties feeling of moral ambivalence, of America in the wrong.

Our unilateral move in Iraq, with the justifications on WMD and Qaeda links to Saddam getting shakier each month, has made us more hated around the world than ever.

September 11, 2003

We're Not Happy Campers

■

T he Saudi religious police are harassing Barbie.

The Commission for the Promotion of Virtue and Prevention of Vice is warning that the "Jewish" dolls—banned in Saudi Arabia for a decade—are a threat to Islam.

The A.P. reported that a message posted on the *mutawwa*'s Web site chided: "Jewish Barbie dolls, with their revealing clothes and shameful postures, accessories and tools are a symbol of decadence to the perverted West. Let us beware of her dangers and be careful."

This, from a hypocritical desert kingdom with more lingerie stores in its malls than Victoria has secrets.

It's probably useless to start correcting the inbred Saudis on facts, but just for the record, Barbie was a knockoff of a German floozy doll.

The place so eager to protect itself from "Jewish" toys and "the perverted West," the breeding ground of the 9/11 hijackers, is still the Bush administration's close ally.

Osama bin Laden is urging the Muslim world to pursue a jihad against America, even as America pursues a GWOT in the Muslim world. (GWOT is how some Pentagon documents refer to the "Global War on Terror." They're out to get us, and we're out to get them.)

Far from being the swift and gratifying lesson in U.S. dominance that Cheney & Co. predicted, our incursion into Iraq is turning into a spun-out, scary lesson in the dangers of hubris. Democrats are combing through the $20 billion part of the White House request involving rebuilding Iraq, trying to make sure there isn't any Halliburton hanky-panky.

I've actually gotten to the point where I hope Dick Cheney is embroiled in a Clancyesque conspiracy to benefit Halliburton. Because if it's not a conspiracy, it's naïveté and ideology. And that means our leaders have used goofball logic and lousy assumptions to trap the country in a cockeyed replay of the Crusades that could drain our treasury and strain our military for generations, without making us any safer from terrorists and maybe putting us more at risk.

On 9/11's second anniversary, seven in ten Americans still believe Saddam had a role in the attacks, even though there is no evidence of it, according to a *Washington Post* poll. That is because the president has done his level best to conflate 9/11 and Saddam and did so again in his speech on Sunday night.

Iraq never threatened U.S. security. Bush officials cynically attacked a villainous country because they knew it was easier than finding the real 9/11 villain, who had no country. And now they're hoist on their own canard.

By pretending Iraq was crawling with Al Qaeda, they've created an Iraq crawling with Al Qaeda.

As Donald Rumsfeld finished up an upbeat talk at the National Press Club here yesterday, brushing off hecklers and calling the global war on terror "well begun," cable began airing fresh *Flint-stones* video of Osama bin Laden and Ayman al-Zawahiri encouraging the Iraqi and Islamic fighters to "bury" American troops and send them to their mothers in coffins.

The Bush team's logic before the war was infuriatingly Helleresque, and it still is.

Mr. Rumsfeld, who was so alarmed about Saddam's WMD before the war, is now so nonchalant that he said he did not even bother to ask David Kay, who runs the CIA's search for WMD in Iraq, what progress he'd made when meeting with him in Iraq last week.

"I have so many things to do at the Department of Defense," Rummy told *The Washington Post.*

Asked at the press club why our intelligence analysts did not predict the extent of Iraq's decayed infrastructure, Rummy said dismissively, "They were worrying about more important things." Yeah, like how to get Dick Cheney off their backs.

Testifying before the Senate on Tuesday on the $87 billion request, Paul Wolfowitz, the Pentagon official who pushed so hard to own Iraq and control it, said, "We have no desire to own this problem or to control it." There may not be much choice, given Colin Powell's pessimistic warning to Congress yesterday that no allies want to help us pick up the tab for rebuilding a country full of people who revile us.

I never thought I'd say this, but watching Dan Quayle's marble bust, unveiled yesterday at the Capitol—soon to join John Adams, Thomas Jefferson and Spiro Agnew—I was nostalgic for the days when Murphy Brown's baby amounted to a serious mess.

Gunsmoke and Mirrors

■

This is how bad things are for George W. Bush: He's back in a dead heat with Al Gore.

(And this is how bad things are for Al Gore: He's back in a dead heat with George W. Bush.)

One terrorist attack, two wars, three tax cuts, four months of guerrilla mayhem in Iraq, five silly colors on a terror alert chart, nine nattering Democratic candidates, ten Iraqi cops killed by Americans, $87 billion in Pentagon illusions, a gazillion boastful Osama tapes, zero Saddam and zilch WMD have left America split evenly between the president and former vice president.

"More than two and a half years after the 2000 election and we are back where we started," marveled John Zogby, who conducted the poll.

It's *plus ça change* all over again. We are learning once more, as we did on 9/11, that all the fantastic technology in the world will not save us. The undigitalized human will is able to frustrate our most elaborate schemes and lofty policies.

What unleashed Shock and Awe and the most extravagant display of American military prowess ever was a bunch of theologically deranged Arabs with box cutters.

The Bush administration thought it could use scientific superiority to impose its will on alien tribal cultures. But we're spending hundreds of billions subduing two backward countries without subduing them.

After the president celebrated victory in our high-tech war in Iraq, our enemies came back to rattle us with a diabolically ingenious low-tech war, a homemade bomb in a truck obliterating the UN offices, and improvised explosive devices hidden in soda cans, plastic bags and dead animals blowing up our soldiers. Afghanistan has mirror chaos, with reconstruction sabotaged by Taliban assaults on American forces, the Afghan police and aid workers.

The Pentagon blithely says that we have 56,000 Iraqi police and security officers and that we will soon have more. But it may be hard to keep and recruit Iraqi cops; the job pays O.K. but it might end very suddenly, given the rate at which Americans and guerrillas are mowing them down.

"This shows the Americans are completely out of control," First Lieutenant Mazen Hamid, an Iraqi policeman, said Friday after angry demonstrators gathered in Falluja to demand the victims' bodies.

Secretary Pangloss at Defense and Wolfie the Naif are terminally enchanted by their own descriptions of the world. They know how to use their minds, but it's not clear they know how to use their eyes.

"They are like people in Plato's cave," observed one military analyst. "They've been staring at the shadows on the wall for so long, they think they're forms."

Our high-tech impotence is making our low-tech colony sullen.

"It's 125 degrees there and they have no electricity and no water and it doesn't make for a very happy population," said Senator John McCain, who recently toured Iraq. "We're in a race to provide the services and security for people so the Iraqis will support us rather than turn against us. It's up for grabs."

Senator McCain says that "the bad guys" are reminding Iraqis that America "propped up Saddam Hussein in the '80s, sided with Iraq in the Iraq-Iran war, told the people in Basra in '91 we'd help them get rid of Saddam and didn't, and put economic sanctions on them in the '90s."

He says we have to woo them, even though we are pouring $87 billion—double the amount designated for homeland security—into the Iraqi infrastructure when our own electrical grid, and port and airport security, need upgrading.

"If anyone thinks the French and Germans are going to help us readily and rapidly," he says, "they're smoking something very strong."

Mocking all our high-priced, know-nothing intelligence, Osama is back in the studio making his rock videos.

The cadaverous caveman has gone more primitive to avoid electronic detection, operating via notes passed by couriers.

We haven't forgotten all Mr. Bush's bullhorn, dead-or-alive pledges.

But he's like a kid singing with fingers in his ears, avoiding mentioning Saddam or bin Laden, or pressing the Pakistanis who must be protecting Osama up in no man's land and letting the Taliban reconstitute (even though we bribed Pakistan with a billion in aid). He doesn't dwell on nailing Saddam, either.

His gunsmoke has gone up in smoke.

October 2, 2003

The Spy Who Loved Him

■

It was like a movie scene. But instead of meeting cute, they met covert.

Valerie Plame and Joseph Wilson both happened to alight in Washington, their jet-set schedules intersecting, and spotted each other across a cocktail party filled with foreigners.

"I saw this striking blonde," he recalled, still sounding smitten six years later. At first she said she was an energy analyst, but confided sometime around the first kiss that she was in the CIA. "I had a security clearance," grinned Mr. Wilson, then a political adviser to the commander of U.S. forces in Europe.

Now Washington is consumed with the saga of how the glamorous CIA officer and the dashing California surfer-turned-ambassador went from wedding cake to yellowcake.

The former diplomat sparked the White House shame spiral when he wrote a *Times* op-ed piece questioning whether the Bush administration had manipulated intelligence to justify the war in

Iraq and buried his report debunking the allegation that Iraq had tried to buy Niger uranium.

Unable to find weapons of mass destruction, the Bush team has turned to weapons of personal destruction. It's bad enough that the administration hasn't come up with any plausible reason for not having uncovered any WMD, even as it's requesting $600 million more to find them; now it's practicing Crawford McCarthyism.

At his office yesterday, a block from the White House that he has turned into Bleak House, Mr. Wilson was calm, even as Republicans continued to rip him. For Bush officials, who have wielded patriotism as a bludgeon on critics, you'd think that doing something as unpatriotic as outing Mr. Wilson's wife and endangering the lives of her CIA contacts would be enough. Nah.

The group that fights so ferally to keep everything secret, from the cronies who met with Dick Cheney to the identities of the people it has tossed into the brig at Gitmo, had no problem spilling the beans on its own spy when self-preservation was at stake.

The issue is the administration's credibility, not Joe Wilson's.

The men who won the 2000 election by promising to restore honor and integrity to the White House spent yesterday doing a pretty good imitation of O. J. Simpson, looking for the culprit. You could just picture President Bush with his Sherlock Holmes deerstalker, magnifying glass and bloodhound Barney. Silly. The White House knows who did it. All Mr. Bush has to do is roll heads.

Mr. Wilson spent yesterday at his office, wondering if he could return the forty-nine messages on his relentlessly vibrating cell phone before going off to a Dave Brubeck concert. His desk was covered with pictures of his wife—one in a straw hat, one with a toddler on her hip. (They have three-year-old twins, a boy and a girl.)

Nearby was a photo of Mr. Wilson, acting ambassador in Baghdad during Desert Shield, with Saddam Hussein. And a framed letter praising his work for the country from the senior President Bush, strategically left facing out toward reporters who come to ask Mr. Wilson if Republicans have a point when they decry him as a politically motivated Democrat who has counseled John Kerry and contributed to his campaign. He and his wife also gave $1,000 each to the Bush-Cheney campaign "before South Carolina," he said, "which was a real rude awakening about the way Ralph Reed & Co. went after John McCain's wife and kid."

Mr. Wilson, fifty-three, refers to his forty-year-old third wife as "the real-life Jennifer Garner," the actress who plays an intrepid CIA officer on TV and who will star in an agency recruitment video. He teased his wife that she would be better cast: " 'You should get out there.' "

His wife, he said, "sees this as an out-of-body experience."

Ms. Plame and Karl Rove attend the same Episcopal church, and she joked to her husband that she should just go up to the president's strategist and ask if he really considered her "fair game" to be outed—a phrase Mr. Wilson says reporters told him Mr. Rove had used.

At his wife's request, Mr. Wilson has toned down his call to see Mr. Rove "frog-marched out of the White House in handcuffs." But he still holds the man the president calls "Boy Genius" accountable.

"The act of leaking my wife's name was clearly a political act," he says. "The White House has a political office that's headed by one Karl Rove. That's where I would look. He certainly condoned it."

■

Uncle Dick of the Underworld

■

In Which the Dark Father Shows Himself in the Least Amiable Light

■

A Tale of Two Fathers

■

I t's a classic story line in myth, literature and movies: a man coming into his own is torn between two older authority figures with competing worldviews; a good daddy and a bad daddy; one light and benevolent, one dark and vengeful.

When Bush the Elder put Bush the Younger in the care of Dick Cheney, he assumed that Mr. Cheney, who had been his defense secretary in Desert Storm, would play the wise, selfless counselor. Poppy thought his old friend Dick would make a great vice president, tutoring a young president green on foreign policy and safeguarding the first Bush administration's legacy of internationalism, coalition building and realpolitik.

Instead, Good Daddy has had to watch in alarm as Bad Daddy usurped his son's presidency, heightened its conservatism and rushed America into war on the mistaken assumption that if we just acted like king of the world, everyone would bow down or run away.

Bush I officials are nonplussed by the apocalyptic and rash Cheney of Bush II, a man who pushed preemption and peered over the shoulders of CIA analysts, as compared with the skeptical and cautious Cheney of Bush I (who did not even press to march to Baghdad in the first gulf war, when Saddam Hussein actually possessed chemical weapons).

Some veterans of Bush I are so puzzled that they even look for a biological explanation, wondering if his two-year-old defibrillator might have made him more Hobbesian. Mr. Cheney spent so much time in his bunker reading gloomy books about smallpox, plague, fear and war as the natural state of mankind.

Last week, for the first time, W.—who tried to pattern his presidency as the mirror opposite of his real father's—curbed his surrogate father's hard-line crony Rummy (Mr. Cheney's mentor in the Ford years).

The incurious George, who has said he prefers to get his information from his inner circle rather than newspapers or TV, may finally be waking up to the downside of such self-censorship. You can end up hearing a lot of bogus, self-serving garbage from Ahmad Chalabi, via Mr. Cheney and Paul Wolfowitz, instead of unpleasant reality.

I hope Mr. Bush at least read the news coverage of his vice president's Iraq speech on Friday, which was a masterpiece of demagogy.

On a day when many Republicans were finding a lesson of moderation in Arnold Schwarzenegger's victory in California, Mr. Cheney once more chose a right-wing setting, the Heritage Foundation, to regurgitate his rigid ideology. While Arnold was saying to voters, "You know best," Mr. Cheney was still propounding "Father Knows Best."

Even after the president was forced to admit after Mr. Cheney's last appearance on *Meet the Press* last month that the link the vice president drew between Saddam and 9/11 did not actually exist, that did not deter Mr. Cheney. He repeatedly tied Saddam and 9/11 and said, all evidence to the contrary, that the secular Iraqi leader "had an established relationship with Al Qaeda."

He characterized critics as naive and dangerous when his own arguments were reductive and disingenuous. In justifying the war, he created a false choice between attacking Iraq and doing nothing.

The war in Iraq and its aftermath have proved that Mr. Cheney was wrong to think that a show of brute strength would deter our enemies from attacking us. There are improvements in Iraq, but it is still a morass, with 326 soldiers dead as of Friday. It's hard to create security when we are the cause of the insecurity.

Mr. Cheney lumped terrorists and tyrants into one interchangeable mass, saying that Mr. Bush could not tolerate a dictator who had access to weapons of mass destruction, was allied with terrorists and was a threat to his neighbors. Sounds a lot like the military dictator of Pakistan, not to mention the governments of China and North Korea.

To back up his claim that Saddam was an immediate threat, the vice president had to distort the findings of David Kay, the administration's own weapons hunter, and continue to overdramatize the danger of Saddam. "Saddam built, possessed and used weapons of mass destruction," Mr. Cheney said. Yes, but during the first Bush administration.

Perhaps the president now realizes the Cheney filter is dysfunctional. If Mr. Bush still needs a daddy to tell him what to do, he should call his own.

October 30, 2003

Eyes Wide Shut

■

I n the thick of the war with Iraq, President Bush used to pop out of meetings to catch the Iraqi information minister slipcovering grim reality with willful, idiotic optimism.

"He's my man," Mr. Bush laughingly told Tom Brokaw about the entertaining contortions of Muhammad Said al-Sahhaf, aka "Comical Ali" and "Baghdad Bob," who assured reporters, even as American tanks rumbled in, "There are no American infidels in Baghdad. Never!" and, "We are winning this war, and we will win the war. . . . This is for sure."

Now Crawford George has morphed into Baghdad Bob.

Speaking to reporters this week, Mr. Bush made the bizarre argument that the worse things get in Iraq, the better news it is. "The more successful we are on the ground, the more these killers will react," he said.

In the Panglossian Potomac, calamities happen for the best. One could almost hear the double-talk echo of that American officer in

Vietnam who said: "It was necessary to destroy the village in order to save it."

The war began with Bush illogic: false intelligence (from Niger to nuclear) used to bolster a false casus belli (imminent threat to our security) based on a quartet of false premises (that we could easily finish off Saddam and the Baathists, scare the terrorists and democratize Iraq without leeching our economy).

Now Bush illogic continues: The more Americans, Iraqis and aid workers who get killed and wounded, the more it is a sign of American progress. The more dangerous Iraq is, the safer the world is. The more troops we seem to need in Iraq, the less we need to send more troops.

The harder it is to find Saddam, Osama and WMD, the less they mattered anyhow. The more coordinated, intense and sophisticated the attacks on our soldiers grow, the more "desperate" the enemy is.

In a briefing piped into the Pentagon on Monday from Tikrit, Major General Raymond Odierno called the insurgents "desperate" eight times. But it is Bush officials who seem desperate when they curtain off reality. They don't even understand the political utility of truth.

After admitting recently that Saddam had no connection to 9/11, the president pounded his finger on his lectern on Tuesday, while vowing to stay in Iraq, and said, "We must never forget the lessons of September 11."

Mr. Bush looked buck-passy when he denied that the White House, which throws up PowerPoint slogans behind his head on TV, was behind the "Mission Accomplished" banner. And Donald Rumsfeld looked duplicitous when he acknowledged in a private memo, after brusquely upbeat public briefings, that America was in for a "long, hard slog" in Iraq and Afghanistan.

No juxtaposition is too absurd to stop Bush officials from insisting nothing is wrong. Car bombs and a blitz of air-to-ground missiles turned Iraq into a hideous tangle of ambulances, stretchers and dead bodies, just after Paul Wolfowitz arrived there to showcase successes.

But the fear of young American soldiers who don't speak the language or understand the culture, who don't know who's going to shoot at them, was captured in a front-page picture in yesterday's *Times*: two soldiers leaning down to search the pockets of one small Iraqi boy.

Mr. Bush, staring at the campaign hourglass, has ordered that the "Iraqification" of security be speeded up, so Iraqi cannon fodder can replace American sitting ducks. But Iraqification won't work any better than Vietnamization unless the Bush crowd stops spinning.

Neil Sheehan, the Pulitzer Prize–winning author of *A Bright Shining Lie*, recalls Robert McNamara making Wolfowitz-like trips to Vietnam, spotlighting good news, yearning to pretend insecure areas were secure.

"McNamara was in a jeep in the Mekong Delta with an old Army colonel from Texas named Dan Porter," Mr. Sheehan told me. "Porter told him, 'Mr. Secretary, we've got serious problems here that you're not getting. You ought to know what they are.' And Mc-Namara replied: 'I don't want to hear about your problems. I want to hear about your progress.' "

"If you want to be hoodwinked," Mr. Sheehan concludes, "it's easy."

The Chicago Way

■

In the movie *The Untouchables*, Sean Connery, a cop named Malone, instructs a naive Eliot Ness on going up against gangsters.

"If you open the can on these worms you must be prepared to go all the way, because they're not gonna give up the fight until one of you is dead," he says. "You wanna know how you do it? They pull a knife, you pull a gun. He sends one of yours to the hospital, you send one of his to the morgue. That's the Chicago way, and that's how you get Capone. Now do you want to do that? Are you ready to do that?"

As the president offered his lofty "vision thing" for spawning democracy in the Middle East, America was at a rough juncture. The administration opened the can on these worms in Iraq. Are Americans now prepared to do what it takes?

The Bush crowd hurtled into Baghdad on the law of Disney: Wishing can make it so. Now they're ensnared in the law of the jungle: The rules of engagement don't apply with this scary cocktail of Saddam loyalists, foreign fighters and terrorists, who hold nothing sacrosanct, not human rights organizations, humanitarian groups or Iraqi civilians.

The gangsters are getting ever bolder about picking off our soldiers on land and out of the sky. With three Army helicopters hit in the last two weeks, killing twenty-two Americans, soldiers are reduced to flying low and fast, as they scan for the glint of sunlight coming off the rockets of the invisible guerrillas. It's an eerie flashback to the ten-year war of attrition Afghans waged against the mighty Soviets, when worn-down Soviet soldiers complained that the Afghan fighters were "ghosts" who would shoot down their helicopters with American Stinger surface-to-air missiles and fade back into the mountains.

On Wednesday, Senator John McCain offered a vinegary critique of the Bush team, urging the president to be more engaged on Iraq, and not leave decisions to subordinates. He also swatted Donald Rumsfeld's assertion that troop levels are fine, saying 15,000 more troops should be dispatched to avoid risking "the most serious American defeat on the global stage since Vietnam."

Senator McCain, nervous about both Army morale and Iraq shattering, believes we must get in deeper to make progress.

Administration officials, nervous about President Bush's election chances shattering, believe we must show progress by starting to pull out.

That is why the Pentagon announced last week it would reduce the number of troops by next summer, replacing them with Iraqis.

But some fret that the Pentagon—growing desperate as the Turks, the Indians, the Pakistanis and other allies refuse to send reinforcements—has been turning out new Iraqi police officers and guards as swiftly and sloppily as Lucy and Ethel turned out chocolates on the assembly line.

The Washington Post reported that tens of thousands of Iraqis were being shoved into action "with little or no formal training in democratic standards and relevant job skills."

Many diplomats were shocked to read the *Times* report that the back-channel attempt of Iraqis to avert war, with Richard Perle as go-between, was blown off with the CIA message, "Tell them that we will see them in Baghdad."

But the Bush brigade had many dovetailing reasons not to be dovish.

Mr. Rumsfeld thought the war could showcase his transformation of the military to be leaner and more agile. Paul Wolfowitz thought the war could showcase his transformation of Iraq into a democracy. Dick Cheney thought the war could showcase his transformation of America into a dominatrix superpower. Karl Rove thought the war could showcase his transformation of W. into conquering hero. And Mr. Bush thought the war could showcase his transformation from family black sheep into historic white hat.

But now Wolfie's messianic vision of growing democracy in the Middle East is at odds with Rummy's stubborn desire to shrink the Army.

Our military around the globe is tapped out, so strained by Iraq and Afghanistan, as the *Times* military correspondent Michael Gordon discovered, that a unit from the Army's Old Guard is even being dispatched overseas. The guard is best known for ceremonial duties such as standing vigil at the Tomb of the Unknowns at Arlington National Cemetery and serving in color guards for visiting dignitaries.

The Old Guard has not been deployed abroad since Vietnam.

Their Master's Voice

■

I t must be the voice.

It is the basso pretendo profundo voice of the dean of boys in a strict private school. At the tables of power, he speaks so sparsely and softly in that low hypnotic monotone, with that lower jaw tilting to the side in a self-assured "I only talk out of one side of my mouth" kind of way, that others at the table have no choice but to listen up. He is the one who must be obeyed.

Dick Cheney's dry Wyoming voice has the same effect on some male Republicans, starting at the very top, and even some journalists, that a high-pitched whistle has on a dog. How else to explain the vice president's success in creating a parallel universe inside the White House that is shaping the real universe.

Congressman Charles Rangel of New York introduced a resolution this week urging President Bush to fire Donald Rumsfeld for misleading the American public about how well the war and the occupation are going, and for sending American forces into battle "without adequate planning" and showing "a lack of sensitivity" about U.S. casualties.

Certainly, Rummy is a worthy target. But maybe Mr. Rangel should aim higher. If the Pentagon is responsible for mismanaging the occupation in Iraq, it is the vice president's office that is responsible for the paranoid vision—the with-us-or-against-us biceps flex against the world—that got us into this long, hard slog.

This week's *Newsweek* cover story on the vice president characterized a recent article by Seymour Hersh in *The New Yorker* as raising the question of whether "Cheney had, in effect, become the dupe of a cabal of neoconservative full-mooners, the Pentagon's mysteriously named Office of Special Plans, and the patsy of an alleged bank swindler and would-be ruler of Iraq, Ahmad Chalabi."

Mr. Cheney's parallel universe is a bizarro world where no doubts exist. He indulges in extremes of judgment, overpessimistic about our ability to contain Saddam and overoptimistic about the gratitude we would encounter as "liberators" in Iraq.

In Cheneyworld, the invasion of Iraq has made the world a safer place (tell it to the Italians), WMD are still concealed in all those Iraqi basements, every Iraqi insurgent is a card-carrying member of Al Qaeda, and the increase in attacks on Americans reflects the guerrillas' desperation, not their strengths. Guerrilla attacks on American soldiers are labeled acts of terrorism rather than acts of war, even though the official U.S. definition describes terrorism as attacks on civilians.

As Eric Schmitt reported in the *Times* this week, Mr. Cheney has implied in recent speeches that Al Qaeda is responsible for the major attacks in Iraq this past summer, even though senior military and intelligence officials say there is no conclusive evidence for that. Clearly, Mr. Cheney remains oblivious to the fact that the president has already had to correct the vice president's previous assertion that the government did not know whether Saddam Hussein had a connection to the 9/11 attacks. Mr. Bush conceded that "no, we've had no evidence that Saddam Hussein was involved with September the 11th."

But while some have suggested that the president feels let down by Mr. Rumsfeld, he still seems seduced by the siren call of that deep Cheney voice and lugubrious Cheney worldview. As *Newsweek* suggested, quoting those who know him: "Cheney has always had a Hobbesian view of life. The world is a dangerous place; war is the natural state of mankind; enemies lurk."

Mr. Cheney's darkness ends up dominating Mr. Bush's lightness.

As *Newsweek* noted, the vice president cherry-picks the intelligence, then feeds his version of reality to Mr. Bush. The president leaves himself open to manipulation because, by his own admission, he doesn't read the papers and relies on his inner circle to filter information to him.

The Philadelphia Inquirer reported yesterday that the CIA had issued a top-secret report from Iraq, endorsed by Paul Bremer, warning that growing numbers of Iraqis are concluding that the U.S. can be defeated and are supporting the insurgents.

The question is whether other voices can ever break through that sonorous ominous murmuring in the president's ear.

The Buck House Stops Here

■

President Bush thought he had at last found someplace even more sequestered from the real world than the Republican fund-raisers and conservative think tanks where he makes his carefully controlled "public" appearances.

Swaddled in the $8.5 million security blanket of reinforced concrete, wire mesh and fourteen thousand bobbies designed to protect him from the ungrateful citizens of our one—I mean, our closest—ally, Mr. Bush was a blithe spirit in his rented tails with his English cousins behind the high gates of Buckingham Palace.

Even sheltered in the bosom of the British royal family, however, Mr. Bush wasn't entirely safe.

Wearing a blue sash and a tiara with enough diamonds to pay for a year of the Iraqi occupation, the British queen gave the American president a bit of a poke, a light sideswipe with her handbag, as it were.

In her remarks honoring Mr. Bush at the state dinner last night,

Queen Elizabeth unleashed a barrage of favorable references to the most dreaded words in the Bush-Cheney lexicon: "multilateral order," "trans-Atlantic partnership," "other allies" and "effective international institutions."

"At the very core of the new international and multilateral order, which emerged after the shared sacrifices of that last terrible world war, was a vital dynamic trans-Atlantic partnership working with other allies to create effective international institutions," she said. This, to a president who has never met an international institution he did not try to wreck and who's darting around like a fugitive in the land of the "special relationship," using Buck House as a safe house.

Her Majesty barely mentioned the pesky colonial mess in Iraq—where U.S. occupiers are also surrounded by razor wire, concrete barricades and armed guards—and spent more time praising the first President Bush's leadership than the second's.

Everything Mr. Bush did in London reinforced the idea that this was a trip made not so much to thank the British people for their friendship, but to send a message to the voters back home that he was at ease as a world leader.

The White House spared Mr. Bush from having to endure a session with the rowdy Parliament and flew him by helicopter over the protesting rabble, who think a bullying Bush administration dragged Britain into the war under false pretenses. (Scotland Yard even wanted to keep the president in a "mobile-free bubble" that would block cell phone calls in his vicinity, but the phone companies refused, calling it "Bush hysteria.")

The White House packaged the visit for the viewers at home.

How else to explain the same Bush advance geniuses who brought us the "Mission Accomplished" banner putting up a blue Power-

Point-ish backdrop for the president's speech at Whitehall Palace that hiccuped, "United Kingdom," "United Kingdom," "United Kingdom."

The people in the United Kingdom already knew he was in the United Kingdom. And the kingdom isn't very united at the moment.

Ken Livingstone, the mayor of London, captured the spirit of the moment when he told NPR that the Republican National Committee should foot the bill for Mr. Bush's extraordinary security, the largest police operation ever in Great Britain. All this, he harrumphed, "just so George Bush can use a few clips of him and the queen in his campaign advertisements for re-election next year."

There was a dispiriting contrast between GWB shutting out the world and avoiding the British public, and the black-and-white clips this week of JFK reaching out to the world and being adored by Berliners.

There was also a dispiriting contrast between the Bush administration, hiding the returning coffins of U.S. soldiers and avoiding their funerals, and the moving pictures of the Italian politicians and people honoring their dead with public ceremonies and a week of mourning.

The bubble in London is just an extension of the bubble the Bush team lives in at home. It superimposes its reality on the evidence for war, the ease of the occupation, the strength of the insurgency and the continuing threat from Saddam and Osama.

Isolationism has been a foreign policy before. But for this administration, it seems to be a way of life.

January 29, 2004

Dump Cheney Now!

■

T he awful part is that George W. Bush and Saddam Hussein were both staring into the same cracked spook-house mirror.

Thanks to David Kay, we now have an amazing image of the president and the dictator, both divorced from reality over weapons, glaring at each other from opposite sides of bizarro, paranoid universes where fiction trumped fact.

It would be like a wacky Peter Sellers satire if so many Iraqis and Americans hadn't died in Iraq.

These two would-be world-class tough guys were willing to go to extraordinary lengths to show that they couldn't be pushed around. Their trusted underlings misled them with fanciful information on advanced Iraqi weapons programs that they credulously believed because it fit what they wanted to hear.

Saddam was swept away writing his romance novels, while President Bush was swept away with the romance of rewriting the end of the 1991 Persian Gulf war to finish off the thug who tried to kill his dad.

The two men both had copies of *Crime and Punishment*—Condi Rice gave Mr. Bush the novel on his trip to Russia in 2002, and Saddam had Dostoyevsky down in the spider hole—but neither absorbed its lesson: that you can't put yourself above rules just because you think you're superior.

When Dr. Kay spoke these words on WMD—"It turns out we were all wrong, probably, in my judgment, and that is most disturbing"—both America and Iraq learned that when you try too hard to control the picture of reality, you risk losing your grasp of it.

In interviews, Dr. Kay defended the war with Iraq, saying that the U.S. "has often entered the right war for the wrong reason," and he defended Mr. Bush, saying, "if anyone was abused by the intelligence, it was the president." He also told Congress "there's no evidence that I can think of, that I know of" that Saddam collaborated with Al Qaeda.

Testifying before the Senate Armed Services Committee yesterday, the ex-CIA weapons sleuth used a metaphor that was perhaps inspired by Martha Stewart, comparing the CIA with a lousy stockbroker.

"If I were your broker," he told Senator Jack Reed, "and you were investing on my advice . . . and at the end of the day, I said Enron was the greatest company in the world, and you had lost a substantial amount of money on it because it turned out differently, you would think I had abused you."

Certainly the CIA has a lot to answer for. For a bargain price of $30 billion a year, our intelligence aces have been spectacularly off. They failed to warn us about 9/11 and missed the spectacle of a deranged Saddam, hoodwinked by his top scientists.

They were probably relying too much on the Arabian Nights tales of Ahmad Chalabi, eager to spread the word of Saddam's imaginary nuclear-tipped weapons juggernaut because it suited his own ambitions—and that of his Pentagon pals.

But while he is skittering away from his claims about Iraqi weapons, President Bush is not racing toward accountability. It's an election year.

The *Times*'s David Sanger wrote about an administration debate "over whether Mr. Bush should soon call for some kind of reform of the intelligence-gathering process. But the officials said Mr. Bush's aides were searching for a formula that would allow them to acknowledge intelligence-gathering problems without blaming" the CIA or its chief.

The president wants to act as though he has a problem but not a scandal that he can fix without rolling heads—of those who made honest mistakes or dishonest ones by rigging the intelligence.

Dick Cheney, who declared that Saddam had nuclear capability and who visited CIA headquarters in the summer of 2002 to make sure the raw intelligence was properly interpreted, is sticking to his deluded guns. (And still trash-talking those lame trailers.)

The vice president pushed to slough off the allies and the UN and go to war partly because he thought that slapping a weakened bully like Saddam would scare other dictators. He must have reckoned there would be no day of reckoning on weapons once Saddam was gone.

So it had to be some new definition of chutzpah on Tuesday, when Mr. Cheney, exuding more infallibility than the pope, presented him with a crystal dove.

The Mirror Has Two Faces

■

W hy is the foreign-policy nanny acting like a foreign-policy ninny?

Hitting the morning shows to do damage control after David Kay's scalding admission that we flew to war on a false premise, Condi Rice made a tyro error. She mirrored.

Saddam, she told Matt Lauer, had secretively refused to account for missing stockpiles of botulinum toxin and anthrax, even though he knew he would face serious consequences: "I don't know how you could have come to any other conclusion but that he had weapons of mass destruction."

A conservative, ice-skating Brahms aficionada from Birmingham had assumed that a homicidal, grenade-fishing Sinatra aficionado from Tikrit reasoned just like her.

Bush officials, awash in the vice president's Hobbesian gloom, deduced that Saddam would not hide if he had nothing to hide. Even after all their talk about a Bernard Lewis clash of civilizations and a battle of good versus evil, they still projected a Western mind-set on Saddam.

Ms. Rice argued that the U.S. was right to conclude that Saddam had WMD and attack him because the dictator was not behaving rationally. But why did she think someone President Bush deemed "a madman" would behave rationally?

Cheney & Co. were so consumed with puffing the intelligence to try to connect Saddam with 9/11, Al Qaeda and nuclear material, they failed to challenge basic assumptions.

The closer the inspectors got to the truth that Iraq didn't have weapons, the more the Bush hawks asserted that only war would uncover weapons. Their threats to Saddam made him bluff that he had the weapons that they said he had.

"Most intelligence failures are about missing something happening," said a former Bush official. "What's so bizarre about this is, they thought something was happening that wasn't. This is right up there with Pearl Harbor and Bay of Pigs."

Even Paul Wolfowitz observed last May that it was important not to assume that foes like Saddam "will be rational according to our definition of what is rational." Interviewed by Sam Tanenhaus for *Vanity Fair*, Mr. Wolfowitz said bad intelligence came from mirror imaging—assuming people would behave like us: "The kind of mistake that, in a sense, I think we made implicitly in assuming that anyone who was intelligent enough to fly an airplane wouldn't commit suicide with it."

Saddam's old lieutenants have said that the dictator did not admit his paucity of weapons because he wanted his Arab neighbors to see him as a great leader and he hoped to deter America from war.

Jerrold Post, a former CIA psychological profiler who calls Saddam messianic but not irrational, speculates that he may have built a Potemkin arsenal after his conventional arsenal was decimated in the first Persian Gulf war. "If he came across as an impotent leader capitulating to the West," Dr. Post said, "he might have been pushed out of power or killed."

Besides, according to Dr. Kay, Saddam was both finagling and finagled. "Did he really think he had the stuff because scientists were scared to tell him he didn't?" wondered a GOP foreign-policy expert.

Saddam was isolated. And the Bush hawks wanted to isolate themselves from less-paranoid allies. They had come into office itching to replay the '91 war and try out their democracy domino theory in the Middle East—mirror imaging writ large. They grabbed 9/11 as an opening, yanked power away from Colin Powell and persuaded the popular diplomat to compromise his integrity by touting sketchy evidence at the UN, with the puppet Tenet as his wingman.

The moral of Vietnam was supposed to be that we would never again go to war without understanding the culture of our antagonists, or exaggerate their threat to us.

Some of those involved in running the '91 Iraq war think the U.S. should cut its losses, forget about Iowa-style caucuses (mirroring again), get the UN in there and let Kofi Annan and the Iraqi Governing Council negotiate with Ayatollah Sistani, who won't talk to the U.S. anyway.

The White House will have a lot of explaining to do if Iraq exchanges one form of dictatorship for another, or if it takes on a fundamentalist Islamic cast that sets Iraqi women's rights back forty years.

"These guys created the exact can of worms we tried to avoid," said a Bush 41 official. "Guess what? Baghdad is ours."

Murder Most Fowl

■

D adburn," Rummy fumed, squinting through his wireless glasses and waving his shotgun in the air. "A trained ape could have found a little something in that stinking cesspool. Can you believe that tweedy blabbermouth David Kay came back without even a germ? Goodness gracious, wasn't he working for us?"

Dick Cheney didn't answer. He was even more immobile than usual, in his jungle cammies in the field of the Rolling Rock Club in Pennsylvania. Nino, his partner in electoral manipulation and fowl assassination, was at his side, smoking and sipping Montepulciano from a silver thermos.

One thing Rummy admired about Dick. He never cracked under pressure. Look at Martha Stewart. When her story fell apart, she turned into a trembly bowl of Jell-O, something she would never be caught dead serving.

Now, with the White House looking untrustworthy and desperate; with the national security team flapping around and pointing fingers at each other and, of course, Bill Clinton; with even the placid Laura getting testy; and with *Newsweek* reporting that the Justice Department is reviewing whether Halliburton was involved in paying $180 million in kickbacks to get contracts in Nigeria at a time when Dick Cheney was chairman, anybody else would be sweating.

Not deadeye Dick. His heavy lids didn't blink when it turned out he'd blown up a half century of American foreign-policy alliances on a high-level hallucination.

Here he was, fresh from presenting a crystal dove to an obviously perplexed pope, stolidly waiting for the club's pheasant wranglers to shoo the doomed birds into his line of fire. He had killed only seventy or so the last time out. But this time he was convinced that the bird population could sustain more casualties. Quack and Awe.

"This is our due," Dick said. He fired a shot: *BLAM!*

Dick loved Nino Scalia, even if he didn't understand how a justice so horrified by gay marriage could be so enchanted by *La Boheme*. Nino was always there to protect Dick's due—from his presidency, er, vice presidency, to his absolute right to secrecy in all matters of public policy.

"Sometimes," Rummy said, in a growl that sent the five hundred pheasants trapped in the net aflutter, "when I watch the news and see another training film of Al Qaeda warriors in Saudi Arabia, I wonder if we should have just gone after them instead. But your pheasant-hunting pal Prince Bandar wouldn't have liked that. Heck, I'm too old for regrets.

"Here's how I see it: It's just as hard to connect the dots after as before. Intelligence is not perfect. Sometimes intelligence is not even intelligent. Analysts can only know what they think they know, what they know that they don't know, and what they think. Right, Dick?"

BLAM!

"The WMDs were just a decoy anyhow, not a smoking duck," Rummy ruminated. "We knocked off Saddam to show we were the biggest, baddest junkyard dog around. We shouldn't be investigating ourselves with all these dagnab, goldarn, nosy Parker commissions. We should just tell everybody to buzz off."

"Buzz off," said Dick. "This is our due." *BLAM!*

The pheasants were scattered across the field like Plantagenets at the end of a Shakespearean tragedy.

"Dick," Rummy rumbled, "I hear Rove and your daughters are putting you on a charm offensive, trying to humanize you. Why in the dickens would you want to be human?

"The Kid should have come with us today. He's home hugging his feather pillow. He's worried about fancy-pants Kerry pushing his overblown heroics in Vietnam while Junior was occasionally showing up to fly jets defending Texas against Oklahoma. But my lord, it will be like shooting birds in a pen. Kerry's just Dukakis on stilts. All we need are a few gay nuptials outside the Boston convention hall and we're home free."

Nino mumbled something bitter about states' rights and took another swig of Montepulciano.

"Rove needs to toughen up. Why fret over some JFK wannabe who thinks he's going to sail to the White House on a sea of ketchup? Sure, he'll say you brainwashed Junior, exploded the deficit, let Halliburton fleece the government, let big business write environmental policy, turned the White House into a secret society, rewarded your rich friends and went to war on a wild surmise. But, golly, so what?"

"Yeah," Dick agreed. "This is our due." *BLAM!*

The Thief of Baghdad

■

In the Ford White House, Dick Cheney's Secret Service name was Backseat, because he was the model of an unobtrusive staffer, the perfect unflashy deputy chief of staff for that lord of the bureaucratic dance, Donald Rumsfeld.

As James Mann writes in his new book, *The Rise of the Vulcans: The History of Bush's War Cabinet,* Mr. Cheney started out supervising such lowly matters as fixing a stopped-up drain in a White House bathroom sink; getting a headrest for Betty Ford's helicopter seat; and sorting out which salt shakers—the regular ones or, as he put it, the "little dishes of salt with funny little spoons"—would be best for stag dinners in the president's private quarters.

Rummy's alter ego rose quickly, though, because he seemed to have no ego. Good old Dick could be counted on to be the man behind the man, a butler to power. The new President Bush, a tabula rasa in foreign affairs, put himself in Mr. Cheney's hands.

But W. had barely settled into the Oval when Backseat clambered into the front seat. Retracing the rush to war, the names Cheney and Chalabi are entwined in bold relief.

Back when Dick Cheney was fiddling with salt shakers, Ahmad Chalabi, a smooth-talking and wealthy young Iraqi MIT graduate, was founding the Petra Bank in Jordan.

As Mr. Cheney moved up in the capital, Mr. Chalabi was tripped up in Jordan by a small matter of embezzlement from his own bank. Jordanian officials have said that the crime rocked their economy and that they paid $300 million to depositors to cover the bank's losses. By the time Mr. Chalabi was convicted and received a sentence of twenty-two years of hard labor, he was a fugitive in London.

During the early nineties, when Mr. Cheney was a fellow at the American Enterprise Institute, Mr. Chalabi was in a full courtship press with Washington's conservative and journalistic elites. He saw them as a springboard for his triumphant return to Iraq.

After 9/11, his passionate desire to take out Saddam coincided with that of conservatives. All they needed for their belli was a casus, so Mr. Chalabi obligingly conned the neocons.

He hoodwinked his pals Dick Cheney, Paul Wolfowitz and Richard Perle into believing Iraq would be a flowery cakewalk to democracy.

A wily expert in the politics of the bazaar, he knew he had to sell his scheme on what was good for Americans and their security. He was happy to funnel information to the vice president that painted a picture of Saddam hunkered on a hair-raising stockpile of WMD. His group, the Iraqi National Congress, tried to spin our government and media through its "information collection program." Intelligence officials now say that the prewar information provided to Washington by this group was suspect and useless, even disinformation.

But here's the wild thing: The propaganda program was underwritten by U.S. government funds. So Americans paid Ahmad Chalabi to gull them into a war that is costing them a billion a week—and a precious human cost. Cops dealing with their snitches check out the information better than the Bush administration did.

Mr. Chalabi's séances swayed the political set, the intelligence set and the journalistic set. In an effect Senator Bob Graham dubs "incestuous amplification," the bogus stories spewed by Iraqi exiles and defectors ricocheted through an echo chamber of government and media, making it sound as if multiple, reliable sources were corroborating the same story. Rather, one self-interested source was replicating like computer spam.

The CIA was stung to find out its analysts had mistakenly thought that Iraq weapons information had been confirmed by multiple sources, when it came from only a single source; that analysts had relied on a fabricating Iraqi defector and spin material from Iraqi exiles; and that this blather made its way into documents and speeches used by the Bush administration to justify war. George Tenet ordered a major change in procedure last week, removing barricades so that analysts can know more about the identities of clandestine agents' sources, and their possible motives.

But even incestuous amplification could not have drowned out reality if Bush officials had not glommed onto the Chalabi flummery for their own reasons—to feed their fantasies about refashioning America's power, psyche and military, and making over the Middle East in our image.

Swept up in big dreams, the foreign-policy dream team became dupes in Ahmad Chalabi's big con.

Sorry, Right Number

■

estifying before the Senate Intelligence Committee on Tuesday, George Tenet was asked why the CIA never picked up the trail of Marwan al-Shehhi, the pilot who crashed Flight 175 into the south tower on 9/11.

Thirty months earlier, German intelligence had passed on a hot tip to the CIA—the Al Qaeda terrorist's first name and phone number.

"The Germans gave us a name, Marwan—that's it—and a phone number," the director of central intelligence replied, adding: "They didn't give us a first and a last name until after 9/11, with then additional data."

For crying out loud. As one guy I know put it: "I've tracked down women across the country with a lot less information than that."

Mr. Tenet is not in any trouble for that sorry answer, of course, just as he hasn't had to pay any penalty for building up the phantom arsenal that Saddam only dreamed he had.

The catchphrase du jour is Donald Trump's snappy, "You're

fired." But no one has lost a job over the intelligence failures that led to 9/11 or the war that was trumped up and velcroed to 9/11. In fact, the only people the president and vice president are trying to put out of business are the members of the commission charged with figuring out how 9/11 happened and how to prevent another one.

The White House seems more worried about the public's finding out how much it knew and how little it did before 9/11 than it does about identifying and fixing security weaknesses.

After trying to kill the commission and then trying to put Dr. Strangelove-Kissinger in charge, President Bush and Dick Cheney have done their best to hamper the panel that's the best hope of the 9/11 widows, widowers and orphans to get justice.

"This is not no-fault government," said Lorie Van Auken, a 9/11 widow. "You don't just let people go on doing what they're doing wrong."

It is a triumph of chutzpah for Mr. Bush to thwart the investigation into 9/11 at the same time he seeks reelection by promoting his handling of 9/11 and scaring us with the specter of more terrorism. He's even using 9/11 memorials as the backdrop for his convention in New York.

Last week, the president played it sly, acting as though he was willing to extend the commission's deadline to finish the work that was taking longer because the administration was stonewalling. But the House speaker, J. Dennis Hastert, was clearly helping out the White House, answering the "Who will rid me of this meddlesome panel?" call.

Senators John McCain and Joseph Lieberman, who helped create the commission, played hardball, threatening highway funds and federal jobs if the commission didn't get two extra months. Mr. Hastert caved.

Mr. McCain said he's expecting the same administration "obfuscation and delay" when he sits on Mr. Bush's handpicked intelligence review board. "That's why I made sure I got subpoena power," he said. "No bureaucracy will willingly give you information that may be embarrassing to them."

Especially not such a secretive, paranoid and high-handed administration. Bush officials act as though they own 9/11, even while refusing to own up to any 9/11 mistakes.

Because of 9/11, they think they can suspend the Constitution, blow off investigators, attack nations preemptively, and keep Americans afraid by waging a war against terrorism that can never be won.

As Bob Kerrey, a frustrated member of the 9/11 commission, told Chris Matthews, the U.S. should have declared war on Osama as soon as it became apparent that he had an army with a "tremendous, sophisticated capability" and an ideology that dictated killing Americans.

"To declare war on terrorism, it seems to me to have the target wrong," he said. "It would be like after the 7th of December, 1941, declaring war on Japanese planes. We declared war on Japan. We didn't declare war on their tactic. . . . Terrorism is a tactic."

A Bush 41 official agreed: "You can't fight terrorism conventionally like a war. Any 16-year-old kid can strap on dynamite and take down any building. It must be fought clandestinely, dealing with the underlying causes and taking security measures in our own country."

Here's a hot tip: If you think the White House should be more cooperative with the 9/11 commission, call George at (202) 456-1111.

I'm sure everyone outside the CIA can take it from there.

Truth as a Weapon

■

As the White House was sliming Richard Clarke, the 9/11 families were stroking him.

Several relatives of victims surrounded the ex–counterterrorism chief after his testimony yesterday and reached out to pat him. After being condescended to, stonewalled, led on and put off by the White House, they were glad to hear somebody say: "Those entrusted with protecting you failed you. And I failed you."

"Mr. Clarke is the first person who has apologized to the families and held himself accountable," said the lovely Kristen Breitweiser of New Jersey, whose husband died in the south tower. "I am enormously grateful for that." She and other widows left the hearing room to protest Condoleezza Rice's lame no-show.

If only Sandy Berger had told the incoming Bush officials that Al Qaeda was no big deal, they might have gotten alarmed about it. They were determined to disdain all things Clinton, including what they considered his overemphasis on terrorism.

Dick Cheney, Rummy et al were on amber alert, "preserved in amber," as Mr. Clarke put it, obsessing on old GOP issues that had been hot when they were last in power, like a menacing Saddam and a Star Wars missile shield to protect America from the awesome might of the Evil Empire.

Terrorism wasn't really their cup of tea anyhow.

As Mr. Clarke writes, the ascension of Al Qaeda and the devolution of Iraq were topics that called for nuance: "Bush and his inner circle had no real interest in complicated analyses; on the issues that they cared about, they already knew the answers, it was received wisdom."

The Bush crew was thinking big, and Osama seemed puny to them.

Donald Rumsfeld told the 9/11 panel that there had been no point retaliating for the *Cole* bombing in October 2000, "four months after the fact," because that might have sent a signal of weakness.

So it was too late to whack Osama four months later, but not too late to rewhack Saddam twelve years later?

As he admitted to the commission on Tuesday, the defense secretary didn't like the idea of going after Osama in Afghanistan because "it didn't have a lot of targets." You just ended up bombing rocks instead of palaces. "Afghanistan was something like 8,000 miles from the United States. . . . You can pound the rubble in an Al Qaeda training camp 15 times and not do much damage; they can put tents right back up."

So, not showy and not convenient? Crummy excuses, Rummy.

Paul Wolfowitz was completely uninterested in Al Qaeda unless he could use it as a rationale to invade Iraq as part of his grandiose dream to remake the Middle East in his image. (And John Ashcroft was just too busy covering up immodest statues and trying to cut counterterrorism funds.)

In the Clarke book, Mr. Wolfowitz fidgets as Mr. Clarke urges that armed Predators target Osama at a meeting in April 2001. "Well," Wolfie whines, "I just don't understand why we are beginning by talking about this one man, bin Laden."

Besides confirming what we already knew—that national security in this White House has been as ideologically driven as the domestic agenda—the Clarke book and the commission hearings are most chilling in describing how clueless the agencies charged with sorting through clues were under Clinton and Bush.

Reprising the scene in the White House on 9/11, Mr. Clarke says Dale Watson, the FBI's counterterrorism chief, called him. "We got the passenger manifests from the airlines," Mr. Watson said. "We recognize some names, Dick. They're Al Qaeda."

Mr. Clarke recalled: "I was stunned, not that the attack was Al Qaeda but that there were Al Qaeda operatives on board aircraft using names that FBI knew were Al Qaeda." Mr. Watson told Mr. Clarke that "CIA forgot to tell us about them."

Mr. Clarke's argument that the Bush team's misguided adventurism in Iraq has actually spawned more terrorism and diverted resources has panicked the Bushies, who are running as heroic terror warriors.

It's always gross to see a White House stoop to smearing the character of someone seen as a threat. It was sickening when the Clinton White House smeared Monica Lewinsky, and it's sickening now.

Charlie McCarthy Hearings

■

*F*ollowing is the text of a letter sent yesterday to Thomas H. Kean *and Lee H. Hamilton of the September 11 commission from Al-berto R. Gonzales, counsel to President Bush.*

While we continue to hold to the principles underlying the constitutional separation of powers, that the appropriate and patriotic action for the commission is to shut down and stop pestering us, the president is prepared, in the interest of comity and popularity, to testify, subject to the conditions set forth below.

The president at all times, even on trips to the men's room, will be accompanied by the vice president.

The commission must agree in writing that it will not pose any questions directly to the president. Mr. Bush's statements will be restricted to asides on Dick Cheney's brush-offs, as in "Just like he said," "Roger that" and "Ditto."

Another necessary condition, in keeping with the tenets of executive privilege: Mr. Cheney will require that the commission observe the rules of his favorite show from the Eisenhower administration, *What's My Line?* The panelists, in the manner of Dorothy Kilgallen and Bennett Cerf, must try to guess what the president and vice president didn't know and when they didn't know it through questions that elicit a "yes" or "no."

After ten "no" answers, the panel will not be allowed to question Mr. Cheney or anyone else in the administration ever again. In the mystery guest round, Richard Ben-Veniste, Bob Kerrey and other Democrats on the commission will be blindfolded.

(Or Mr. Cheney is willing to follow the precedent of Garry Moore and Bess Meyerson, using *I've Got a Secret* rules: The vice president will whisper a secret about the administration's inadequate response to terrorism in the president's ear and each panelist will have thirty seconds to question Mr. Cheney in an attempt to guess the secret, which he will not reveal even if they guess right.)

As an additional accommodation, the president and vice president have now agreed to take a "pinkie oath," looping little fingers with each other, while reserving the right to cross the index and middle fingers of their remaining hands and hide them behind their backs.

We must deny your request that Mr. Cheney bring along a Power-Point presentation depicting who was in and out of the loop, in accordance with separation of PowerPoint principles. The vice president has decreed that the loop of influence is under the cone of silence.

The White House is taking the extraordinary step of bowing to public opinion—even though Mr. Cheney states that he doesn't give two hoots about public opinion. Therefore, the vice president will only entertain questions about negligence in fighting terrorism concerning the critical period between January 21, 1993, and January 20,

2001. As President Bush stated on Tuesday, March 30, the commission must gain "a complete picture of the months and years before September 11."

The vice president will not address any queries about why no one reacted to George Tenet's daily hair-on-fire alarms to the president about a coming Al Qaeda attack; or why the president was so consumed with chopping and burning cedar on his Crawford ranch that he ignored the warning in an August 6, 2001, briefing that Al Qaeda might try to hijack aircraft; or why the president asked for a plan to combat Al Qaeda in May and then never followed up while Richard Clarke's aggressive plan was suffocated by second-raters; or why the president was never briefed by his counterterrorism chief on anything but cybersecurity until September 11; or why the administration-in-amber made so many cold war assumptions, such as thinking that terrorists had to be sponsored by a state even as terrorists had taken over a state; or why the president went along with the vice president and the neocons to fool the American public into believing that Saddam had a hand in the 9/11 attacks; or why the administration chose to undercut the war on terrorism and inflame the Arab world by attacking Iraq, without a plan to protect our perilously overextended forces or to exit with a realistic hope that a democracy will be left behind.

The commission must not, under any circumstances, ask the vice president why American soldiers and civilians in Iraq are being greeted with barbarous infernos rather than flowery bouquets.

Finally, we request that when the president finishes with this painful teeth-pulling visit, the commission shall offer him a lollipop.

■

Drunk on Rummy

■

In Which

the Boy Emperor

Has No Clothes (or Weapons)

■

April 4, 2004

Mired in a Mirage

■

A ll White Houses spin and lots of presidents stray into fiction. Johnson on Vietnam. Nixon on Watergate. Bill Clinton trying to squeeze through silly semantic loopholes on his sex life. And when Ronald Reagan made statements that turned black into white—trees caused pollution or welfare queens drove Caddys—his aides said that authenticity was irrelevant because the Gipper was sharing "parables" or "notions," reflecting larger truths as he saw them.

The Bush White House does not merely aim to put the most appealing gloss on truth. By holding back documents, officials, information, images and the sight of returning military coffins, by twisting and exaggerating facts to fit story lines, by demonizing anyone who disagrees with its version of reality, this administration strives to create an optical delusion.

There was always something of the boy in the bubble about George W. Bush, cosseted from the vicissitudes of life, from Vietnam to business failure, by his famous name.

In the front yard of the Kennebunkport estate, he blithely announced his run for president knowing virtually nothing about foreign affairs, confident that Poppy would surround him with the protective flank of his own Desert Storm war council.

But now Mr. Bush is trying to pull America and Iraq into his bubble.

In briefings delivered in the bubble of their own security bunkers, Paul Bremer and military officials continue to insist that democracy and stability are taking root in Iraq. The occupation administrator travels Iraq surrounded by armed guards while attacks get scarier, culminating in last week's bestial block party in Falluja.

American commanders in Iraq have claimed the violence is primarily the work of outsiders, Islamic terrorists with at least loose links to Al Qaeda. They said, as the *Times*'s John Burns wrote, that "the worst of the 'Saddamist' insurgency was over, its power blunted by a wide American offensive that followed the former dictator's capture."

The administration does not want to admit the extent of anti-American hatred among Iraqis. And even if some of the perpetrators are outsiders, they could never succeed without the active help of Iraqis.

Just as they once conjured a mirage of a Saddam sharing lethal weapons with Osama, now the president and vice president make the disingenuous claim that Al Qaeda is on the run and that many of its capos are behind bars. Meanwhile, counterterrorism experts say terrorism has become hydra-headed, and one told *Newsweek* that the spawned heads have perpetrated more major terror attacks in the thirty months since 9/11 than in the thirty months before. Experts agree that the nature of the threat has shifted, with more than a dozen regional militant Islamic groups reflecting growing strength.

Senator Bob Graham compared the new, decentralized Al Qaeda to a blob of mercury that "you slam your fist into and it suddenly bursts into a hundred small pieces."

Mr. Bush also likes to brag that the Taliban is no longer in power. But the Taliban roots are deep. At least a third of Afghanistan is still so dicey that voters there cannot be registered, and the Kabul government has postponed June elections.

The president did not want to mar the gay mood of his fundraiser here Wednesday night, so he did not mention the ghoulish slam dance in Falluja. As the *Times*'s David Sanger wrote, "In the Bush campaign, casualties are something to be alluded to obliquely, if at all." In the Bush alternative universe of eternal sunshine, where the environment is not toxic and Medicare is not a budget buster, body bags and funerals just muddy the picture.

Bush strategists say that good or bad Iraq news is still good for Mr. Bush; they think scenes of desecration will simply remind voters of his steely presidential resolve.

The Bushies are busy putting a retroactive glow on their terrorism efforts, asserting that their plan was more muscular and "comprehensive" than Mr. Clinton's. To support that Panglossian view, they held back a load of Clinton documents on terrorism from the 9/11 commission.

If we can't take a cold, hard look at reality, how can we protect ourselves from terrorists? And how can we rescue Iraq from chaos? Now we're told the military is preparing an "overwhelming" retaliation to the carnage in Falluja. You can hear the clammy blast from the past: We're going to destroy that village to save it.

The Iraqi Inversion

■

Maybe after high-definition TV, they'll invent high-dudgeon TV, a product so realistic you can just lunge through the screen and shake the Bush officials when they say something maddening about 9/11 or Iraq, or when they engage in some egregious bit of character assassination.

It would come in handy for Karen Hughes's Bush-nannying book tour and Condoleezza Rice's Clarke-riposting 9/11 commission testimony.

And I was desperately wishing for it yesterday, when Donald Rumsfeld held forth at a Pentagon briefing.

Even though the assumptions the Bush administration used to go to war have now proved to be astonishingly arrogant, naive and ideological, Mr. Rumsfeld is as testy and Delphic as ever about the fragility of Iraq.

"We're trying to explain how things are going, and they are going as they are going," he said, adding: "Some things are going well and some things obviously are not going well. You're going to have good days and bad days." On the road to democracy, this "is one moment, and there will be other moments. And there will be good moments and there will be less good moments."

Calling the families of more than thirty young Americans killed this week in the confusing hell of Iraq must be a less good moment.

Our troops in Iraq don't know who they're fighting and who they're saving. They don't know when they're coming home or when they're being forcibly re-upped by Rummy. Our diplomats in Baghdad don't know who they're handing the country over June 30. And Bush officials don't know where to go for help, since the military's tapped out, the allies have cold feet, the Arab world's angry and the rest of the globe is thinking, "You got what you deserved."

Before heading out to Iraq last spring, Marine commanders explained that they would try to take a gentler approach than the Army. They would avoid using military tactics that would risk civilian casualties, learn Arabic and take off their sunglasses when talking with Iraqis. "If to kill a terrorist we have got to kill eight innocent people, you don't kill them," Major General James Mattis told the *Times*'s Michael Gordon.

But in the wake of the Falluja horror and Shiite uprising, civility must take a backseat to stomping.

The Marines had to fire rockets at a mosque in Falluja, and the hospitals are filled with civilians. Instead of playing soccer with kids, now the Marines have to worry that the kids are the enemy, spotting targets or wielding guns. The farmers and taxicab drivers, wearing their own clothes and driving their own cars, try to murder the Marines before melting back into the populace.

Paul Wolfowitz assumed that the Shiites, tormented by Saddam over their religion, would be grateful, not hateful. Wrong. It isn't a cakewalk; it's chaos.

Every single thing the administration calculated would happen in Iraq has turned out the opposite. The WMD that supposedly threatened us did not exist. The dangerous dictator was deluded and writing romance novels. The terrorism that would be thwarted has mushroomed in Iraq and is feeding Arab radicalism.

Mr. Rumsfeld thought invading Iraq would exorcise America's Vietnam syndrome, its squeamishness about using force. Instead, it has raised the specter of another Vietnam, where our courageous troops don't understand the culture, can't recognize the enemy and don't have an exit strategy. And the administration spins the war every day.

Rummy also thought he could show off his transformation of the military, using a leaner force. Now even some Republicans say he is putting our troops at risk by stubbornly refusing to admit he was wrong.

Dick Cheney thought fear was better than weak-kneed diplomacy, that if America whacked one Arab foe, all the others would cower. Wrong. The Iraq invasion has multiplied and emboldened our enemies.

Mr. Cheney and Mr. Rumsfeld thought America should flex its hyperpower muscles, castrating the UN and blowing off multilateral arrangements. Now the administration may have to crawl back for help.

The hawks thought they could establish a democracy that would produce a domino effect in the Arab world. Wrong. The dominoes are falling in a scarier direction.

The president thought he could improve on the ending to his father's gulf war. Wrong again.

April 11, 2004

Our New No-Can-Do Nation

■

Young Americans are bravely fighting and dying in Iraq, try-ing to fulfill the audacious vision of George W. Bush and Dick Cheney to remold Iraq in the image of America.

But while we try to turn them into us, who have we become?

The president presents himself as an avatar of American values, plainspoken cowboy and tough flyboy.

But Condi Rice's testimony on Thursday raises the depressing possibility that we've lost the essence of our frontier spirit: the in-genious individualist who gets around the system and faces down the drones.

From Abigail Adams to Tom Sawyer to Bugs Bunny to Jimmy Stewart's Jefferson Smith to Indiana Jones, the best American char-acter is plucky, nimble, clever, inventive.

So it's disturbing to see our government reacting to crises with a jaded shrug and lumbering gait, especially since we are up against such a creative, chameleon-like enemy.

Consider the pathetic performance of NASA, which inverted its motto to "Failure is an option" by shrugging off warnings about the safety of the seven *Columbia* astronauts who burned up coming back to earth, and not trying to send up a rescue shuttle.

This no-can-do spirit marked George Tenet's lame excuses to senators in February who wanted to know why the CIA never picked up the trail of Marwan al-Shehhi, the pilot who crashed Flight 175 into the south tower on 9/11, even though the Germans gave the agency his name and phone number. "They didn't give us a first and a last name until after 9/11," Mr. Tenet said.

And what would Eliot Ness say about an FBI that is less computer savvy than American preschoolers and Islamic terrorists? The FBI is only halfway through modernizing its computers, which could not, before 9/11, do two searches at once, such as "Al Qaeda" and "flight schools." Can't we draft Bill Gates for duty?

This ominous passivity was threaded through the testimony of Ms. Rice, a brainy and accomplished woman who should represent the best of America. She blamed "systemic" and "structural" impediments that prevented the CIA and the FBI from sharing. She complained that other people hadn't recommended what she should do; even the terrorists were faulted for not giving specifics.

The screeching chatter in the spring and summer of 2001—"There will be attacks in the near future"—did not yank Mr. Bush and his team from their Iraq fixation. "But they don't tell us when," Ms. Rice protested. "They don't tell us where, they don't tell us who, and they don't tell us how." Paging Nancy Drew.

Inconclusive intelligence did not bother the Bush team when it wanted to be "actionable" on Iraq, or engage in "tit for tat" with Saddam.

The August 6, 2001, presidential daily briefing—remarkably

headlined "Bin Laden Determined to Attack Inside the United States"—mentioned Al Qaeda's wanting to hijack planes and the seventy FBI field investigations into suspected Al Qaeda sleeper cells in the U.S.

The briefing had three-month-old information that Al Qaeda was trying to sneak into the country for an explosives attack. No wonder the CIA chief and counterterrorism czar were running around with their hair on fire.

What should have made Condi hysterical, she deemed "historical."

W. kept fishing and denouncing Saddam, while Condi sat for a glam *Vogue* photo shoot and interview.

On Iraq, they ran roughshod over the system. On Al Qaeda, Condi blamed the system, saying she couldn't act on Richard Clarke's plan until there was a strategy, a policy, "tasking," meetings, etc.

The FBI officials who ignored Coleen Rowley as she tried to break through the obtuse leadership of Louis Freeh's FBI to get evidence on Zacarias Moussaoui, and Kenneth Williams, the Phoenix agent who outlined the Al Qaeda plot to train Arab terrorists in our flight schools, have not been held accountable. Why aren't the heroic Ms. Rowley and Mr. Williams running something?

Dick Clarke has struck a chord because his passionate efforts reflected those great American virtues of ingenuity and brashness. Even if he was a bit of a cowboy, loading up his .357 sidearm to return to the West Wing the night after 9/11, at least he was not dozing through High Noon.

From Osama with Hate

■

If only Osama had faxed an X-marks-the-spot map to the Crawford ranch showing the Pentagon, the Capitol, the twin towers and the word "BOOM!" scrawled in Arabic.

That might have sparked sluggish imaginations. Or maybe not.

Only a couple of weeks after the endlessly vacationing President Bush got his August 6, 2001, briefing with the shivery headline "Bin Laden Determined to Strike in U.S.," the CIA chief, George Tenet, and other top agency officials received a briefing about the arrest of Zacarias Moussaoui after his suspicious behavior in a Minnesota flight school. And that had another shivery headline: "Islamic Extremist Learns to Fly."

"The news had no evident effect" on prompting the CIA to warn anyone, according to the dryly rendered report of the 9/11 commission's staff, which faults the agency for management miasma and Al Qaeda myopia, citing a failure to make a "comprehensive estimate of the enemy."

Asked by the commission member Timothy Roemer about whether he had shared this amazing news at a September 4 meeting with Condi Rice, Colin Powell, Donald Rumsfeld and Richard Clarke— the meeting on Al Qaeda that Mr. Clarke had been urgently begging for since January—Mr. Tenet said no. Asked if he had ever mentioned it to Mr. Bush in August, during a month of "high chatter and huge warnings," Mr. Tenet said no.

The Man Whose Hair Was Allegedly on Fire told the commissioners that he had not talked to the president at all in August. Mr. Bush was in Texas, and he was in Washington. Or he was on vacation, and the president was in Texas. *Quel* high alert.

After the hearing, Mr. Tenet had an aide call reporters to say he had misspoken, that he had briefed the president twice in August, in Crawford on August 17 for a morning briefing he deemed unexceptional and again in Washington on August 31.

I'm not sure whether Mr. Tenet—a mystifyingly beloved figure even though he was in charge during the two biggest intelligence failures since Pearl Harbor and the Bay of Pigs—has a faulty memory, which is scary. Or if he's fuzzing things up because he told the president more specifics than he wants to admit. But in a town where careers are made on face time with the president, it's fishy that the head spook can't remember a six-hour trip to Crawford for some.

In a commission staff report, there is a stark juxtaposition of Sandy Berger's approach before the millennium and Condi Rice's before 9/11.

"Berger, in particular, met or spoke constantly with Tenet and Attorney General Reno," the report said. "He visited the F.B.I. and the C.I.A. on Christmas Day 1999 to raise the morale of exhausted officials."

Condi and her deputy, Steve Hadley, did not stoop to mere domestic work. "Rice and Hadley told us that before 9/11, they did not feel they had the job of handling domestic security." They left that up to Dick Clarke to broker, the same guy Dick Cheney said "wasn't in the loop."

Maybe Condi's confusion about her job—that it entailed national security as well as being the president's foreign-policy governess and workout partner—explains why so many critical clues went into the black holes of the FBI and the CIA.

After the Bay of Pigs, President Kennedy spoke to newspaper publishers and said: "This administration intends to be candid about its errors. For as a wise man once said, 'An error does not become a mistake until you refuse to correct it.' . . . Without debate, without criticism, no administration and no country can succeed—and no republic can survive."

Compare Kennedy with Mr. Bush, who conceded no errors and warned that any Vietnam analogy with Iraq—in this acid flashback moment when sixty-four U.S. troops were reported to have died last week and when McNarummy is forcing up to twenty thousand troops to stay in Iraq—"sends the wrong message to our troops and sends the wrong message to the enemy."

He reiterated that his mission is dictated from above: "Freedom is the Almighty's gift to every man and woman in this world."

Given the Saudi religious authority's fatwa against our troops, and given that our Marines are surrounding a cleric in the holy city of Najaf, we really don't want to make Muslims think we're fighting a holy war. That would only further inflame the Arab world and endanger our overstretched military, so let's hope that Mr. Bush's reference to the Almighty was to Dick Cheney.

April 18, 2004

House of Broken Toys

■

When Colin Powell decided that Dick Cheney's crazy "fever," as he called the vice president's obsession with linking 9/11 and Saddam, was leading the country into a war it did not need to fight, he should have bared his heart to the president and made his case using the Powell doctrine—with overwhelming force.

Mr. Bush probably wouldn't have listened. He was in Mr. Cheney's gloomy sway, and Rummy's bellicose sway. And W. felt competitive with his more popular top diplomat.

But Mr. Powell should have tried. And if the president didn't listen, the secretary should have quit—not let himself be used by the vice president and his "Gestapo office" of Pentagon neocons, as Mr. Powell referred to them, to put a diplomatic fig leaf on a predetermined war plan and to present bogus intelligence to the UN.

He knew his word held enormous weight around the world. And he knew he was the only one, out of all the officials in on the clandestine rush to war, who had fought in a war. He should have spoken up for all those soldiers who would fight and die and be maimed for Dick Cheney's nutty utopian dream of bombing the world into freedom, and W.'s dream of being so forceful with Saddam, the slimebag who survived his father's war, that he would forever banish his family's bête noire—the wimp factor.

It would have been much more honorable than playing Achilles sulking in his Foggy Bottom tent, privately pouting to Bob Woodward that he had warned the president about the Pottery Barn effect—break Iraq and "you know you're going to be owning this place"—and tattling that his colleagues were engaged in "lunacy."

"At times, with his closest friends, Powell was semidespondent," his pal Mr. Woodward writes in *Plan of Attack*. "His president and his country were headed for a war that he thought might just be avoided, though he himself would not walk away."

Mr. Woodward, who is clearly channeling Mr. Powell, as he has done to present Mr. Powell's side of the story in past books, re-creates his innermost thoughts: "He saw in Cheney a sad transformation. The cool operator from the first gulf war just would not let go. Cheney now had an unhealthy fixation. Nearly every conversation or reference came back to Al Qaeda and trying to nail the connection with Iraq. He would often have an obscure piece of intelligence. Powell thought that Cheney took intelligence and converted uncertainty and ambiguity into fact. It was about the worst charge that Powell could make about the vice president. But there it was."

Everyone in Washington has been puzzling over how Mr. Cheney, a reasonable, cautious, popular man in the first Bush administration, turned into Pluto, king of the underworld and proponent of worst-case scenarios and preemption.

But Mr. Powell shared his dread, Cassandra-like, with Mr. Woodward: "The more Powell dug, the more he realized that the human sources were few and far between on Iraq's WMD. It was not a pretty picture."

George Tenet comes across in the book as another profile in cravenness. On December 21, 2002, the CIA chief went to the Oval Office with an aide to present "The Case" on WMD. Even Mr. Bush, already deeply enmeshed in war plans, was taken aback at the paucity of it. "Nice try," Mr. Bush said. "I don't think this is quite— it's not something that Joe Public would understand or would gain a lot of confidence from." Turning to Mr. Tenet, he added: "I've been told all this intelligence about having WMD and this is the best we've got?"

When the president asked how confident he was, Mr. Tenet, premier apple polisher, gave Mr. Bush the answer he wanted to hear: "Don't worry, it's a slam dunk!"

Just as the Democratic president ducked behind the parsed line, "I did not have sexual relations with that woman," so the Republican president ducked behind the parsed line, "I have no war plans on my desk."

The plans for invading Iraq (with the help of "The House of Broken Toys," as the CIA referred to the Iraqi operations group) may not have been sitting on his desk, but he secretly started planning with Rummy for war with Iraq in November 2001, and with Tommy Franks starting the next month. Once they were thick into the planning, the president couldn't turn back, of course. That would make him like the loathed Bill Clinton—a lot of bold talk and not much action—not like "The Man," as Mr. Cheney called his warrior president.

The Body Politic

■

Not since Jane Goodall lived with chimps in Tanzania has there been such a vivid study of the nonverbal patterns of primates engaged in a dominance display.

Bob Woodward's new book, *Plan of Attack*, reveals that President Bush decided to go to war based mostly, believe it or not, on body language.

Like his father, Mr. Bush prefers more elemental means of self-expression than the verbal. (Not long before the first gulf war, Bush senior's masseuse told a client that the president's neck was so tight, she assumed we were going to war.)

The younger Bush, suspicious of Clintonesque dialectical fevers and interminable analyses, did not bother to ask most of his top advisers what they thought. The less Dick Cheney talked, the more power Mr. Bush entrusted in him.

Like the silent, cool-hand cowboy he aspires to be, who would shoot a man just because he didn't like the way the varmint was looking at him, the president preferred doing gut checks, visually sizing up advisers and Saddam, rather than dwelling on pesky facts.

He did not probe deeply to reconcile advisers' assessments. He cared only about their spine, figuratively and literally. There was no skeptical debate in the Oval Office like the one before the Cuban missile crisis in 1962.

The president explained to Mr. Woodward that he had wanted to talk to Tommy Franks in person about the Iraq war plan. "'I'm watching his body language very carefully,' Mr. Bush recalled. He emphasized the body language, the eyes, the demeanor. It was more important than some of the substance. . . . 'Is this good enough to win?' he recalled asking Franks, leaning forward in his chair and throwing his hand forward in a slicing motion at my face to illustrate the scene."

As the president studied the physio-semiotics of those around him, they studied his. " 'I knew my relationship with the president and the access and his interest and how he feels and his body language on things,'" a typically cocky Donald Rumsfeld said.

The author writes of the Cheney aide and Iraq hawk Scooter Libby: "He was watching the president carefully, noting the body language and the verbal language ordering war planning for Iraq, the questions, attitudes and tone."

When the CIA briefers told Mr. Bush that to recruit sources inside Iraq, they would have to say the U.S. was coming with its military— putting him in the awkward position of simultaneously pursuing diplomatic and military solutions—Condoleezza Rice watched the president. "The president's body language suggested he had received the message, but he didn't make any promises."

Nick Calio, the White House legislative affairs director, realized the endgame by September 2002: "Judging from Bush's side comments and body language, Calio assumed that the question on Iraq was not if but when there would be a war."

When George Tenet was telling a dubious president that the WMD "evidence" would be there when he needed it, he knew how to physically underscore his point. "Tenet, a basketball fan who attended as many home games of his alma mater Georgetown as possible, leaned forward and threw his arms up again. 'Don't worry, it's a slam dunk!'"

When the president at long last informed his top diplomat that he was going to war, Colin Powell could tell from the president's body language that there was no point in arguing: "It was the assured Bush. His tight, forward-leaning, muscular body language verified his words."

After a while, the usually literal Mr. Woodward also began dipping into the science of kinesics. When he greeted Mr. Bush at a White House Christmas party in 2002, he interpreted the president's body language as blessing the prospect of a sequel to his last book, *Bush at War*.

The end of *Plan of Attack* says that when Mr. Woodward asked the president how history would judge his Iraq war, Mr. Bush smiled. "'History,' he said, shrugging, taking his hands out of his pockets, extending his arms out and suggesting with his body language that it was so far off. 'We won't know. We'll all be dead.'"

Soon, these people had the problem of the body language of more than seven hundred dead soldiers. Some persuasive non–body language is way overdue.

Shocking and Awful

■

D onald Rumsfeld and Paul Wolfowitz were swanning around in black tie at the White House Correspondents' dinner on Saturday night, mingling with *le hack* Washington and a speckling of shiny imports, like John Kerry's former Tinseltown gal pal Morgan Fairchild, Ben Affleck, a Victoria's Secret model who was not Gisele and several *Apprentice* alumni who were not Omarosa.

The Pentagon potentates seemed unburdened by the spreading storm kicked up by the torture pictures shown on *60 Minutes II* and about to appear in *The New Yorker*—the latest example of a dysfunctional and twisted occupation warped by arrogance over experience, ideology over common sense.

When a beaming Mr. Wolfowitz stopped at my table to greet an admiring Republican, I wanted to snap, "Get back to your desk, Mr. Myopia from Utopia!" Shouldn't these woolly headed warriors burn the midnight Iraqi oil—long enough for Wolfie to learn the body count for dead American troops and for Rummy to read General Antonio Taguba's whole report on "horrific abuses" at Abu Ghraib?

Sure, the secretary of defense has had two months to read the report, but as he complained to Matt Lauer, it's awfully thick: "When I'm asked a question as to whether I've read the entire report, I answer honestly that I have not. It is a mountain of paper and investigative material." Goodness gracious, where is Evelyn Wood now that we need her?

Can't the hawks who dragged us into this hideous unholy war at least pay attention to a crisis of American credibility that's exposing Iraq and the world to more dangers every day? For the defense chief and the president to party two nights in a row, Friday at Rummy's house and Saturday at the Washington Hilton, is, to borrow a Rummy line, "unhelpful in a fundamental way."

President Bush also seemed in a buoyant mood on Saturday. But he might think about getting just a tad more involved so he doesn't have to first see on TV, as he clicks around between innings, the pictures sparking a huge worldwide, American reputation–shattering military scandal. And so he doesn't keep nattering about how we had to go to war to close Iraq's torture chambers, when they are "really not shut down so much as under new management," as Jon Stewart dryly put it.

Most Republicans seemed in a "Party on, Garth" mood, less concerned with Humpty-Dumpty Iraq or Unjolly Green Giant John Kerry than with the unfairness of a world where Jeb Bush would probably not be able to succeed his brother. "By 2008," a wistful Republican fund-raiser said, "there'll probably be Bush fatigue."

It seems nothing can make hard-core hawks criticize the war (even the request for $25 billion more). Rush Limbaugh compared the prison torture to "a college fraternity prank," like a Skull and Bones initiation.

Michael Eisner evidently also feels the Bush dynasty will survive because he is balking at distributing a new documentary by Michael Moore that criticizes President Bush's 9/11 actions and ties with the Saudis, probably out of fear that Jeb will come after his Disney World tax breaks.

Senator Kerry jumped on the president yesterday for saying nothing about Crown Prince Abdullah's "outrageous anti-Semitic comments" that terrorists in Saudi Arabia get funds from "Zionists." The prince's remarks—and arrests of reformers—show that, far from transforming the Mideast into democracies that flower with love of America and Israel, the bumbling neocons have unleashed a rash of racism, revenge and hate.

Colin Powell's chief of staff, Larry Wilkerson, tells *GQ* magazine that Wolfie is "a utopian" like Lenin: "You're never going to bring utopia, and you're going to hurt a lot of people in the process of trying to do it."

Just when you thought things couldn't get worse, the A.P. reports from London that "U.S. soldiers who detained an elderly Iraqi woman last year placed a harness on her, made her crawl on all fours and rode her like a donkey."

And Douglas Feith, the defense undersecretary who was in charge of Iraqi postwar planning and the secret unit that furnished prêt-à-porter intelligence to back up Dick Cheney's doomsday scenarios, told conservatives that the administration might set up an office to plan postwar operations for future wars.

Well, on the one hand, it would be refreshing to have a postwar plan. On the other: future wars???

May 9, 2004

A World of Hurt

■

Good golly, you knew Rummy wasn't going to pretend to stay contrite for long. Not with lawmakers bugging him about the Pearl Harbor of PR, as Republican Tom Cole called it.

The flinty seventy-one-year-old kept it together as John McCain pounced and Hillary prodded. But soon he was once more giving snippy one-word answers to his inquisitors, foisting them on his brass menagerie or biting their heads off himself.

By Friday evening, when the delegate from Guam, Madeleine Bordallo, pressed him on whether "quality of life" was an issue in the Abu Ghraib torture cases, you could see Donald Duck steam coming out of his ears.

"Whether they have a PX or a good restaurant is not the issue," he said with a veiled sneer.

Rummy was having a dickens of a time figuring out how a control-freak administration could operate in this newfangled age when GIs have dadburn digital cameras.

In the information age, he complained to senators, "people are running around with digital cameras and taking these unbelievable photographs and then passing them off, against the law, to the media, to our surprise, when they had not even arrived in the Pentagon."

Senator Lindsey Graham, a Republican, mourned that America was in a "world of hurt." If General Richard Myers knew enough to try to suppress the CBS show, Mr. Graham asked, why didn't he know enough to warn the president and Congress?

Donald Rumsfeld, a black belt at Washington infighting, knew the aggrieved lawmakers were most interested in an apology for not keeping them in the loop. He no doubt was sorry—sorry the pictures got out.

The man who promised last July that "I don't do quagmires" didn't seem to be in trouble on Friday, despite the government's blowing off repeated Red Cross warnings.

But who knows what the effect will be of the additional "blatantly sadistic and inhuman" photos that Mr. Rumsfeld warned of. Or the videos he said he still had not screened.

Dick Cheney will not cut loose his old mentor from the Nixon and Ford years unless things get more dire.

After all, George Tenet is still running the CIA after the biggest intelligence failures since some Trojan ignored Cassandra's chatter and said, "Roll the horse in." Colin Powell is still around after trash-talking to Bob Woodward about his catfights with the Bushworld *Mean Girls*—Rummy, Cheney, Wolfie and Doug Feith. The vice president still rules after promoting a smashmouth foreign policy that is more Jack Palance than Shane. And the president still edges out John Kerry in polls, even though Mr. Bush observed with no irony to Al Arabiya TV: "Iraqis are sick of foreign people coming in their country and trying to destabilize their country, and we will help them rid Iraq of these killers."

The only people who have been pushed aside in this administration are the truth tellers who warned about policies on taxes (Paul O'Neill); war costs (Larry Lindsey); occupation troop levels (General Eric Shinseki); and how Iraq would divert from catching the ubiquitous Osama (Richard Clarke).

Even if the secretary survives, the Rummy Doctrine—using underwhelming force to achieve overwhelming goals—is discredited. Jack Murtha, a Democratic hawk and Vietnam vet, says "the direction's got to be changed or it's unwinnable," and Lieutenant General William Odom, retired, told Ted Koppel that Iraq was headed toward becoming an Al Qaeda haven and Iranian ally.

By the end, Rummy was channeling Jack Nicholson's Colonel Jessup, who lashed out at the snotty weenies questioning him while they sleep "under the blanket of the very freedom I provide, then question the manner in which I provide it."

Asked how we can get back credibility, Rummy bridled. "America is not what's wrong with the world," he said, adding: "I read all this stuff—people hate us, people don't like us. The fact of the matter is, people line up to come into this country every year because it's better here than other places, and because they respect the fact that we respect human beings. And we'll get by this."

Maybe. But for now, the hawks who wanted to employ American might to scatter American values like flower petals all across the world are reduced to keeping them from being trampled by Americans. As Rummy would say, not a pretty picture.

May 13, 2004

Clash of Civilizations

■

T estifying before the Senate yesterday, General Richard Myers admitted that we're stalemated in Iraq.

"There is no way to militarily lose in Iraq," he said, describing the generals' consensus. "There is also no way to militarily win in Iraq."

Talk about the sound of one hand clapping. And they say John Kerry is on both sides of issues.

Sounding like Mr. Kerry, General Myers summed up: "This process has to be internationalized. The UN has to play the governance role. That's how we're, in my view, eventually going to win."

The administration's demented quest to conquer Arab hearts and minds has dissolved in a torrent of pornography denigrating other parts of the Arab anatomy. George Bush, who swept into office on a cloud of moral umbrage, now has his own sex scandal—one with far greater implications than titillating cigar jokes.

The Bush hawks, so fixated on making the Middle East look more like America, have made America look un-American. Should we really be reduced to defending ourselves by saying at least we don't behead people?

Gripped in a "I can't look at them—I've got to look at them" state of mind, lawmakers grimly filed into private screening rooms on the Hill to check out the eighteen hundred grotesque images of sex, humiliation and torture.

"They're disgusting," Senator Dianne Feinstein told me. "If somebody wanted to plan a clash of civilizations, this is how they'd do it. These pictures play into every stereotype of America that Arabs have: America as debauched, America as hypocrites.

"Cheney and Rumsfeld and Wolfowitz act like they know all the answers, almost like a divine right," she said. "They don't have a divine right, and they are wrong."

After 9/11, America had the support and sympathy of the world. Now, awash in digital evidence of uncivilized behavior, America has careered into a war of civilizations. The pictures were clearly meant to use the codebook of Muslim anxieties about nudity and sexual and gender humiliation to break down the prisoners.

Senator Ben Nighthorse Campbell said some photographs seemed to show Iraqi women being commanded to expose their breasts— such debasement, after a war that President Bush partly based on women's rights.

The problem, of course, is that the war in Iraq started with lies— that Saddam's WMD were endangering our security and that Saddam was linked to Al Qaeda and 9/11.

In a public relations move that cheapens the heroism of soldiers, the Pentagon merged the medals for the wars in Afghanistan and Iraq, giving the GWOT medal, for Global War on Terrorism, in both wars to reinforce the idea that we had to invade Iraq to quell terrorism. The truth is that our invasion of Iraq spurred terrorism there and around the world.

That initial deception—and headlong rush to throw off international conventions and old alliances, and namby-pamby institutions like the UN and the Red Cross—led straight to the abuse of Abu Ghraib. Now the question is whether the CIA tortured Al Qaeda operatives.

Officials blurred the lines to justify ideological decisions, calling every Iraqi who opposed us a "terrorist"; conducting rough interrogations, perhaps to find the nonexistent WMD so they would not look foolish; rolling all opposition into one scary terrorist ball that did not require sensitivity to the Geneva Conventions or "humanitarian do-gooders," to use the phrase of Senator James Inhofe, a Republican.

Senator Fritz Hollings made it clear yesterday that Rummy has left us undermanned and undertrained in Iraq—another factor in the torture scandal. "Now, in a country of 25 million, you're trying to secure it with 135,000," he scolded Mr. Rumsfeld, adding: "We're trying to win the hearts and minds as we're killing them and torturing them." At least, he said sarcastically, General William Westmoreland never asked a Vietcong general to take the town, "like we have for Falluja. We've asked the enemy general to take the town."

The hawks, who promised us garlands in Iraq, should have recalled the words of the historian Daniel Boorstin, who warned that planning for the future without a sense of history is like planting cut flowers.

May 16, 2004

The Springs of Fate

■

Oblivious of the consequences, the impetuous black sheep of a ruling family starts a war triggered by a personal grudge.

The father, a respected veteran of his own wars, suppresses his unease and graciously supports his son, even though it will end up destroying his legacy and the world order he envisioned.

The ferocious battle in the far-off sands spirals out of control, with many brave soldiers killed, with symbols of divinity damaged, with graphic scenes showing physical abuse of the conquered, and with devastatingly surreptitious guerrilla tactics.

Aside from dishing up a gilded Brad Pitt with a leather miniskirt and a Heathrow duty-free accent as he tosses about ancient insults, such as calling someone a "sack of wine," *Troy* also dishes up some gilded lessons on the Aeschylating cost of imperial ambitions and personal vendettas.

The Greek warriors question their sovereign's reasons for war, knowing that he has taken an incendiary pretext (Paris' stealing

Helen from Sparta) to provide emotional acceleration to his real reasons—to settle old scores and forge an empire through war.

When Mars rushes into Achilles' soul in his battle with Hector, as
Alexander Pope wrote in his translation of Homer's *Iliad*, "the
springs of fate snap every lock tight."

But Barbara Tuchman, in her book *The March of Folly: From
Troy to Vietnam*, observes that while the Trojans reject advice to
keep that dagnab nag, as Rummy might put it, out of the walled city,
"the feasible alternative—that of destroying the Horse—is always
open."

Cassandra and others warned them. (The always-ignored Cassandra is left out of the movie, but she must have sensed that was coming.)

"Notwithstanding the frequent references in the epic to the fall
of Troy being ordained, it was not fate but free choice that took the
Horse within the walls," Ms. Tuchman writes. " 'Fate' as a character
in legend represents the fulfillment of man's expectation of himself."

A State Department official noted last week that if any of the
Bush hawks had read Ms. Tuchman's dissection of war follies, her
warning about leaders who get an "addiction to the counterproductive," they might have been less rash.

"The folly" in Vietnam, she writes, "consisted not in pursuit of a
goal in ignorance of the obstacles but in persistence in the pursuit
despite accumulating evidence that the goal was unattainable, and
the effect disproportionate to the American interest and eventually
damaging to American society, reputation and disposable power in
the world."

The Bush team, working on divine right, doesn't bother checking
human precedent.

The president and secretary of defense boast about not reading
newspapers, presumably because they don't want any contrary opin-

ion or fact to shake their faith in the essential excellence of their policies.

It's astonishing the amount of stuff these guys don't bother to read, preferring to filter their information through their ideology. They certainly didn't read enough Iraqi history. They delayed looking at photos and reports on Americans abusing Iraqi prisoners. Paul Wolfowitz clearly wasn't bothering to read updated casualty reports.

The deputy defense secretary got cuffed around at a Senate hearing on Thursday when he admitted that he had first read a document that morning detailing questionable rules of engagement for confronting Iraqi prisoners.

As Ms. Tuchman notes, wooden heads are as dangerous as wooden horses: "Wooden-headedness, the source of self-deception, is a factor that plays a remarkably large role in government. It consists in assessing a situation in terms of preconceived fixed notions while ignoring or rejecting any contrary signs."

President Bush's Achilles' heel is his fear of wimpiness, and Dick Cheney and Rummy played on that, making him think he had to go to war once the war machine was revved up, or he would lose face and no longer be "The Man."

Maybe the president and vice president will catch *Troy* on their planes as they jet around to fund-raisers. But the antiwar message will probably be lost, except on the official who is both a snubbed Cassandra and a sulking Achilles, Colin Powell. "Wooden-headedness," Ms. Tuchman said, "is also the refusal to benefit from experience."

May 20, 2004

What Prison Scandal?

■

Maybe anyone who was once married to Liz Taylor at a time when she favored tiger-striped pantsuits and Clyde's chicken wings—would not flinch at wrangling with another aging sex symbol and demanding diva: Rummy.

Or maybe, at seventy-seven, Senator John Warner is at a stage in life where he can't be intimidated into putting a higher value on Republican reelection prospects than on what he sees as the common good.

In a bracing display of old-fashioned public spiritedness, the courtly Virginian joined up with the crusty Arizonan, John McCain, to brush back Rummy and the partisan whippersnappers in Congress who are yelping that the Senate Armed Services Committee's public hearings into prison abuse by American soldiers are distracting our warriors from taking care of business in Iraq.

"I think the Senate has become mesmerized by cameras, and I

think that's sad," said a California Republican, Representative Duncan Hunter.

Then Senator John Cornyn of Texas weighed in, suggesting that Mr. Warner, a Navy officer in World War II, a Marine lieutenant in the Korean War and a Navy secretary under Nixon, and Mr. McCain, who lived in a dirt suite at the Hanoi Hilton for five years, were not patriotic. Their "collective hand-wringing," Mr. Cornyn sniffed, could be "a distraction from fighting and winning the war."

Rummy had a dozen Republican senators over to the Pentagon for breakfast on Tuesday, and Mr. Cornyn said the secretary was exasperated by the "all-consuming nature" of the congressional hearings.

The man who David Plotz of *Slate* says is widely "considered one of the dumbest members of Congress" chimed in, dumbly. Following up on his inane rant defending the soldiers accused of abuse at Abu Ghraib and whining about "humanitarian do-gooders," Senator James Inhofe of Oklahoma wondered whether Mr. Warner was trying to help the Democrats with public hearings.

The most absurd cut was delivered by Speaker Dennis Hastert, who responded to Mr. McCain's contention that Congress should not enact tax cuts during wartime because it prevented a sense of shared sacrifice by barking: "John McCain ought to visit our young men and women at Walter Reed and Bethesda. There is sacrifice in this country."

It just shows how completely flipped out the Republicans are about how the Iraq occupation is going that they are turning on a war hero and POW, and on a man who enlisted in not one war but two.

It's hard to believe that even if the generals weren't testifying here, they could do much to stop the spiral into anarchy there, with each day bringing some new horror.

General John Abizaid told the panel that the hearing helped establish an image in the Arab world that Americans face up to their problems and handle them in the open. Certainly, he wasn't echoing the often Panglossian view of Donald Rumsfeld yesterday. He predicted that "the situation will become more violent" after the June 30 transfer of power and that he might then require more than the 135,000 troops now in Iraq.

Senator McCain, who has long advocated more troops, said that the Pentagon and its cheerleaders were silly to think they could throw a blanket over incendiary developments. "It's only a matter of time before the Pentagon's new disc of abuse pictures starts bouncing around the Internet," he said.

When I asked about Mr. Hastert's crack about visiting Walter Reed, the man whose temper used to be so close to the surface just laughed. "My," Mr. McCain murmured, "they certainly are angry. There has been some obvious resentment because of my 'independence' for a long time."

He reiterated that he would never run with John Kerry. "I'm a loyal Republican," he said. "A lot of their resentment goes back to campaign finance reform."

I asked whether Mr. Warner, who helped Mr. McCain, as a shattered POW, reorient to America after Vietnam, was a good example of the exemplars he writes about in his new meditation, *Why Courage Matters.*

Agreeing that his colleague had shown strength, Mr. McCain concluded: "I believe from my experience that the only way you get one of these things behind you is to get everything out as quickly as possible."

Open and sharing Bushies. Now, there's a novel concept.

May 23, 2004

Bay of Goats

■

S o let me get this straight:

We ransacked the house of the con man whom we paid millions to feed us fake intelligence on WMD that would make the case for ransacking the country that the con man assured us would be a cinch to take over because he wanted to run it.

And now we're shocked, shocked and awed to discover that a crook is a crook and we have nobody to turn over Iraq to, and the Jordanian embezzler-turned-American puppet-turned-accused-Iranian-spy is trying to foment even more anger against us and the UN officials we've crawled back to for help, anger that may lead to civil war.

The party line that Paul Bremer was notified about the raid on Ahmad Chalabi's house after the fact is absurd. The Iraqi police, who can't seem to do anything without us, were just proxies. We were going after the very guy who persuaded us to go after Saddam, the con man the naive neocons cast as de Gaulle; the swindler who sold himself to Dick Cheney and Paul Wolfowitz as Spartacus.

One diplomat from the region grimly cited an old Punjabi saying: "It's very bad when grandma marries a crook, but it is even worse when she divorces the crook."

Mr. Chalabi's wealthy family was swept out of Iraq in a coup in 1958 and he spent much of his life plotting a coup to take back his homeland, a far-fetched scheme that took on life when he hooked up with Mr. Wolfowitz, Richard Perle and Doug Feith, who had their own dream of staging a coup of American foreign policy to do an extreme Middle East makeover.

The hawks dismissed warnings from their own people—such as the Bush Middle East envoy General Anthony Zinni—that the Iraqi National Congress was full of "silk-suited, Rolex-wearing guys in London." As General Zinni told the *Times* in 2000: "They are pie in the sky. They're going to lead us to a Bay of Goats, or something like that."

The CIA and State Department, too, grew disgusted with Mr. Chalabi, even though State paid his organization $33 million from 2000 to 2003.

Cheney & Co. swooned over Mr. Chalabi because he was telling them what they wanted to hear, that it would be simple to go back and rewrite the Persian Gulf war ending so that it was not *bellum interruptus.*

The president and his hawks insisted that only a "relatively small number" of "thugs," as Mr. Perle told George Stephanopoulos last month, were keeping the country from peace. Mr. Perle said the solution was "to repose a little bit of confidence in people who share our values and our objectives . . . people like Ahmad Chalabi." The neocons still think he can be Churchill.

On Thursday, an Iraqi judge, Hussain Muathin, also lamented the actions of "a small number of thugs." But he was announcing warrants for the arrest of thugs around Mr. Perle's own George Washington, Chalabi henchmen suspected of kidnapping, torture and theft. Didn't we sack Saddam to stop that stuff?

Now we're using Saddam's old generals to restore order—reversing the de-Baathification approach that Mr. Chalabi championed—while Mr. Chalabi snakes around like a bus-and-truck Tony Soprano, garnering less trust than Saddam in polls of Iraqis.

A half-dozen dunderheads who thought they knew everything assumed they could control Mr. Chalabi and use him as the instrument of their utopian fantasies. But one week after getting cut off from the $335,000-a-month Pentagon allowance arranged by his neocon buddies, he glibly accepts the street cred that goes with bashing America. And he still won't give us all of Saddam's secret files, which he confiscated and is using to discredit his enemies.

Going from Spartacus to Moses, he proclaims to America, "Let my people go"—even as he plays footsie with the country that once denounced the U.S. as the Great Satan.

On Friday at Louisiana State University, President Bush told graduates: "On the job and elsewhere in life, choose your friends carefully. The company you keep has a way of rubbing off on you—and that can be a good thing, or a bad thing. In my job, I got to pick just about everybody I work with. I've been happy with my choices—although I wish someone had warned me about all of Dick Cheney's wild partying."

Mr. Bush thought he was kidding, but too bad he didn't get that warning before Dick Cheney took the world on such a wild ride.

■

In Which the Skull and Bones Scions, One Who Saucily Sloughed Off and One Who Pompously Strived Up, Face Off

■

Gotta Lotta Stigmata

■

John Kerry is going to announce his candidacy for the presidency next week (who knew?) standing in front of an aircraft carrier.

That's a relief. If he had used the usual town square or high school gym backdrop, what would we have thought about his manliness?

Dropping his heroic military service into almost every speech has not been enough, nor has mounting his Harley in a bomber jacket whenever a TV camera's near.

Three Purple Hearts, a Silver Star and a Bronze Star in Vietnam should trump one lackadaisical Texas National Guard record, but we live in an age when "reality" is defined by ratings. So the issue is illusion: Can Senator Kerry match President Bush's ability to appropriate an aircraft carrier as a political prop?

Mr. Kerry, a Boston Democrat, had thought about announcing in front of a warship, wrote *The Boston Globe*'s Glen Johnson, but felt the need for something bigger, to stage a more chesty confrontation with Mr. Bush.

Even though his "Mission Accomplished" backdrop turned out to be woefully premature, W.'s Top Gun moment is immortalized with an action figure in a flight suit and the leg-hugging harness that made Republican women's hearts go *boom-boom*.

In presidential races, voters look for the fatherly protector. In the nineties, contenders showed softer sides, crying, wearing earth tones, confessing to family therapy.

But 9/11 and the wars that followed have made pols reluctant to reveal feminine sides. Howard Dean struts and attacks like a bantam, and wonky Bob Graham paid half a mil to plaster his name on a Nascar truck.

Out-he-manning the cowboy in chief, Arnold Schwarzenegger strides into the arena in a cloud of cordite, cigar smoke, Hummer fumes and heavier bicep reps.

Spike TV, the first men's channel, offers *Baywatch*, a Pamela Anderson cartoon called *Stripperella, The A-Team, American Gladiators, Car and Driver* and *Trucks*!

Conservatives want to co-opt all this free-floating testosterone and copyright the bravery shown on 9/11. They disparage liberals as people who scorn "traditional" male traits and sanction gay romance.

The cover of the American Enterprise Institute's magazine bellows: "Real Men: They're Back."

A roundtable discussion by conservative women produced the usual slavering over W. in his flight suit and Rummy in his gray suit.

"In George W. Bush, people see a contained, channeled virility," said Erica Walter, identified as "an at-home mom and Catholic writer." "They see a man who does what he says, whose every speech and act is not calculated."

Yeah. Nothing calculated about a president's delaying the troops from getting home and renting stadium lights so he can play dress up and make a movie star landing on an aircraft carrier gussied up by his image wizards, at a cost of a mil.

Kate O'Beirne of the *National Review* gushes: "When I heard that he grew up jumping rope with the girls in his neighborhood, I knew everything I needed to know about Bill Clinton. . . . Bill Clinton couldn't credibly wear jogging shorts, and look at George Bush in that flight suit."

On the men's roundtable, David Gutmann, a professor emeritus of psychology at Northwestern, notes that Mr. Bush "bears important masculine stigmata: he is a Texan, he is not afraid of war, and he sticks to his guns in the face of a worldwide storm of criticism."

Stigmata, schtigmata. Shouldn't real men be able to control their puppets? The Bush team could not even get Ahmad Chalabi and the Iraq Governing Council to condemn the UN bombing or feign putting an Iraqi face on the occupation. The puppets refused because they didn't want to be seen as puppets.

Shouldn't real men be able to admit they made a mistake and need help? Rummy & Co. bullied the UN and treated the allies like doormats before the war, thinking they could do everything themselves, thanks to the phony optimistic intelligence fed to them by the puppet Chalabi. No wonder they're meeting with a cold response as they slink back.

Shouldn't real men be reducing the number of Middle East terrorists rather than increasing them faster than dragon's teeth?

Could the real men please find some real men?

April 29, 2004

Guns and Peanut Butter

■

S o let's see. What's our swell choice here?

A guy who mimed being a fighter pilot on a carrier versus a guy who mimed throwing his medals over a fence?

An incumbent who sticks with the wrong decisions based on the wrong facts versus a challenger who seems unable to stick to one side of any decision, right or wrong?

A Republican who's a world-class optimist, despite making the world more dangerous and virulently anti-American, versus a Democrat who looks like a world-weary loner, even as he pledges to make the world safer and more pro-American?

A president who can't go anywhere without his vice president to give him the answers versus a candidate who can't go anywhere without his campaign butler/buddy to give him peanut butter and jelly sandwiches?

Bush campaign strategists don't seem worried that every positive development the administration predicted would happen if we invaded Iraq has soured into the opposite.

As an article on Monday in the *Times* noted about the growing ranks of angry Muslims: "The call to jihad is rising in the streets of Europe, and is being answered."

Communing with the Higher Father and the Almighty, President Bush has either stumbled into a holy war or swaggered into one.

In their new book, *The Bushes*, Peter and Rochelle Schweizer, who interviewed many Bushes, including the president's father and his brother Jeb, quote one unnamed relative as saying that W. sees the war on terror "as a religious war": "He doesn't have a PC view of this war. His view of this is that they are trying to kill the Christians. And we the Christians will strike back with more force and more ferocity than they will ever know."

Bush strategists seem to believe that the worse Mr. Bush makes things, the better off he is, because nervous Americans will cling to the obstinate president they know over the vacillating challenger they don't know.

Senator Kerry's talent for turning a winning proposition into a losing one is disturbingly reminiscent of Al Gore, who somehow managed to lose an election he won. So is Mr. Kerry's sometimes supercilious manner, and his habit of exacerbating a small thing with an answer that is not quite straight.

When the senator was asked last week whether he owned a gas-scarfing Chevy Suburban SUV, he replied, "I don't own an SUV," only to have to admit, when pressed further by reporters, that his wife owns the SUV. "The family has it," he said lamely. "I don't have it."

The White House pounds Mr. Kerry for not playing straight on small-bore stuff, even as they don't play straight on huge-bore stuff.

The House Democratic leader, Nancy Pelosi, pronounced the administration "in denial" yesterday, after hearing Condi Rice's briefing for House Democratic lawmakers.

"This is an administration that told us that our troops would be welcomed with roses," Representative Pelosi said. "Instead, it's rocket-propelled grenades. This is an administration that told us that the Iraqi government would be able to pay for its own reconstruction, and soon. And now it's costing nearly $200 billion to the American people."

She added: "And it was expressed by the national security adviser now that yes, there was disappointment—disappointment?—about the Iraqi security forces not being able to secure the region that they were assigned to. And this is the judgment that the American people have placed their confidence in?"

Mr. Kerry errs on the side of giving the answer he thinks people want to hear, even as Mr. Bush errs on the side of giving the answer he expects people to accept as true.

When the president was asked yesterday by a reporter whether it would take an all-out military offensive to put down the violence in Falluja, and whether this would impede the transfer of power on June 30, he was reassuring, despite news of the aerial bombardment of Falluja by U.S. gunships and the seventy-ton battle tanks being rushed in to aid Marines in the escalating fight.

"Most of Falluja is returning to normal," the president said, presumably defining normal as flattened.

Anyway, is that ten minutes to normal, as Karen Hughes would say? Or ten years to normal? And what on earth is normal, when you're talking about Iraq chaos theory?

I Read, I Smoke, I Spin

■

Laura Bush does not want that Chanel-wearing, shawl-draping, senator-marrying Teresa Heinz Kerry to get her house.

It's a swell house, with doting servants, fresh flowers and grand paintings.

And she does not want her Bushie to be tarred for lacking character, after he ascended by promising to restore character to an Oval Office still redolent of thongs and pizza.

So the reserved librarian who married the rollicking oilman on the condition that she would never have to make a political speech has suddenly transformed herself into a sharp-edged, defensive protectrix of her husband's record.

Many White House reporters, including ones the first lady has been testy and sarcastic with, say they are thrilled with the new Laura. They found the old Laura "plastic" and "unreal," limited to treacly concerns about children, reading and being George's rock. The new Laura, they say, has "juice."

But I kind of miss the old Laura, the one who long ago shocked W.'s paternal grandmother by describing her interests in a way that sounded, heaven forfend, French: "I read, I smoke and I admire." The new Laura reads polls, fumes and admonishes. A cool Marian the Librarian morphed into a hot Mary Matalin, running around the country spinning reporters, slicing and dicing Democrats, and raking in dough at fund-raisers.

I always had a cozy image of Laura Bush curled up in a window seat in the White House solarium, reading Dostoyevsky and petting a cat dozing beside her. She seemed beyond politics, an estimably private, utterly classy presence unsullied by the nasty edge that Bush family politics takes on when a Bush pol gets in trouble, not the sort to needle political rivals and the press or rigorously catalog injustices the way Barbara Bush did.

Not that Laura was bland. I liked the confidence with which this champion of literacy blew off the poets she'd invited to the White House last year, once she realized they planned to do to her husband what Eartha Kitt did to Lyndon Johnson—turn a cultural event into an antiwar protest. It was her party, and she could cry foul if she wanted.

During the 2000 campaign, she was content to be the serene counterpoint to her husband's boyish bouncing off the walls. She rejected Hillary's two-for-the-price-of-one mantra and told the *Times*'s Frank Bruni, "I'm not that knowledgeable about most issues. . . . And just to put in my two cents to put in my two cents—I don't think it's really necessary."

Bush advisers liked her detachment from the messy arena. They thought she made her husband seem grounded, moderate and down to earth, a contrast with the obsessive, egoistic ambition of the Clintons and Al Gore.

But this time around, it is Mr. Bush who is getting attacked on credibility and do-whatever-it-takes ambition. His strategists, panicked about chaotic Iraq, confused economic policy, cascading deficits and incoherent National Guard records, needed to draw, if you'll pardon the expression, the most unimpeachable person in the White House into the fray. They pitched her as Mr. Bush's secret weapon. Maybe, after the David Kay debacle, the White House just needed to unearth a weapon—any weapon.

The woman known for telling her husband to tone it down is now telling his critics to get lost. In an interview with the A.P. on Thursday, she said of the National Guard flap: "I think it's a political, you know, witch hunt, actually, on the part of Democrats."

Speaking to the *Times*'s Elisabeth Bumiller, a prickly Mrs. Bush defended her husband on Iraq and shared the chip on his shoulder about the East Coast elite, apparently resentful that they might consider her a fifties throwback, doing women's work.

Talking to ABC's Terry Moran, Mrs. Bush harshly responded to Terry McAuliffe's AWOL charge: "I don't think it's fair to really lie about allegations about someone." She stated flatly that W. was pulling Guard duty in Alabama. When Mr. Moran asked how she knew, she replied, "Well, because he told me he was."

The last time a powerful man from Texas got into trouble and sent his wife out to defend him, it was W. contributor Kenny Boy Lay.

The president can't skirt the issues by hiding behind Laura's skirts forever. One way of showing character is to come out from behind all her protestations about his character.

See Dick Run

■

You've got to admire the Bush reelection ads being rolled out today. With up to $60 million to spend by convention time, the campaign is plotting the most expensive political advertising seduction in history, and you can see the money on the screen.

In scary/gauzy images, the president does his best to shift the blame, take the credit and transmit concern about regular folks—waitresses, welders, firefighters, black children, black seniors, middle-class families—when he really spends more time helping his fat-cat corporate friends.

Mr. Bush keeps implying that we should be scared because we're not safe, so we need to keep him to protect national security. Which seems like a weird contradiction. If he's so good at protecting us, why aren't we safe?

The president doesn't hesitate to exploit 9/11 in his ads, even as he tries to keep 9/11 orphans and widows in the dark about what really happened.

President Bush's ad flashes a shot of firefighters removing some flag-draped remains of a victim from the wreckage at ground zero even as he prohibits the filming of flag-draped remains of soldiers coming home from Iraq and Afghanistan. You might call the Bush ads, an homage to Ronald Reagan's famous ads, "Mourning in America."

Nothing like hypocrisy with high production values.

I'm assuming that the second phase of the ad blitz will highlight the man with the plan: Dick Cheney. The Cheney ads could appeal to the base, featuring rich white men in the backseats of limos, showing how hard it is to make the tough decisions for you.

Consider the possibilities:

ON THE SCREEN: The spot lingers on a shot of the vice president's office door, closed and padlocked.

THE SCRIPT: "Big enough to tell you to butt out. Sensitive enough to know that special interests are truly special."

■

ON THE SCREEN: A tightly focused shot of a headless pheasant dissolves into a shot of a big Dick Cheney putting a miniature Antonin Scalia into the pocket of his Elmer Fudd hunting jacket.

THE SCRIPT: "Man enough to hunt with all the big dogs."

■

ON THE SCREEN: The spot opens with Mr. Cheney checking his mailbox for his annual deferred compensation check for $150,000 from Halliburton.

THE SCRIPT: "Bighearted enough to forgive and forget Halliburton's pesky overcharges in Iraq for oil, and food for American troops."

ON THE SCREEN: A picture of Mr. Cheney beaming at his family.

THE SCRIPT: "Strong enough to put his base above his daughter and support a constitutional amendment against gay marriage."

∎

ON THE SCREEN: A close-up of Mr. Cheney with a huge NRA check.

THE SCRIPT: "Protective enough to safeguard the firearms industry from liberal potshots."

∎

ON THE SCREEN: While "Pink Panther" music plays, a cartoonish vice president, with an Inspector Clouseau trench coat and a mustache, wanders the desert with a spyglass.

THE SCRIPT: "Steely enough to ignore the administration's intelligence on the absence of WMD and an Al Qaeda link to Saddam. Farsighted enough to know that one of these decades, the rocks and trash Iraqis throw at U.S. forces will be replaced by flowers and palm fronds."

∎

ON THE SCREEN: A doctored photo of John Kerry, his war medals airbrushed out, canoodling with Jane Fonda at an antiwar rally.

THE SCRIPT: "After getting four student deferments himself during Vietnam so he could attend to 'other priorities,' he's still gritty enough to paint John Kerry as a spineless wimp on Vietnam and Iraq."

∎

ON THE SCREEN: An ominous close-up of Mr. Cheney's spider hole.

THE SCRIPT: "Brazen enough to say deficits don't matter, and to send Dennis Hastert out to chide Kerry as a big-time deficit spender."

■

ON THE SCREEN: A shot of Mr. Cheney driving the Nascar Viagra race car.

THE SCRIPT: "Audacious enough to shred the American Constitution, even while he imposes one on Iraq."

■

Instead of saying he approved the message, as Mr. Bush does in his ads, Mr. Cheney comes on at the end of his spots with a paper bag over his head and says, "It's none of your beeswax who approved this message." Except in one, where a rotund man comes on and says, "I am Ahmad Chalabi, and I approved this message."

Cultural Drifter

■

Here are some things you might not know about George W. Bush:

- He hasn't gone out to see a movie in the last five years.
- He likes Van Morrison.
- The last actress who made his heart race was Julie Christie in *Doctor Zhivago.*
- He doesn't identify with any literary heroes, but is drawn to Paul Newman's defiance in *Cool Hand Luke* and Jack Nicholson's irreverence.
- He loved *Cats.*

In an interview about culture, W. gamely concedes there are yawning gaps. Baseball, he says, is his favorite "cultural experience." (Like his father, he views cultural questions as some kind of psychoanalysis.)

We're in a van on the way to Reagan Airport after his speech to the Christian Coalition.

He has one word for opera: "No." He likes "nice, quiet jazz on the radio." He went to one ballet "and was amazed by the athleticism."

Although some of the Bushes are musical—his uncle Jonathan was in a Bronx revival of *Oklahoma* in 1958 and his uncle Bucky plays the guitar and sings—W. is not.

"I loved *Cats*," he says brightly.

He said he doesn't watch TV series, just news and sports. "Culturally adrift," he says, making a funny face. "Occasionally, I'll cruise into an A&E biography. The last one I saw was about me."

He avoids cable chat. "Now that I'm the subject, there's no telling what you'll hear about yourself. So I've just chosen not to listen."

He says he's usually asleep by Leno and Letterman, but adds: "They're actually very funny. Even at my own expense."

I asked if he and his wife, Laura, ever fight over the clicker. He says he's mostly doing work stuff or falling asleep. "We're both usually reading instead of battling over flickers."

He did not try to impress his librarian wife when they were dating by reading more. "Our first date was to go play putt-putt golf," he says.

As to literary preferences, he said: "I've always liked John La Care, Le Carrier, or however you pronounce his name. I'm mainly a history person." He's just finished *Isaac's Storm*, a history of the Galveston hurricane of 1900, and reads Robert Parker's detective-for-hire stories.

Asked if he likes movies, he says: "Not too much. I like 'em O.K. I haven't been to a movie theater since I've been governor. We occasionally rent movies. We've got a Blockbuster card the girls use more than Laura and me. The last movie I saw I really liked was *Saving Private Ryan*.

"But prior to getting elected I did go to movies. Laura and I were talking the other day about the last time we'd gone to a movie. I think it was the day Ann Richards called me a jerk. It was *Forrest Gump*."

Has he ever censored his twin seventeen-year-old daughters' movie picks? "I can't think of anything. Uh-oh, a giant hole in the net of censorship."

In an interview with *GQ*, the fifty-three-year-old governor said that when he was at Yale in the sixties, he did not share the musical tastes of the counterculture. He said he liked the Beatles before their "weird, psychedelic period."

I asked who was his favorite Beatle. "The first drummer," he joked. "As you know I was a fraternity man at Yale. I had parties. We had a lot of groups come in. I just was not, I mean, I like music. But I'm not a great aficionado of music."

Asked if he would set a cultural tone in the White House closer to Jackie's Pablo Casals or Bill's Kenny G, W. replied: "I imagine it would be eclectic. You know we've had Lyle Lovett come to the mansion to play. I probably won't be spending a lot of time making the list up. I'll delegate."

W. sometimes waggles his hips when he's on a stage. Does he like to dance?

"No," he said. "It's not a religious thing. I just don't dance. At the last inauguration, I did the box step for about 25 seconds and declared my dancing over for the year. . . . I don't go to dances and I don't socialize very much."

Asked about Warren Beatty's presidential flirting, W. asks something that probably hasn't even dawned on the Hollywood star: "The question is, Can he survive the Iowa caucuses?"

The governor's perfect day would include running, fishing and watching sports on TV, followed by dinner with friends with Van Morrison playing in the background. Then, bed by ten.

Is this a great country or what?

JFK, Marilyn, "Camelot"

■

Here are five things you might not know about John F. Kerry:

- Like W., he loved *Cats*.
- Like his hero JFK, he was crazy about the musical *Camelot* and Marilyn Monroe (but only on screen).
- Like that other earnest Massachusetts liberal, Michael Dukakis, he is drawn to the sultry tango. (Then again, tango is called the dance of "vertical solitude.")
- Like Dennis Kucinich, he writes soulful poetry.
- Like my older brother Michael, he never got over the image of Elizabeth Taylor in a white bathing suit in *A Place in the Sun*.

It's not often that you get a presidential candidate to recite poetry to you, especially in a year when W. and JFK are going macho a macho. But there was Mr. Kerry flying from Boston to New Orleans on

Friday, sipping tea for his hoarse throat and reeling off T. S. Eliot's *Love Song of J. Alfred Prufrock.*

"There are so many great lines in it," he said. " 'Do I dare to eat a peach?' 'Should I wear my trousers rolled?' 'Let us go, through certain half-deserted streets/The muttering retreats/Of restless nights in one-night cheap hotels/And sawdust restaurants with oyster-shells.' "

Then he started on *Gunga Din* and " 'talk o' gin and beer.' "

When I gave George W. Bush a culture quiz in 2000, he gamely struggled to come up with one answer in each category, calling baseball his favorite "cultural experience."

Mr. Kerry, on the other hand, struggled to stop coming up with a cascade of things in each category, rarely settling on a definite favorite.

In what may be an interesting harbinger for their debates, W. raced through his whole interview in the same time Mr. Kerry took to answer the first question about his favorite movie. After he had roamed through thirty-seven movies, ranging from his "Fellini stage" to his Adam Sandler period, from *National Velvet* to *The Deer Hunter* to *Men in Black*, and nine favorite actors, Mr. Kerry's aides began to hover.

The Republicans would denounce it as film flip-flopping, no doubt. But in culture, as in policy, the senator and the president proved very different creatures—the complicated versus the concrete, the "insatiable," as Teresa Heinz Kerry calls her husband's interests, versus the incurious.

Mr. Kerry is not a simple brush-clearing, ESPN-watching fellow. Just as he has an almost comically vast palette of aggressive masculine sports and hobbies, with costumes and gear, he has a vast palette of cultural preferences.

He not only reads poetry—"I love Keats, Yeats, Shelley and

Kipling"—he writes it. "I remember flying once; I was looking out at the desert and I wrote a poem about the barren desolation of the desert," he said. "I wrote a poem once about a great encounter I had with a deer early in the morning that was very moving."

Still showing his phantom Irish side, he pronounced Leon Uris's *Trinity* his favorite novel, and said he once explored making it into a movie. Then he tacked on Huck Finn, Tom Sawyer and the Hardy Boys—"all those good dudes." Then, remembering he's in an alpha race, he added portentously: "We all were affected by Hemingway."

Dan Rather may have been skeptical in the last debate about whether Mr. Kerry has enough Elvis in him, but the senator said he learned the guitar and played in a band because he loves Elvis, Buddy Holly, the Beatles, the Rolling Stones, the Grateful Dead—not to mention classical, opera and, yes, folk music.

Though he dated Morgan Fairchild, Mr. Kerry has no interest in prime time now: "*Saturday Night Live*'s my favorite show."

Though critics paint him as pompous, Mr. Kerry dares to be corny. He says he's a "sap" for movies like *It's a Wonderful Life, Miracle on 34th Street* and *Braveheart*, and a "sucker" for musicals like *Les Miserables, Phantom of the Opera* and *My Fair Lady*. He says he likes airport mysteries and thrillers as well as biographies of Teddy Roosevelt and Lincoln.

The Republicans cast Mr. Kerry as dour and angry, but he likes comedies like *The Blues Brothers* and *Animal House* and old-fashioned romantic epics, like *Scaramouche, Ivanhoe* and *Indiana Jones*.

And finally, dancing. "I can rock and roll," he said. "And I'd love to learn to tango." With trousers rolled, no doubt.

Whence the Wince?

■

A few years back, some Hollywood TV producers I know were thinking about making a sitcom with Cher. Before they committed, they wanted to be sure that, after all the work she'd had done on her face, Cher could still actually move it.

They went to her house and secretly tested her ability to react, asking questions to elicit various emotions.

With all the fuss about the sixty-year-old John Kerry going from Shar-Pei to whippet, I figured a physiognomic quiz might be in order. The candidate's more serene visage has spurred rampant speculation that his attractive sixty-five-year-old wife, Teresa, a Botox aficionado, turned him on to the wrinkle diffuser, which paralyzes the muscles that deepen wrinkles.

How could we elect a president who couldn't show his emotions? After all, the leader of the free world has even more reason to frown, wince and be startled than a sitcom star.

I tracked down Senator Kerry on Tuesday in Evanston, Illinois.

My plan was to start by needling him into a frown. (Dermatological entrapment.)

I observe that the Republicans have cast him as the melancholy, indecisive Hamlet to President Bush's vigorous Prince Hal.

Nary a Kerry glower. "They'll try to be destructive," he says. "I'm a tough fighter." (Yesterday, he called them "the most crooked, you know, lying group I've ever seen.")

I press on, trying for an extreme facial expression: "Do you think that you were rolled on Iraq by the administration?" "There was a sense of that at first," he replies placidly. "But the answer is no because then Scowcroft and Jim Baker went very public in their dissent about the UN and not doing this properly."

Desperate for furrows, I recite unflattering depictions: Roger Simon saying he put the "grave" into gravitas; *The New Yorker* calling him "sepulchral"; the Republican pollster Kellyanne Conway saying he looks as if he "sucked on a lemon."

"Sometimes it's been my own fault," he says, his voice, and face, stubbornly affectless. "I can be as wild and crazy as the next person."

O.K., I think, I'll go for a wince. I've been struck by the nasty Republican habit of portraying opponents as less than fully masculine. They called John Edwards the "Breck girl" and John Kerry French-looking.

I figure that the skin on Senator Kerry's face will certainly rise at the mention of Dick Cheney's Gridiron speech, teasing that since Botox is related to botulism toxin, maybe David Kay should search for missing biowarfare agents in Senator Kerry's forehead. Is this a way to mock him for an effeminate vanity?

"No, I don't have it," he says coolly. "Vanity or Botox?" I ask, grimacing. "I don't have Botox, but whatever their game is, I don't care," he replies without a wisp of a wince. "That sort of thing is so childish. In the end, people will care about real choices that affect their lives."

O.K., I decide, I'll escalate. I broach Hillary Clinton's plans for 2008, with the implication that she and her gang can't be genuinely committed to a Kerry victory. I tell him that after Rudy Giuliani joked at the Gridiron that the one thing he and Hillary had in common was that they were both voting for George W. Bush, Hillary grinned and playfully high-fived him.

Mr. Kerry does not rise to the bait. "I have confidence that Hillary and the president will be part of this team," he says without excess emotion, adding that, unlike Al Gore, he wants Bill Clinton's help.

This isn't working. I have to shock him. I mention Skull and Bones, in the hope that it will show on his skull and bones. But instead of bolting from the room in horror, he simply smiles and notes that he and W. had a "nice" phone conversation.

On the other hand, maybe a poker face could be an advantage in the Oval Office. After all, Hollywood agents get Botox so they can be expressionless while making big deals.

And think of all the pols who could have benefited from modern cosmetic techniques. William Howard Taft could have been liposuctioned. Richard Nixon could have used Botox to stop his sweating, as Fortune 500 execs do now. And Al Gore could have frozen those condescending eyebrows during the 2000 debate.

Finally, I give up. The interview ends with a frown—not John Kerry's.

The Politics of Self-Pity

■

Republicans relished their philosophy of personal responsibility last week with John Belushi's famous mantra: Cheeseburger-cheeseburgercheeseburger.

When the House passed the "cheeseburger bill" to bar people from suing fast-food joints for making them obese, Republican backers of the legislation scolded Americans, saying the fault lies not in their fries, but in themselves.

"Look in the mirror, because you're the one to blame," said F. James Sensenbrenner, Jr., of Wisconsin, home of brats and beer bellies.

So it comes as something of a disappointment that the leader of the Republican Party, the man who epitomizes the conservative ideal, is playing the victim. President Bush has made the theme of his reelection campaign a whiny "not my fault."

His ads, pilloried for the crass use of the images of a flag-draped body carried from ground zero and an Arab-looking everyman with the message, "We can fight against terrorists," actually have a more fundamental problem. They try to push off blame for anything that's gone wrong during Mr. Bush's tenure on bigger forces, supposedly beyond his control.

One ad cites "an economy in recession. A stock market in decline. A dot-com boom gone bust. Then a day of tragedy. A test for all Americans."

Mr. Bush's subtext is clear: If it weren't for all these awful things that happened, most of them hangovers from the Clinton era, I definitely could have fulfilled all my promises. I'm still great, but none of my programs worked because, well, stuff happens."

It's as if his inner fat boy is complaining that a classic triple cheeseburger from Wendy's (940 calories and 56 grams of fat, 25 of them saturated, and 2,140 milligrams of sodium) jumped out of its wrapper and forced its way down his unwilling throat, topped off by a pushy Frosty (540 calories and 13 grams of fat, 8 of them saturated).

Mr. Bush has been in office over three years. It's time to start accepting some responsibility.

Republicans have a bad habit of laying down rules for other people to follow while excluding themselves. Look how they beat up Bill Clinton for messing around with a young woman, while many top Republicans were doing the very same thing.

Mr. Bush's whining was infectious. The very House Republicans who greased the skids for the cheeseburger bill got in a huff over John Kerry's overheard comment to some supporters in Chicago that his Republican critics were "the most crooked, you know, lying group" he'd ever seen.

These tough-guy Republicans, who rule the House with an iron fist, were suddenly squealing like schoolgirls at being victimized by big, bad John Kerry. J. Dennis Hastert, the House speaker, said Mr.

Kerry would have his "upcomeance coming." Tom DeLay sulked that the public was getting "a glimpse of the real John Kerry." The hammer was talking like a nail.

Marc Racicot, Mr. Bush's campaign chairman, accused Mr. Kerry of "unbecoming" conduct and called on him to apologize.

Oh, the poor dears. The very Bush crowd that savaged John McCain in South Carolina, that bullied and antagonized the allies we need in the real war on terror, that is spending $100 million on ads that will turn Mr. Kerry into something akin to the Boston Strangler; these guys are suddenly such delicate flowers, such big bawling babies, that they can't bear to hear Mr. Kerry speak of them harshly.

Mr. Bush is not believable in the victim's role. He and Dick Cheney have audaciously imposed their will on Washington and the world.

We are not yet sure who is behind the horrendous bombings in Spain, but they have already underscored how vulnerable our trains and subways are. And they have reminded us that the administration diverted resources from the war on terror and the search for Osama to settle old scores in Iraq, building a case for war with hyped and phony claims on weapons.

In an interview with *The Guardian*, the weapons sleuth David Kay said it's time for Mr. Bush to take personal responsibility: "It's about confronting and coming clean with the American people. . . . He should say: 'We were mistaken and I am determined to find out why.'"

In other words, Mr. Bush, look in the mirror.

March 18, 2004

Pride and Prejudice

■

House Republicans haven't suggested an embargo on olives and paella yet, but it's probably just *pocos minutos* away. By the time these guys are through, it will be unpatriotic to consume any ethnic food but fish and chips and kielbasa, washed down with a fine Bulgarian wine.

Republicans like Dennis Hastert were ranting yesterday about the Spaniards. "Here's a country who stood against terrorism and had a huge terrorist act within their country," Mr. Hastert said, "and they chose to change their government to, in a sense, appease terrorists."

The Republicans prefer to paint our old ally as craven rather than accept the Spanish people's judgment—which most had held since before the war—that the Iraq takeover had nothing to do with the war on terror.

The Spanish were also angry at Jose Maria Aznar because they felt he had misled them about the bombings, trying to throw guilt on ETA and away from Al Qaeda. The Republicans certainly don't want anyone here to think about throwing somebody out of office because he was misleading about Al Qaeda.

During a photo op with Prime Minister Jan Peter Balkenende of the Netherlands on Tuesday, Mr. Bush did his *Beavis and Butt-head* snigger as a Dutch reporter noted that most of his countrymen want to withdraw Dutch troops from Iraq because they think the conflict "has little to do with the war against terrorism, and may actually encourage terrorism." (Uh-oh, looks like no tulips on the Capitol grounds this spring.)

"I would ask them," the president replied, "to think about the Iraqi citizens who don't want people to withdraw because they want to be free."

Now that he hasn't found any weapons, Mr. Bush says the war was worth it so Iraqis could experience democracy. But when our allies engage in democracy, some Republicans mock them as lily-livered.

The Republicans treat John Kerry as disdainfully as they do the European allies who have disappointed the White House, painting him as a French-looking dude who went to a Swiss boarding school, as an effete Brahmin who would rather cut intelligence and military spending than face down terrorists.

The election is shaping up as a contest between Pride and Prejudice.

Mr. Kerry is Pride.

He has a tendency toward striped-trouser smugness that led him to stupidly boast that he was more popular with leaders abroad than President Bush—playing into the Republican strategy to depict him as one of those "cheese-eating surrender monkeys."

Even when he puts on that barn jacket over his expensive suit to look less lockjaw—and says things like, "Who among us doesn't like

NASCAR"—he can come across like Mr. Collins, Elizabeth Bennet's pretentious cousin in *Pride and Prejudice*. Mr. Collins always prattles on about how lucky people would be to be rewarded by his patron, Lady Catherine de Bourgh, with "some portion of her notice" and to receive dollops of her "condescension."

Speaking to Chicago union workers last week, Mr. Kerry happily informed them that on the ride over, his wife, Teresa, had said she could live in Chicago. What affability, as Mr. Collins would say, what condescension.

Mr. Bush is Prejudice.

Like Miss Bennet, who irrationally arranged the facts to fit her initial negative assessment of Mr. Darcy, Mr. Bush irrationally arranges the facts to fit his initial assessment that 9/11 justified blowing off the UN and some close allies to invade Iraq.

The president and vice president seem incapable of admitting any error, especially that their experienced foreign policy team did not see through Saddam's tricks. As Hans Blix told a reporter, Saddam had put up a "Beware of Dog" sign, so he didn't bother with the dog. How can they recalibrate the game plan when they won't concede that they called the wrong game plan to start?

When he challenged Mr. Kerry to put up or shut up on his claim of support from foreign leaders, Mr. Bush said, "If you're going to make an accusation in the course of a presidential campaign, you've got to back it up with facts."

If you're going to make an accusation in the course of a presidency, you've got to back it up with facts, too.

■

In Memoriam

■

April 6, 2003

"The Best Possible Life"

■

Michael Kelly was a lucky guy.
When he stumbled upon a column of Iraqi troops during Desert Storm, they surrendered to him, piling into his car with their white flags.

He was the only reporter to find passion in the Dukakis campaign; he met his future wife, Max Greenberg, a beguiling CBS producer, on the bus.

Michael always seemed to be in the right place at the right time to get the best quote and the best story, the best jobs and the best life.

"I've had one good break after another," he told *The Boston Globe*, in an interview last year about how he'd revived *The Atlantic Monthly* in just two years as its editor. Cruising in his 1966 baby blue Mustang convertible, he said he'd had "a long series of lucky breaks and good jobs and stories and a life I like living."

He did many things well enough to provoke envy: He was a dazzling writer, editor, dancer, cook. Except he wasn't the sort you'd envy; he was too generous. He'd had his share of donnybrooks, in print and out, but he was, to use one of his own terms of endearment, a "lambikins."

When I had boyfriend troubles or work troubles, I would show up at his house in Washington. He would always be sprawling on the chaise longue I gave him as a wedding present, reading Orwell or A. J. Liebling or John O'Hara. And he would always get up and make a gourmet meal, with wine he'd chosen and herbs he'd grown, for Max and me.

He liked to say he'd had "an unusually seamless life." He was crazy about his parents, Tom and Marguerite, and wanted to become a reporter because his dad had been a reporter at *The Washington Daily News*.

"My father would bring me in on Saturdays to the newsroom—an old-fashioned one with the bookie in the corner, reporters bringing in beer—and I would hang out," he told our friend Diana McLellan.

Even at forty-six, the father of two little boys, Michael never lost the raffish air of an altar boy who'd just talked a nun into letting him smoke a cigar in the sacristy.

He looked like a Dead End Kid, an Irish imp with blue eyes, pug nose, round face and round glasses. He was wickedly funny, a great mimic who made people laugh so hard that the section where we worked at the *Times* was dubbed "Happy Valley."

He had many important jobs but no phony airs. He went to parties at his local firehouse way before 9/11. He was deeply sentimental about ordinary working-class people—and maintained an angry outsider posture in his column even as he was embraced by the conservative mandarins of Washington.

"He had enviable eyes," said Leon Wieseltier, his colleague at *The New Republic*. "He observed more in a glance than other reporters did in a week."

The boy could write.

On the decline of liberalism: "Its animating impulse is . . . to make itself as unattractive to as many as possible: if it were a person, it would pierce its tongue."

On Ross Perot: "H. Ross Perot made his way onto the national stage, barking like a dog and occasionally biting off small pieces of himself."

On the first gulf war's bombing of Baghdad: "The tracer rounds made lines of incandescent beauty, lovely arcing curves and slow *S*s and parabolas of light."

He said war reporters were people "who did not want to get in harm's way but merely close enough to record the fate of those who did."

But he put himself in harm's way because he wanted to go back to Baghdad and see America kick out Saddam. "Tyranny truly is a horror. . . . It is, as Orwell wrote, a jackboot forever stomping on a human face."

Michael was the first American reporter to die in Iraq, when the Army Humvee he was riding in came under Iraqi fire and rolled into a canal south of Baghdad airport.

At an impromptu wake at his parents' house on Capitol Hill Friday, Marguerite Kelly, who writes a *Washington Post* column about raising children, put out her usual spread of food. And Tom told friends his son was lucky: He had had the best possible life for a journalist and died well, better than full of tubes in a hospital somewhere.

Michael died for two things he believed in: journalism and ridding the world of jackboots.

And as Pat Moynihan said when he learned JFK was dead: "I don't think there's any point in being Irish if you don't know that the world is going to break your heart eventually."

Death Be Not Loud

■

W ho can blame poor President Bush? Look at his terrible dilemma.

There are those who say the chief executive should have come out of his Texas ranch house and articulated and assuaged the sorrow and outrage and anxiety the nation was feeling on Sunday after the deadliest day in Iraq in seven months. An attack on a Chinook helicopter had killed fifteen American soldiers, thirteen men and two women, and wounded twenty-one.

There are those who say Mr. Bush should have emulated Rudy Giuliani's empathetic leadership after 9/11, or Dad's in the first gulf war, and attended some of the funerals of the 379 Americans killed in Iraq. Or one. Maybe the one for Specialist Darryl Dent, the twenty-one-year-old National Guard officer from Washington who died outside Baghdad in late August when a bomb struck his truck while he was delivering mail to troops. His funeral was held at a Baptist church three miles from the White House.

But let's look at it from the president's point of view: If he grieves more publicly or concretely, if he addresses every instance of bad news, like the hideous specter of Iraqis celebrating the downing of the Chinook, he will simply remind people of what's going on in Iraq.

So it's understandable why, going into his reelection campaign, Mr. Bush wouldn't want to underscore that young Americans keep getting whacked over there, and we don't know who is doing it or how to stop it.

The White House is cleverly trying to distance Mr. Bush from the messy problem of flesh-and-blood soldiers with real names dying nearly every day, while linking him to the heroic task of fighting global terror.

It's better to keep it vague, to talk about the "important cause" and the "brave defenders" of liberty.

If he gets more explicit, or allows the flag-draped coffins of fallen heroes to be photographed coming home, it will just remind people that the administration said this would be easy, and it's teeth-grindingly hard. And that the administration vowed to get Osama and Saddam and WMD, and hasn't. And that the Bush team that hyped the presence of Al Qaeda in Iraq has now created an Al Qaeda presence in Iraq. And that there was no decent plan for the occupation or for financing one, no plan for rotating or supporting troops stretched too thin to guard ammunition caches or police a fractious society, and no plan for getting out.

As the White House points out, Mr. Bush cannot fairly pick and choose which memorial services to go to, or which deaths to speak of.

"If a helicopter were hit an hour later, after he came out and spoke, should he come out again?" Dan Bartlett, the White House communications director, told the *Times*'s Elisabeth Bumiller, explaining Mr. Bush's silence after the Chinook crash. The public, he added, "wants the commander in chief to have proper perspective, and keep his eye on the big picture and the ball."

The ball for fall is fund-raising. President Bush has been going full throttle since summer, spending several days a week flying around the country, hitting up rich Republicans for $2,000 checks. He has raised $90 million so far out of the $175 million he plans to spend on a primary campaign in which he has no opponent.

At fund-raisers, Mr. Bush prefers to talk about the uptick in the economy, not the downtick in Iraq. On Monday, arriving for a fund-raiser in Birmingham, he was upbeat, not somber. As Mike Allen of *The Washington Post* reported in his pool report, "The president, who gave his usual salute as he stepped off Marine One, appeared to start the day in a fabulous mood. . . . An Alabama reporter who was under the wing shouted, 'How long will U.S. troops be in Iraq?' The president gave him an unappreciative look."

Raising $1.8 million at lunch, he stuck to the line that "we are aggressively striking the terrorists in Iraq, defeating them there so we will not have to face them in our own country." He didn't want to depress the donors by mentioning the big news story, the loss of fifteen American soldiers, or sour the mood by conceding the obvious, that the swelling horde of terrorists fighting us there will not prevent terrorists from coming after us here. Maybe we should all be like President Bush and not read the papers so we don't get worn down either.

Perhaps the solution to Mr. Bush's quandary is to coordinate his schedule so he can go to cities where he can attend both fund-raisers and funerals.

The law of averages suggests it shouldn't be hard.

Wolfie's Fuzzy Math

■

T his administration is the opposite of *The Sixth Sense.*
They don't see any dead people.

Beyond the president's glaring absence at military funerals; beyond the Pentagon's self-serving ban on photographing the returning flag-draped coffins at Dover; beyond playing down the thousands
of wounded and maimed American troops and the thousands of hurt
and dead Iraqi civilians, now comes the cruel arithmetic of Paul
Wolfowitz.

What can you say about a deputy defense secretary so eager to invade Iraq he was nicknamed Wolfowitz of Arabia, so bullish to remold the Middle East he froze the State Department out of the
occupation and then mangled it, who doesn't bother to keep track of
the young Americans who died for his delusion?

Those troops were killed while they were still trying to fathom
the treacherous tribal and religious beehive they were never pre-

pared for, since they thought they'd be helping build schools and hospitals for grateful Iraqis.

Asked during a congressional budget hearing on Thursday how many American troops had been killed in Iraq, Mr. Wolfowitz missed by more than 30 percent. "It's approximately 500, of which—I can get the exact numbers—approximately 350 are combat deaths," he said.

As of Thursday, there were 722 deaths, 521 in combat. The number two man at the Pentagon was oblivious in the bloodiest month of the war, with the number of Americans killed in April overtaking those killed in the six-week siege of Baghdad last year.

This is, of course, an administration that refuses to quantify or acknowledge the cost of its chuckleheaded empire policies, in bodies, money, credibility in the Arab world, reputation among our allies or the reinvigoration of militant Muslims around the globe. Duped themselves, they duped Americans into thinking it would be easy, paid for with Iraqi oil. But Donald Rumsfeld's vision of showing off a slim, agile military was always at odds with the neocons' vision of infusing enough security into Iraq to turn it into an instant democratic paradise.

Crushed in the collision of these two grandiose dreams are all the smaller dreams of fallen soldiers, to raise kids and watch baseball and grill hot dogs on the Fourth of July.

Now things have deteriorated to the point that the administration is pathetically begging for help from the very people it was trying to roll over—the UN, Saddam's Baathist generals and the Iranians.

When Ted Koppel decided to devote his Friday *Nightline* to showing the faces and reading the names of the men and women killed in action, Bill Kristol of *The Weekly Standard* denounced it as "a stupid statement" and the conservative Sinclair media company, one of the country's largest owners of local stations, said it would pre-empt the program on its ABC affiliates. Sinclair, a big Republican donor, felt Mr. Koppel was undermining the war effort.

Bill O'Reilly suggested that CBS, by breaking the news of the grotesque pictures of American soldiers gaily tormenting Iraqi prisoners, had put American lives at risk.

But it's unhealthy to censor the ugly realities of war. The real danger is when the architects of war refuse to rethink bad assumptions, wrapping themselves in the blindly ideological nobility of their mission.

Senator John McCain let Sinclair have it with both barrels, noting that the public needed "to be reminded of war's terrible costs, in all their heartbreaking detail" and calling the preemption "unpatriotic." (Shouldn't John Kerry be running as John McCain's vice president?)

Mr. Koppel told me that he neither wanted to beat the drums for war nor "encourage flower children to come back." He said war is "a bitter, bitter business and we need to keep talking to each other about where the war goes from here." The tolerance for casualties, he said, shortly before the start of his wrenching roll call of all those baby-faced and smiling soldiers and marines, will be in direct relation to faith in the motivation for war.

The WMD reason vanished. And, with the re-Baathification of the de-Baathification, the American idealism rationale is not panning out.

Hiding the faces of the war dead makes the motivation seem like saving face in an election year.

Americans won't take casualties for the credibility of the Bush administration. That's not a good enough reason for people to die.

Epitaph and Epigone

■

S ometimes I feel as if I'm watching a nation mourn. And sometimes I feel as if I'm watching a paternity suit.

At every opportunity, as the extraordinary procession solemnly wended its way from California to the Capitol, W. was peeping out from behind the majestic Reagan mantle, trying to claim the Gipper as his true political father.

Finally, there's a flag-draped coffin and military funeral that President Bush wants to be associated with, and wants us to see. (It's amazing they could find enough soldiers, given Rummy's depletion of the military.)

"His heart belongs to Reagan," Ken Duberstein declared about Mr. Bush on CNN, in a riff on the old Cole Porter ditty "My Heart Belongs to Daddy." W. "is that bold-stroked, primary-colors leader that—somebody who has this big vision and wants to stick to it." (Well, the two presidents do share a middle initial.)

The Bush-Cheney reelection Web site was totally given over to a Reagan tribute, with selected speeches, including "Empire of Ideals"—too bad we didn't just stick to ideals—and "The Boys of Pointe du Hoc," President Reagan's 1984 Normandy speech, played so often last Sunday that it eclipsed W. at Normandy.

Bush hawks were visibly relieved to be on TV answering questions that had nothing to do with prison torture, phantom WMD or our new CIA-operative-turned-prime-minister in Iraq. What a glorious respite to extol a strong, popular, visionary Republican president who spurred democracy in a big backward chunk of the world— even if it isn't W., and it's the Soviet bloc and not the Middle East.

Showing they haven't lost their taste for hype, some Bushies revved up the theme that Son of Bush was really Son of Reagan.

Never mind that back in 1989, the deferential Bush *père* couldn't wait to escape the Gipper's Brobdingnagian shadow. Though he liked Ronald Reagan, 41 had a secret disdain for 40's White House. He was dismayed by the way media wizards treated the president like a prop and the Oval Office like an MGM set. He and Barbara, who divide the world into peers and "the help," also hated being treated like "the help" by the Reagans, who did not have them upstairs at the residence for dinner and who did not always thank them for presents.

The Reagans returned the favor. "Kinder and gentler than who?" Nancy sniffed after 41's convention acceptance speech. (As for Barbara, Nancy had warned her off wearing "Nancy Reagan red.")

For the neocons, ideology is thicker than blood. Bush *père* is the weakling who broke his tax pledge and let Saddam stay in power. Just as Ronnie was a poor kid from Dixon, Illinois, who reinvented himself as a brush-clearing cowboy of grand plans and simple tastes, so W. was a rich kid from Yale and Harvard and a blue-blooded political dynasty who reinvented himself as a brush-clearing cowboy of grand plans and simple tastes.

While W. talks the optimistic talk, he doesn't walk the walk; the Bush crew conducted its Iraq adventurism with a noir and bullying tone.

But Richard Perle and Paul Wolfowitz tried to merge Junior and Gipper. Mr. Perle said on CNN that Mr. Reagan wouldn't have been "pushed out of Iraq before completing the mission," and Wolfie agreed that 9/11 had "changed everything. I think it would have changed it for Ronald Reagan. We've gone from just being concerned with the freedom of other people in the Middle East to the threat to our own country from totalitarian regimes that support terrorism."

These maunderings forget that Mr. Reagan sometimes avoided risk, compromised and retreated; when 241 Marines were blown up in Beirut, he rejected advisers' pleas and pulled out. Mr. Wolfowitz has told friends this was Mr. Reagan's low point.

As Alexander Haig told Pat Robertson yesterday, Mr. Reagan won the cold war without a shot. He championed freedom but didn't impose it at the point of a gun barrel. He had "Peace Through Strength"; Mr. Bush chose Preemption Without Pals.

The Bush crowd's attempt to wrap themselves in Reagan could go only so far. While Laura Bush and Donald Rumsfeld shared memories of fathers who had suffered from Alzheimer's, Mrs. Bush said she could not support Mrs. Reagan's plea to remove the absurd and suffocating restrictions on stem-cell research.

Whether he was right or wrong, Ronald Reagan was exhilarating. Whether he is right or wrong, George W. Bush is a bummer.